In God's Mirror

In God's Mirror

Reflections and Essays

by
HAROLD M. SCHULWEIS

Introduction
by
IRVING GREENBERG

KTAV PUBLISHING HOUSE, INC.
JERSEY CITY, NJ

Copyright ©2003
Harold M. Schulweis
Library of Congress Cataloging-in-Publication Data

Schulweis, Harold M.
  In God's mirror: reflections and essays / Harold M. Schulweis.—New ed.
  p. cm.
  ISBN 0-88125-805-9

  1. Judaism—20th century. 2. Fasts and feasts—Judaism. I. Title

BM565.S362 2003
296'.09'4—dc21

2003047672

Manufactured in the United States of America

Distribution rights:

Rabbi Harold M. Schulweis
Valley Beth Shalom
15739 Ventura Blvd.
Encino, CA 91436
(818) 788-6000

Aytz Chaim Foundation
c/o Congregation Agudas Achim
Jarrell D. Rubinett
7300 Hart Lane
Austin, TX 78731
(512) 477-6309

Distributed by

Ktav Publishing House, Inc.
930 Jersey Avenue
Jersey City, NJ 07306
201-963-9524 Fax 201-963-0102
www.ktav.com

This Book is Dedicated to
The Jewish Foundation for the Righteous

❧

The proceeds from the purchase of this book support the cause of the Jewish Foundation for the Righteous. The Jewish Foundation for the Righteous (JFR) provides monthly financial support to more than 1,700 aged and needy Christian rescuers in twenty-seven countries who risked their lives to protect Jews during the Holocaust, and educates generations to come about their extraordinary acts of courage.

In 1986, the Foundation was created to fulfill the traditional Jewish commitment of *hakarat hatov*, the searching out and recognition of goodness. To this end, JFR is committed to assisting those Righteous Gentiles who are in need. We support and remember with gratitude these extraordinary individuals who were singular lights in the darkness. These unassuming, heroic people are reluctant to ask for help. They acted without expected reward, then or now. Yet they express their appreciation for the Foundation's support.

In addition to providing needed financial assistance to rescuers, the Foundation's education program, "Teaching the Holocaust: History, Perspectives and Choices" focuses on educating middle and high school teachers about the history of the Holocaust, and providing them with the resources to integrate this knowledge into their classrooms. The JFR's: *Voices & Views: A History of the Holocaust* is the cornerstone of the Foundation's outreach education program to teachers throughout the country. Using short selections from leading scholarship, *Voices and Views: A History of the Holocaust* introduces teachers both to the history of the Holocaust and to the scholarly literature in the field. Within that context, it addresses the specific subject of moral courage and the rescue of Jews.

Rescuers serve as role models for us and for future generations. They teach us that, even in the midst of the worst evil in recorded history, each human being had the capacity to act humanely (men and women who had the courage to care and to make a difference. There are always alternatives to passive complicity with evil. Without the example of the rescuers, we are left with the lessons of brutality, hatred, indifference and unspeakable suffering to teach our children.

The Foundation's Board of Trustees has been instrumental in the success of the work of the Foundation. Under the current leadership of Harvey Schulweis and Paul Goldberger and before them E. Robert Goodkind, the Board has become an active national group of business, civic, and lay leaders. Their energy and dedication make it possible for the Foundation to provide aid to so many and to educate generations.

The Jewish Foundation for the Righteous works closely with the Conference on Jewish Material Claims Against Germany (Claims Conference) and The American Jewish Joint Distribution Committee. Both organizations provide significant financial support to the Foundation. The Claims Conference has supported the Righteous for many years, and provided initial funding for rescuers in Poland. Today, the JFR also works collaboratively with Yad Vashem, the Holocaust memorial in Jerusalem, on the critical issues of rescuer documentation and verification.

The section on the Holocaust in this book, specifically the chapter entitled "Letting Go/ Holding On" explains the rationale and motivation of the Jewish Foundation for the Righteous.

Harold M. Schulweis
Founding Chairman, JFR

Contents

IV. RITUALS AND FESTIVALS   215

THE SHABBAT

FESTIVALS

KADDISH, YIZKOR, AND YAHRZEIT

PROLOGUE

I am honored by the decision of the Etz Hayim Foundation to republish the out of print book *In God's Mirror*, and thankful to my good friend Jarrell Rubinett, who convinced me that the essays originally published in 1990 speak to our contemporary human condition and deserve renewal.

The one global event that has transpired in the intervening years since the original publication is the trauma of 9/11. It has shaken the security of Western civilization and has pushed to the forefront the persistent questions of explaining evil within the parameters of conventional theology. I ask the reader and myself whether we are prepared in our thinking to deal with the tragedy of 9/11.

We have changed politically, militarily and diplomatically. We have lost our innocence, naiveté and false sense of security. We have matured politically and militarily, but religiously we have remained stagnant. We ask the same questions and offer the same answers as if nothing has changed. Religion past 9/11 is business as usual. "Why me?" "Why us?" "Where was God in 9/11?" From some in the religious right we hear the kind of responses we have always heard. God lurks behind the catastrophe. If the Towers fell, it was because of the corroded foundations of liberalism or pro-choice advocates or the prominence of gays and lesbians or the activities of the ACLU. More often, religious leaders sidestep the difficult questions and tend to ignore its theological disruptions. They fall back upon yesterday's old rhetoric and find comfort in God's inscrutable will and in reverential agnosticism.

But denial is a short-term salve and long-term infection. The question that gnaws at us, "Where was God on 9/11?" is isolated, oblivious to the deeper grievous questions. "Where was God on 9/10, 9/11, 9/8?" Tens of thousands of parents have watched malnourished infants die every day in the world. Where was God? In Africa every day more people have died of AIDS than were killed in the Twin Towers. Where was God? Arteries and brain cells have stifled vibrant persons with strokes, silences, and stupor. Where was God? A few months ago in India an earthquake left a hundred fifty thousand injured and one million homes destroyed. Where was God?

When I hear this piling up on the Deity, I suspect that God has become a victim of our abuse, that He is being used as a global "kaparah", our cosmic scapegoat. In the biblical past, on Yom Kippur, a scapegoat encumbered with all of our sins, was sent out into the desert to be sacrificed. That ritual became dormant. Today our scapegoat, in a world in which things go radically wrong, is cast upwards. It is He, the Ribbono Shel Olam, the Omniscient, and Omnipotent One who is responsible. How convenient, to wallow in moral indolence.

Victor Frankl, the psychologist of logo-therapy, wrote that while he had met all kinds of people who denied the existence of God, he had never met a person who doesn't want a God.

But what kind of God do we want? After the crisis, we return to the conventional God of mass culture, the God with whom we were raised in and out of school. We revert to the God who is a supernatural combination of Superman, Spiderman and Batman. We want a Divine Hero, "faster than a speeding bullet, more powerful than a locomotive, able to leap tall buildings with a single bound." We want a God who, when a bullet is fired by a villain, turns the cartridge into butter, paralyzes world killers and makes rapists impotent before their crimes are committed. We want a magical God ruling a fantasy world. We revert to a golden calf that will assume the burden of our responsibilities and our freedom.

But that is not the kind of God that mature Jewish minds believe in. That magical thinking violates the reality principle of Judaism that is expressed in the following passage in the Talmud Avodah Zarah (54b): "If an individual should steal some seeds of wheat and plant them in his own field, it would be just if those stolen seeds should not sprout. But nature pursues its own course and in the real world stolen seeds sprout." The Talmud continues: "If a man should rape his neighbor's wife it would be just that the violated woman should not become pregnant. But nature pursues its own course." DNA is not Din, the laws of Newton are not the laws of the Decalogue. The world of natural law is not a rabbinic court of justice

The rabbis understood that the world was created incomplete. They knew that "The mustard seed has to be sweetened, the lupine must be soaked, wheat is to be ground and the human being must be mended. Everything needs repair" (Midrash Tanhuma: Tazria 5).

In Judaism, the created world is a universe of plenitude: sunrise and sunset, forest and ocean, plant and animal, earthquake, hurricane, thunder, sickness and terror, a world full of amoral potentialities. But that real world is not static, and we who live in that world are not impotent. We are gifted with the power to transform, to turn, to change. That capacity lies at the root of our faith. That reality principle of Judaism eschews the split thinking that segregates divinity from humanity, heaven from earth. After 9/11 we have to reclaim the shared covenant that raised us up as partners, co-creators and co-responsible agents with God. That world can and should be repaired. God created us to be custodians of this real world, to care and to guide the trajectory of history. Multiply, fructify, fill the earth and heal its wounds with wisdom and morality.

Some still ask, "Is it so difficult for an omnipotent and omniscient God to create human genes, chromosomes and DNA devoid of evil and apostasy?" No more atheism. No more Gnosticism. No more sin. But others have thought that under those conditions God could not create a human being, a partner with God endowed with the capacity to think, feel, choose and exercise the capacity to enter the real world and transform it. Human beings live in a world of "is" upon which they are morally mandated to impose a world of "ought." The real and the ideal are set before us.

That kind of covenanted God demands much of us. It is easier to drop the human/divine covenant and to ask God alone to come down and send his grace, to fill our calendar with Sabbaths and holidays alone, where we do not have to petition, work or change. But that passivism betrays the reciprocal Covenant, and allows evil, sickness, poverty and war to remain undisturbed.

Judaism will not let us or others sleep. When the children of Israel were caught between the Red Sea and the Egyptian chariots,

Moses prayed to God and urged the people to "stand still and see the salvation of the Lord who will work for you today. The Lord will fight for you and you will hold your peace." God's response to Moses' plea for Divine intervention is arresting and as relevant as 9/11: "Why are you crying to Me? Why do you come to Me with long prayers? Speak to the Jewish people that they go forth" (Exodus 16). This biblical passage reflects the Jewish reality principle.

God answers our questions with His own. The dialogue, the question and answer, is dialectical. It goes both ways. God asks, "Where are you? Why do you perseverate?" You ask, "Where is divinity?" Ask rather, "Where is humanity?" You ask, "Does God really care?" Ask, "Do I really care?" You who ask, "Does God intervene?" Ask rather, "Do I intervene?" You, who are created with the potentiality of the Divine Image, carry the answer in, with and between you. Especially after 9/11, the human question turns reflexive. We must redirect our search for God by turning the question inward. In the time of the prophet Isaiah the people also asked the same old questions and sounded the same stale complaints. "We fast, why don't you respond? We bring sacrifices, why do you slumber in the clouds above? Why, when we fast, do you, God, not see? When we starve our bodies why do You, God, pay no attention?" God replies: "On your fast day, you see to your business and oppress all your laborers. You fast in strife and contention and strike with a wicked fist. Is this the fast that I desire?" God answers with his own questions: "What kind of a God do you think I am? What kind of piety do you imagine I want? Is it that you bow your head like a bulrush and lie in sackcloth and ashes? You call that a fast day? This is the fast that I, God, desire: that you unlock the fetters of wickedness, that you untie the cords of the yoke to let the oppressed go free, that you break off every yoke. This is the imperative I call for, that you share your bread with the hungry and take the wretched poor into your home and that when you see the naked that you clothe him and that you do not ignore you own kin.

With 9/11 we enter a new world and a renewed task. We are at the brink of a global struggle against radical evil. We are called upon to destroy the forces of intolerance, the viruses of xenophobia and hatred in order to defend the helpless victims and to restore their dreams. There is no super-person to do so for us. That is the challenge of the sacred dual covenant between us. God/Elohim has given us "the world as it is" and the Lord/Adonai has given us the vision of "the world as it ought to be." We have the energy, power, mind, heart and soul to combine both sources of Divinity and to actualize the world of possibilities.

After 9/11 the global dialogue must be opened and the questions inflected. We must ask of ourselves, our people, our nation, our religions, and our humanity: "Where are we?" We pray, each in our unique liturgies, not to move God, but to move us out of our pews into the political, social and ethical arena in which we live.

Judaism is a realistic faith and a demanding one. Superficially it may seem easy because it has so few dogmas. But dogmas are not as challenging as ethical mandates to make this a healthier and safer universe. Judaism offers us real freedom in a real world with real responsibility. Judaism does not proffer magic. The doors of illusion lead to the portals of disillusion. The doors of responsibility open the ark of this worldly sanctuary. The global universe after 9/11 calls for global consciousness, beginning with humanity, the moral colleague of divinity.

HMS
April 2003

Addictive Culture" is a searing portrayal of the hedonistic culture and the way it enervates the human condition.

Schulweis is a pioneer in empowering people ("Countering the Attraction of Cult," "Riteless Passages and Passageless Rites"). He is a credible moralist in an age of polarization between "anything goes" and regression ("Sex and the Single God"). He offers a keen and powerful analysis of the moral conundrums of innocent suffering ("Suffering and Evil").

INTRODUCTION

Plain and simple: Rabbi Harold Schulweis is a remarkable person.

Harold Schulweis is the best known pulpit rabbi in America. He has a philosophic mind of first-rate academic quality as evidenced by his book, *Evil and the Morality of God*. His stature as a leading voice of conscience in the American Jewish community has been earned over the course of decades. Just in case you live on a desert island and have not encountered him in any of these aspects of his distinguished career, this book will supply all the evidence you need that he is in fact a remarkable person.

This book exemplifies the extraordinary range of interests and topics on which Harold writes with intelligence, insight and a consistently distinctive voice. How many other rabbis could range from a sophisticated analysis of the polarities of Jewish ideas ("From Either/Or To Both/And") to a folksy critique of the excessive focus on anti-Semitism in modern Jewish identity? Who else could write with such intelligence—nay wisdom—about the Jewish holidays (see "As Children or As Servants," "Creation and Creativity," etc.) and with equal feeling and insight on family and interpersonal relations ("Parents and Pressure on the Child," "Fiddler on a Hot Tin Roof")?

Some pieces reflect the man of conscience and deep human compassion. "Holding On, Letting Go" is an unforgettable call to remember the righteous Gentiles, the rescuers who risked all to save lives in the heart of darkness. His critique of Bar Mitzvahs and Bas Mitzvahs, the distortion of values, the human (should I say, inhuman) pressures on parents, reveals empathy and feeling for the nitty gritty dilemmas of Jewish existence. "Raised in an

Addictive Culture'' is a searing portrayal of the hedonistic culture and the way it enervates the human condition.

Schulweis is a pioneer in empowering people (''Countering the Attraction of Cult,'' ''Riteless Passages and Passageless Rites''). He is a credible moralist in an age of polarization between ''anything goes'' and repression (''Sex and the Single Girl''). He offers a keen and powerful analysis of the moral conundrums of innocent suffering (''Suffering and Evil'').

Through all this, Schulweis consistently shows deep understanding for the other side of the position that he takes. He must be at peace with himself for he has the ability to hear and sympathetically share even while critiquing. The essay, ''Love With A Bear Hug Around My Soul,'' could easily have turned into a caricature of the Lubavitcher movement, making its people look credulous, fanatical, offensive. Instead, it becomes a sensitive interaction, an honest self-revelation, a meditative critique on the limits of love when respect for intellect is absent. No one is made to look bad; there are no easy victories or easy victims.

''The Stranger in Our Memory'' does justice to the two sides of American Jewish reactions to converts. It recognizes that in Jewish history there have been periods in which strangers seeking conversions were welcomed (as a bona fide strategy of survival), even as there have been periods of closing ranks and creating such a powerful ethnocentric atmosphere that outsiders were all but excluded. He manages to combine this open-endedness with a sensitive and moving portrait of the convert today and the need to welcome Jews by choice.

Harold has meditated on pluralism as often and as thoughtfully as almost anyone in Jewish life. The fruits of his reflections show up in essay after essay (see ''The Pendulum of Pluralism,'' ''Havdalah: The Wisdom of Separation'' and many others). He goes beyond truisms, beyond motherhood-and-apple-pie pluralism to new insights about the other side, about what it takes to hear others, about the emotions of pluralism (or of separationism). These essays can be read with profit by *farbrente* pluralists or sworn separationists or anything in between.

Written with grace, with self-awareness, with sensitivity, these essays could be called occasional pieces—except that Schulweis' 'occasional' is not occasional. His writing is instruction, wisdom of life, ethical inspiration.

Over the years, these pieces have been given as lectures or published as essays in a wide variety of media. For that reason, very few people had access to all of them. It was therefore a mitzvah to gather them together and publish them so that their cumulative power can be experienced. Now all of us can have access to all of them, not just for the moment but to come back to for additional insight and for repeated study.

In *Pirkei Avot* we are told that if we learn one thought, one word, even one letter from a scholar, we must treat him as our Rebbe— with all the rights and dignities that that honored title bestows. With these essays, Harold Schulweis becomes the rebbe of an even wider circle in Jewry whose lives he enriches by one concept that illumines the soul, by one vision that moves the heart, by one insight that stimulates the brain. Taste and see how good he is. You will come out a wiser and better person. What more can one ask from an author or from a book.

Irving Greenberg

IN GOD'S MIRROR

The title of this book of essays is derived from a rabbinic legend. Six hundred thousand Jews standing at the foot of Sinai heard One Voice declaring, "I am the Lord *thy* God" (Exodus 20). Remarkably, though the voice addressed an entire people, each individual heard the voice as if it were addressed to him individually. Rabbi Levi explained: "God appeared to them like a mirror in which many faces can be reflected. A thousand may look at it and it reflects each of them. Thus the text does not say, 'I am the Lord *your* God,' addressed to the collective, but 'I am the Lord *thy* God,' addressed to the individual."

Rabbi Yose ben Chanina elaborated: "God spoke with each person according to each person's power. Nor need you marvel at this. The manna tasted differently to each: to the children, to the young, and to the old, according to their power. Now if each and every person was able to taste the manna according to his particular capacity, how much more was each and every person enabled to hear according to his capacity. David said, 'The voice of the Lord with strength.' It does not say 'with God's strength' but 'with strength,' that is according to the strength of each. Therefore the Holy One says, 'Do not think that because you hear many voices there are many gods, for it is always I. I am the Lord thy God' " (*Pesikta de-Rav Kahana piska* 12).

The mirror is one, the reflections many. God is one, the theologies many. The Torah is one, the commentaries many. The people is one, the definitions many. I interpret the rabbinic parable on the Many and the One as an insight into the need for theological modesty. In this world at least there is no immaculate perception.

We cannot jump out of our human skins. Whatever the claim for the origin of revelation, divine disclosures are filtered through our human fallibility, the uniqueness of our moral sensibility. None of this is to deny *ha-Makom,* the Place, the rabbinic term for God, but to remind ourselves that "we live in the description of a place, not in the place itself" (Wallace Stevens).

PLURALISM

The voice is one but there are multiple echoes. It is enriching to listen to what other ears have heard and to respect their hearing. The parable indicates a respect for pluralism, the subject of the essays in our first section. Applied to the religious civilization of the Jewish people, pluralism does not view Judaism as a discrete, simple unit of thought and practice. As the historian of ideas Arthur Lovejoy observed, "The doctrines or tendencies that are designated by familiar names ending in -ism or -ity, though they occasionally may be, usually are not units of the sort which the historian of ideas seeks to discriminate." The suffixes our language uses are names of complexes that stand "not for one doctrine, but for several distinct and conflicting doctrines held by a different individual or groups." It is no diminution of the singularity of Judaism to "go beyond the superficial appearance of singleness and identity, to crack the shell which holds the mass together."

In our times we are experiencing a mounting impatience with pluralism, an intolerance of other voices, other perceptions, alternative readings. There is a call for simple and certain convictions. The qualifications set upon absolutes, the questioning of assumed truths are unnerving to those who are more comfortable with the past, more suspicious of innovations, however rooted in tradition.

To contain its fears neophobia excommunicates. Alternative ways are dismissed as heresies, schools of thought are branded as rival denominations, half-baked analogies are used to denigrate others: the Orthodox are Karaites, the Reformed are alien sects. What is lost is the holistic character of a tradition, the wider vision that recognizes differences as splinters of the same wood. At its core, idolatry is the worship of the part as if it were the whole. All religious movements within Judaism must be wary of the lure of strange worship of the part, *avodah zarah.*

The polarization of ideologies has gone past the theoretical. A felt alienation within Judaism has filtered down to the laity, who are experiencing a loss of their sense of belonging. Even the appeal to the Holocaust, the common existential fate of a people, has exhausted its binding power. If the mirror is shattered into isolated fragments, it will distort the reflections.

THE HOLOCAUST

The second section deals with the Holocaust, the dominant psychic reality in our lives. The commemoration of the Shoah raises questions about the use and abuse of Jewish memory. What lessons about the meaning of the Shoah may be transmitted to our children and with what effect upon their morale?

Elie Wiesel is understandably wary of those who would assign meaning to such a monstrous, irrational phenomenon. Like others, he is concerned lest the search for meaning in the Holocaust be twisted into the justification of its happening, e.g., the Holocaust as the enabling instrument for the establishment of the State of Israel, or as the punishment for a people's transgressions, or as evidence of God's inscrutable will. But while one must be careful not to turn causes into divine purposes, or consequences into divine maledictions or benedictions, there are meaningful lessons to be learned and unlearned from the Holocaust. Without rationalizing evil, is there any hope salvageable from the embers of the crematoria? How is the Jewish belief in the divine image of human beings to be squared with the radical evil experienced in the Shoah? Does the popular interpretation of the Holocaust carry within it a metaphysics that freezes Jewish statesmanship? How should the recollection of the Holocaust affect the Jewish relationship to the gentile world?

FAMILY AND SYNAGOGUE

The little girl asked by her rabbi why she believed in God answered more profoundly than she may have suspected. "I don't know why I believe in God. I guess it just runs in the family." In dealing with a number of the crises affecting Jewish life—ranging from addiction, mixed marriage, the appeal of the cults, and the limitations of educational institutions—I am convinced that all roads lead to Home.

Not only charity begins at home. Theology, morality, the basic attitudes towards authority, the loyalties towards a people begin at home. Begin but do not end there. What happens in the private domain spills over into the public domain of the synagogue, federation, center, organization, the megastructures of the Jewish community. Thus home and synagogue together make up the subject of the third section.

I also sense what some American sociologists have termed the "underinstitutionalization" of the home. The family, faced by rapid and massive moral, social, economic changes, is left on its own to raise its children and to shape its way of living. Here the public institutions have inadvertently bypassed the empowerment of the family. The essays include some experiments within the synagogue community that reject the school and temple surrogation of the roles properly belonging to the family. Havurah, para-rabbinic, family-to-family programs are focused on retrieving the functions and activities of parents that have been assumed by the personnel and programs of public institutions. Without communal support of the family and strengthening of the home, the personnel of school, sanctuary, and Jewish organizations will grow increasingly frustrated. Without the natural, sacred center of the family, the institutional extensions of the Jewish home will remain detached artificial organs. Whatever outreach programs institutions may devise, they will rise or fall with their ability to reach into the home.

RITUALS AND FESTIVALS

The concluding section deals with the body-language of Jewish civilization: the rituals of festivals and fasts that punctuate the time shared within the Jewish community. Rituals give birth to philosophy. However much the sages warned against assigning rationales to ritual ordinances, the hunger of the mind searched for explanations, discovered and invented reasons for observances. The rationale created a literature forming and reflecting Jewish wisdom and values.

Layers of interpretation are born out of the matrix of celebration and commemoration. To the outsider the observance is one. Around the Seder table my grandfather, father, cousins, uncles, and aunts all drank wine, broke matzah, and sang songs. The ritual acts were the same but they had different meanings for the Orthodox, socialist, Zionist and freethinker among them. For some the ritual imperatives came down vertically as divine commandments from above. For others the sanctions rose horizontally from the experiences of a living people. Whether the validation for the ritual derives from a supernatural Person above or from a collective conscience within, observance of the act itself adds a rationale of its own. Before and beyond believing, the sense of belonging is experienced in behaving. I have always been surprised by the fidelity with which even the least believing cling to some rituals. The least contemplative recognize that what they do in common with others is important. "I could never be an atheist," the agnostic declared, "because atheists have no holidays." There is a sacred dimension in the selective celebration of time.

The rabbinic tradition advises that the architecture of the House of Prayer should include a window. Petitioners should be aware of the needs of others so that they can pray more realistically for their own needs. The architecture of rabbinic thought requires a window on the world so that the widsom of the tradition may be responsive to the needs of the people.

The selections in this book were largely occasioned by attention to the questions posed by congregants. Congregants are the windows of the rabbinic world.

I
Pluralism

JEWISH APARTHEID

*The Divine Presence does not dwell among a people with a
divided heart.*

—Numbers Rabbah 15:14

We are one people. That is the underlying predicate of Torah. We
are addressed as one people—elders and officers, men and women
and little ones, priests and proselytes, "from the hewers of thy
wood unto the drawers of thy water." We are all of us covenanted
to each other and to the eternal God.

But there is no guarantee that we Jews will continue to live. No
covenant guarantees our unconditional immortality, no biological
instinct our collective self-preservation. We are what we choose.

We are the choosing people. "I call heaven and earth to witness
against you this day, that I have set before thee life and death, the
blessing and the curse; therefore choose life that thou mayest live,
thou and thy seed" (Deuteronomy 30:19).

These are times when serious thinkers wonder aloud whether
there will be one Jewish people by the year 2000. Indeed, one
might well ask whether we can still speak of one people now.
Given the mounting polarization of the Jewish community, do we
not already stand on the brink of cataclysm? In our midst, today,
vilifying language and behavior urge disassociation from the major
religious groups of our community. We have passed beyond the
stage of stereotypic caricaturing, beyond the depiction of Orthodox Judaism as crazy, Reform as lazy, and Conservative as hazy.

The old stereotypes have been replaced by a fragmentation that
tears at our identity, at the continuity and character of Judaism.

3

Today, the deepest threat to Jewish living does not come from without, from external factors—the anti-Semite, the cultist, the missionary. The threat comes not by way of physical genocide but by spiritual suicide.

We have been warned. Over and again our sages related that the Temple was destroyed not because there was no study of Torah in the land or because no commandments were observed. Instead, they traced the lethal cause of the *churban,* destruction, to *sinat chinam,* causeless hatred, a sin the rabbis weighted as seriously as the three major transgressions of murder, idolatry, and harlotry (*Yevamot* 62b). To avoid these latter sins one is to surrender his or her life rather than transgress.

Another talmudic source explained the destruction of Jerusalem as a consequence of those whose judgments were based strictly upon the law, who did not go beyond the letter of the law (*Bava Metzia* 30b). The disaster of death that befell the disciples of Rabbi Akiva did not come from external forces, but because "the scholars did not treat each other with respect" (*Yevamot* 62b). The tradition reveled in the correlation of the oneness of God—"Hear, O Israel, the Lord our God"—and the oneness of the Jewish people—"one nation in the world" (*Berachot* 71a). Hence the quarrelsome divisions among the people disqualified their testimony to God's unity, leaving God divided, exiled, alone.

Whatever accounts for the origin of the schism, no one religious movement alone is blameworthy for its perpetuation. Caste creates outcaste, and the latter retaliates with its own pariahs.

Blame aside, the existing situation is intolerable. No prior deliberations among the decision-making religious bodies take place, even in matters affecting the status and character of world Jewry. Decisions regarding patrilineal descent, the conversion of the unchurched, the ordination of women, the off-limits to non-Orthodox synagogues are denominationally privatized. They are unilaterally arrived at, and their revelations are communicated to other Jewish religious movements through the Op-Ed section of the *New York Times.* Tragically, there simply is no intramural vehicle through which prior consultations may take place, accommodations be proposed, negotiations be considered. Where there is no true communication, there is no true community. Where *yeder macht Shabbes far zich alayn* ("each person makes Shabbat for him or herself, alone") there is neither Sabbath nor *Havdalah.*

Evidence of the schism comes from small and large incidents, from public statements and private anecdotes. I read with sadness the responsa of the foremost Orthodox *posek* (legal decisor), Rabbi Moshe Feinstein, in his *Iggerot Mosheh.* Asked by a rabbinic colleague whether a professor at the Conservative Jewish Theological Seminary of America may be invited to lecture at an Orthodox synagogue's adult education program, he counsels him not to allow such a lecture to take place because such a person presumably would teach heretical doctrines. In yet another response to a rabbinic question—and the nature of these questions is significant—the distinguished rav is asked whether one may recite "amen" after the blessing over bread spoken by a Conservative or Reform rabbi. He judges that however correct the recitation may be, inasmuch as the rabbi is non-Orthodox, his benedictions are *devarim be-alma,* mere words, invalid blessings, and one is *not* to recite "amen."

Rabbi Feinstein was a profoundly influential decisor, noted for his leniency, and when he once ruled on what amounted to the permissibility of artificial insemination, he was compelled to retract his responsum because of a strong attack by the Satmar Rebbe. Rabbi Feinstein was confronted by many pressures. How, for example, is the Orthodox rabbi to deal with the halachic issue of *mamzerut,* illegitimacy, in our times? A *mamzer,* an illegitimate child, is not a child born out of wedlock, but one born either out of incest or adultery or out of a second marriage performed without a prior religious divorce, a *get.* According to Jewish law (halachah), a woman who remarries without a *get* is considered to be an adulteress, and any child of the subsequent marriage is considered to be a *mamzer.* That *mamzer* cannot "enter the congregation of the Lord" (Deuteronomy 23:3), cannot marry another legitimate Jew; he or she may marry only another illegitimate Jew.

But the Reform movement, for reasons of its own, does not require a religious *get;* it is satisfied with a civil divorce as the legal sanction for the dissolution of marriage. What, then, to do? Rabbi Feinstein's liberal solution to such tragic cases was to nullify the *initial* marriage of the mother on the presumption that the presiding officiant was a Reform rabbi. The marriage is invalid since these rabbis are invalid, "all evil and given to wanton Sabbath violations"; "they violate all the prohibitions in the Torah with contempt."

(There is a strange gallows humor in all this. To be lucky in law is to have an "evil" Reform rabbi officiate at your marriage; an observant rabbi is a valid *mesader kiddushin,* and he could prove disastrous. The situation allowing Jewish illegitimates to marry only other Jewish illegitimates suggest a bizarre satire—a personals ad reading, "*Mamzer* seeking mamzeret—object: matrimony.")

With the best of intentions, Rabbi Feinstin's lenient response nevertheless labels an entire rabbinate. It legitimates the *mamzer* by delegitimizing with one stroke the authority of a major religious movement in Judaism, one with a constituency of more than one million Jewish souls.

This is not the Orthodoxy in which I was brought up, not the Jewish teachings I was taught, teachings that stressed spiritual delicacy in interpersonal relationships, that cautioned against the transgression of shaming others (which the rabbis compared to the shedding of another's blood), that emphasized a Torah whose ways are "the ways of pleasantness." When a yeshiva director in the United States refers to Conservative Judaism as *avodah zarah* (idolatry); when Orthodox high officials in Israel suggest that if Conservative and Reform groups seek religious equality in Israel they ought to declare themselves separate religions like the Armenians, Greek Orthodox, and Druse; when pressures by the Orthodox right are placed upon moderate Orthodox to resign from boards of rabbis and from the Synagogue Council of America because their joint participation confers the appearance of legitimacy upon non-Orthodox rabbis; when this year's Orthodox rabbinic graduates from my alma mater, Yeshiva University, refuse to be interviewed by *Moment* magazine because at the table there will also be rabbinically ordained graduates from other ordaining seminaries—Reform, Conservative, Reconstructionist—we have the threat of genuine fracture.

There are personal experiences that sadden me. I am mortified by the calls I and my colleagues receive from women who have gone through Jewish conversions, been examined by a Beth Din of three rabbis, immersed themselves in the *mikveh* (ritual bath) and, before an open *aron kodesh*, a holy ark, covenanted themselves to God and the people of Israel. They have given birth to sons, called upon qualified *mohelim* (ritual circumcisors)—and then been informed that their conversion was no conversion. The entire process of halakhic conversion is discredited not because of "how" it was preformed but because of "who" performed it—in these instances, Conservative rabbis and the Conservative University of Judaism. The women call in tears—confused, resentful, feeling betrayed. Is there a Jewish community out there? Are we one people?

I am chagrined. The daughter of a congregant is to be married in Israel. The rabbinate there requires proof of the Jewishness of her parents. It will not accept the testimony of a non-Orthodox rabbi. I suggest that the parents speak to an Orthodox rabbi in town. They do not know him and he does not know them. They are embarrassed, but they follow my advice. The rabbi then calls me, asks if I know the family to be Jewish, and is pleased that I do. The matter is concluded. My anonymous testimony is valid—but not as a Conservative rabbi. Halachah has been politicized. The critical criterion is the religious party to which the rabbi belongs.

I attended a Chevrah conference at the Brandeis-Bardin Institute this past summer. It was convened by the National Jewish Resource Center, headed by the courageous and innovative Orthodox rabbi, Yitzhak Greenberg. Chevrah brings together rabbis of many schools of thought—Reform, Orthodox, Conservative, Reconstructionist. At the conference, papers are read and critiqued, an extraordinary meeting of minds and hearts takes place. I have hit it off splendidly with a prominent Orthodox rabbi from the East Coast and am moved to invite him to speak from my pulpit at Friday evening services. He is complimented, but uncomfortable with the invitation. He asks whether the congregation recites the *Borchu* and the *Kaddish* prayers. I am surprised, and do not suspect the meaning of his query. I answer affirmatively—and my colleague informs me that he therefore must decline my invitation. The inclusion of these central prayers proves that ours is a religious service—and he cannot participate in a Conservative service.

Jews universally pounced upon Reverend Bailey Smith, president of the Southern Baptist Conference, when in 1980 he declared,

"With all due respect to those dear people, God does not hear the prayers of a Jew." Smith was called bigot, anti-Semite, forced to offer an apology. A few months later, the chief rabbis of Jerusalem announced publicly that those who prayed in Conservative synagogues on Rosh Hashanah would not be fulfilling the mitzvah of hearing the shofar. Bailey Smith knows that God does not hear the prayers of Jews; Jewish Orthodox authorities know that God does not hear the sound of the shofar when it is blown in the "wrong" place. How deprived the angels of heaven must be, who await the sanctification of God's name on earth.

When Jewish marriages and Jewish divorces are disputed, when converts and their children are not recognized by other Jewish religious bodies as Jews, we have a major internal crisis on our hands. Yitzhak Greenberg, among others, estimates that within only the next two decades, 15 to 20 percent of American Jews will be socially and halachically separated from traditional Jews; nearly a million men, women, and children will have their Jewishness contested and their marriageability denied by a large group of other Jews.

We are a small people, 2.6 percent of the general population; by the year 2000, a precious five million Jewish souls in America will be increasingly diminished. No anti-Semite can do better. We are legislating ourselves out of existence, engaging in a civil war of attrition by definition. This has Jewish wisdom and Jewish conscience against it. Before us is not controversy for the sake of heaven, no religious debate conducted rationally by differing schools of thought. There is no civil dialogue here, only anger, labeling, and threats. There is far more dialogue, more accommodation, more civility, more respect, in Christian-Jewish dialogues than among us. There are more exchanges between Christian and Jewish seminaries than among Jewish yeshivoth and Jewish rabbinical seminaries. The geographic distance between Yeshiva University, the Jewish Theological Seminary, and Hebrew Union College in New York is a subway ride. But the distinguished faculties of the rabbinic institutions are kept apart from each other and from the rabbinical students. What a waste of intellectual, spiritual, and moral stimulation for those who will tomorrow serve the Jewish world!

Jewish apartheid is practiced de facto within the Jewish community. Our children are raised in denominationally separate universes, totally separate Hebrew schools, day schools, summer camps, youth activities programs. A small people is made smaller yet. Our Jewish youth is trifurcated. We who cry against "outmarriage" have shrunk and shriveled the dating and marriage pool. We who cry "survival" have violated the elementary common sense of preserving the critical mass for Jewish survival. We rally behind the twisted motto, "Divided we stand; united we fall." It is easier for schools or youth groups to arrange joint programs with Christian schools and church groups than to arrange such programs between classes or clubs from the different Jewish schools of thought. We may not successfully prevent our children from marrying out of the fold, but the way we function, we surely will succeed in keeping Jewish youth from marrying each other. What is to be done, and by whom? Here I appeal to the Jewish people, to the laity. Institutional leaders are too vulnerable to a variety of pressures to transcend their institutional loyalties. We who have instructed the world in the lessons of Auschwitz need to instruct ourselves. We know, we remember, that in Auschwitz there was no doubt about Jewishness. In Buchenwald there was no denominational segregation. Jews were herded together, banded together, came to each other's aid not as Orthodox or Conservative or Reform or secular Jews. We Jews were defined by ash and fire, by a common fate that transcended all ritual laws and all theological variations. In the darkest hour of Jewish life, while the enemy howled derision, we knew we had each other. It was our comfort and our strength. We were one people, with one fate and one destiny. Who dares now rend this people apart?

We learned from the Holocaust one powerful lesson, the cardinal mitzvah of our times. In the language of Maimonides' *Mishneh Torah* (*Hilkhot De'ot* 6:3): "Duty demands that every one of us love every Jew as him or her own self"—to protect, to respect, every other Jew, for "whoever glorifies himself by humiliating someone else has no share in the future world." The will and talent to overcome "causeless hatred" will not come from historical research, or from debates as to the meaning of divine revelation or the right to apply the law. As Rav Kook understood, causeless hatred can only be overcome by causeless love. And love costs.

A rabbinic legend imagines that just as Jews pray, God prays, and just as Jews wear tefillin (phylacteries), God wears tefillin. In the tefillin of the Jew we find the verse declaring God's oneness: "Hear, O Israel, the Lord our God, the Lord is One." The verse in God's tefillin reads, "Who is like Thy people, one people on earth?" When the tefillin are accidentally dropped, we are obligated to pick them up and kiss them. Once, when Levi Yitzchak of Berditchev prayed, he said to God, "Your tefillin have fallen. Raise them up and kiss them." The prayer is directed towards ourselves.

What can we do to raise us up? We must engage in a serious program to mend the torn Jewish fabric. This means to reach out beyond the four cubits of our synagogues and our movements to Jews from other congregations and other movements—Conservative, Reconstructionist, Reform, and Orthodox. It means to use our havurot as circles of friendship to which other havurot of other movements are invited. We who reach out, but not to our own, have to place the problem of our estrangement on the common agenda. We must meet and talk and listen hard to each other. The purpose of these exchanges is not to convert the other to our interpretation of Judaism; not to dwell upon the faults and failures of each other's movements; not to indulge in one-upmanship. The aim is to listen to each other, to understand each other, to learn from each other.

We are *mishpachah*, family. We must hold before us the whole and steady vision of our children expanding their view of the Jewish people, understanding that they are more than members of a congregation, that they are part of a larger, marvelously heterogeneous people. We must sustain the vision of their Jewish growth, of their meeting and arguing and praying and dating and marrying each other, building Jewish homes together. They must be given the opportunity to celebrate with Jews of other convictions and behaviors the Sabbaths and festivals of their lives.

We are told that you cannot compromise with revealed truth, that halakhic decisions are not negotiable, that especially in matters of marital status and conversions, the tradition cannot countenance concessions. But that is unfair to a tradition that struggles against the false identification of obduracy with principle, a tradition that knows when and how to be as soft as a reed.

There are many precedents for halachic pluralism in Jewish history and in the law itself. In important matters concerning marital status, even those involving illegitimacy, a celebrated *mishnah* reports that nothwithstanding disagreements in philosophy and practice between the School of Shammai and the School of Hillel, these permitting what the others prohibited and these declaring ineligible those whom the others declared eligible, "the men of Shammai did not refrain from marrying women from the families of the School of Hillel, nor did the men of Hillel refrain from marrying the women of Shammai." Between the two schools a spirit of trust and respect prevailed. Each informed the other when practices contrary to the rulings of the other school were being enacted. After three years of dispute between the Houses of Shammai and Hillel, each contending that its rulings were the true halachah, a voice descended from heaven and declared that the utterances of "both are the words of the living God." And if, despite this, the House of Hillel was entitled to have the halachah fixed in agreement with its rulings, that was, according to the account we read in *Eruvin* 13b, due to the kindness and modesty of the House of Hillel. For the House of Hillel studied the arguments of its opponents and even mentioned the words of Shammai before its own.

On the surface of things, the civil war appears to be between Orthodoxy and non-Orthodoxy. But this simplified view misplaces the area of the true Kulturkampf. The struggle is between those with an insulated and insulating view of Judaism and those who will not retreat behind the cultural *mechitzah* (partition); between a Jewish fundamentalism intolerant of alternative views and a Judaism with sufficient modesty to recognize that the whole of revelation is not given to one group alone; between those like the biblical figures Dathan and Abiram, who "will not come up" to reason together, and those principled Orthodox leaders who will not excommunicate but are determined to speak and argue and persuade; between those who confuse stringency and inflexibility with piety, and those for whom accommodation and reasonableness are not apostasy but the genius that preserves Jewish continuity and identity; between those who function by exclusion and those who practice the art of *keruv,* drawing Jews closer together; between those who don't care and those who do.

We who do care must meet and talk and plan to save Jewish life from deadly division. Without denying fidelity to our particular commitments, there is something transcendent, something transdenominational that draws us together. The distinguished Orthodox philosopher Eliezer Berkovits has written unambiguously, "The claim of what is known as Conservative or Reform Judaism to equality with Orthodoxy is morally irrefutable." His Orthodox colleague, Professor Ephraim Urbach, has demonstrated that "any form of coercion in matters of religion is contrary to the concept of Judaism and carries with it no halakhic authority." Rabbi Norman Lamm, the president of Yeshiva University, has warned repeatedly against the coercive homogeneity that ultra-Orthodoxy seeks to impose on Jewish life as "leading to bigotry and shallowness." My beloved teacher at Yeshiva College and the former president of Bar-Ilan University, the late Rabbi Joseph Lookstein, counseled against raising the Orthodox ramparts against "our Conservative and Reform brothers. Is it not wise and Jewish to draw them close to our hearts?"

Jewish-Jewish dialogue begins a long process, involving us all. If we are to arrest the violence of words, the denigration of movements and leaders, our own and not our own, it will require patience, wisdom, and courage. There are matters, judgments, and attitudes with which most of us disagree, both within and without our movements. We are entitled, indeed obligated, to press our views. But that suasion, the very possibility of influencing others to reconsider their judgments, is predicated upon respect, a term that derives from a root meaning "to look again." In the name of the unity and continuity of my people, I acknowledge the right and privilege of Jews of diverse schools of thought to build their own institutions of learning, to support the rabbis they elect to follow, to entrust their children to these rabbis for instruction. For the sake of Zion, I may criticize their method of conversion or their interpretation of the law, but I am pledged to recognize their authority, to accept their marriages, their divorces, their conversions; and with love and reason I am free to seek to persuade them to modify their modes of ritual behavior.

Whoever has studied the history of Jewish religious movements over the past one hundred years alone must be impressed by the capacity of responsible and responsive movements to change. Religious ideologies that once opposed Zionism now build religious kibbutzim in Israel; religious movements that feared Jewish particularism now organize excellent Jewish day schools. Religious movements that regarded a sermon in English and the study of secular subjects as vile "imitations of the gentiles" build yeshivot and produce pious scholars at home in multiple cultures.

A loving, caring laity has more to do than respond to fundraising appeals. It has an obligation to demand from the leaders and institutions it supports that they report on what they are doing to stanch the flow of our hemorrhaging community. Rabbis and institutions may be made accountable to the people. Responsible philanthropy may exercise pressure out of love.

Love for others requires understanding, compassion, self-sacrifice. Every ideology, every movement, every school of thought must yield something of its own for *kelal yisrael,* the whole house of Israel. Through negotiation, Reform will be asked in certain areas to modify its insistence on autonomy, or on freedom of individual conscience, and will have to consider the larger community beyond its movement in matters of conversion and intermarriage. For Reform, ritual immersion and circumcision, for example, may become minimal symbolic acts in the name of *kelal yisrael;* and the proscription of mixed marriage may have to be more carefully enforced—in the name of the love and unity of Israel. Orthodox and Conservative rabbis will be urged to respect the authority of Reform rabbis and accept their judgments in the name of *ahavat yisrael* and *kelal yisrael.*

Ahavah beli tenai—unconditional love for the Jewish people—is today the major Jewish imperative. If there is to be any change, any accommodation of Jews, it will not come from ostracism or delegitimation. It will come from inner resolution.

Our internecine battles drain us of much-needed energy. We are so small in number and so large in purpose. Together we may regain our self-respect and turn our minds to the unaffiliated, the disaffiliated, the untouched, the "untouchables." They constitute the majority of Jews in the world. They are made up of many temperaments, many different dispositions; no one approach can reach them all. They need liberal and traditional, Hasidic and rationalistic approaches. One formula, one doctrine, one mode of halachah will never touch them and never unite them. And coercion will never turn them to deeper feeling or greater practice.

The Jewish community would not have been better off without a Heschel or a Soloveitchik, without a Kaplan or a Buber, without a Leo Baeck or a Shneur Zalman. Not all wisdom or truth is mine; not all revelation is limited to my school, to my movement, to my denomination. We have to think of Judaism with a whole and steady vision, not as in the story of the blind men, each touching one part of the elephant and then claiming his own part as the whole. Judaism cannot be reduced to a set of theological doctrines or ritual practices, or to Zionism, or to Hebrew or Yiddish or to philanthropy. To reduce it so is to break the wholeness and richness of Judaism into sectarian and denominational parts.

In the name of *ahavat yisrael,* four proposals for the Jewish laity of all religious movements are offered.

1. "All real life is meeting" (Martin Buber). In our homes, and in our schools, from within our denominational congregations, we must reach out to our Jewish counterparts, to break down the barriers that estrange us from each other. Michael Wyschogrod, the Orthodox rabbi and philosopher, has set the tone clearly. "There must be no segments of Judaism that are not on speaking terms with each other. . . . Let us realize that the alternative to speaking is violence. There is no such thing as ignoring a fellow human being, much less a fellow Jew."

2. "In time to come, your children might speak unto our children, saying, 'what have ye to do with the Lord God of Israel?' " (Joshua 22:24). Let us bring our children together. Let them periodically break out of the incestuous ties of their own club activities, their own classes, and experience the claim that they are part of one people, sharing a common memory and promise. Speak with our youth directors and our educational directors, to enable our young to explore and celebrate the harmony in their disparity. We must not use Solomon's sword to cut the living child in two.

3. "We will go with our young and with our old, with our sons and with our daughters" (Exodus 10:9). Let us increase our

political effectiveness by quadrupling the strength of our social-action enterprises by joining with other denominations to promote our historic interests, e.g., Israel, Soviet Jewry, Ethiopian Jewry, separation of church and state.

4. There are decrees under which a people cannot, need not, and must not live. We have a right to press upon our leaders, organizations, institutions, seminaries, the will to heal the near-mortal wounds of our people. We the people who "dedicate and maintain synagogues, enter therein to worship, devote ourselves to the needs of the community and the rebuilding of Eretz Yisrael" are mandated to exercise moral and responsible philanthropy, to demand of our leaders that they use their rabbinic wisdom and compassion to form networks of cooperative rabbis to create a decent and respectful *modus vivendi* for Jewish living. It is time to remember Malachi's cry: "Have we not all one father? Has not one God created us all? Why do we deal treacherously, everyone against his brother, profaning the covenant of our fathers?"

THE PENDULUM OF
PLURALISM

We have benedictions for all occasions—on seeing the ocean, a rainbow, the blossoming of trees, an electrical storm. And on beholding a Jewish audience, the Talmud prescribes a special benediction: "Blessed is He who discerns secrets, for the mind of each is different from the other, as is the face of each different from the other." It is a blessing in praise of God, who creates diversity in our world, and rejoices in different minds, perceptions, judgments, visages. It is a blessing over Jewish pluralism.

The benediction is easier said than lived. It is one thing to acknowledge the pluralism among us, it is another to acknowledge it as a blessing. It is one thing to love Jews because we share a common fate, it is another to love Jews who hold different theologies, different modes of ritual and religious practice, different politics. Religious and ethnic parties have entered a stage on the brink of sectarianism, denominationalism, schismatic movements. The signs of aggravating incivility abound. A small Jewish world is made smaller yet by factionalism with impenetrable *mechitzot* (partitions).

The pressures in opposition to pluralism mount. People look about and see older horizons erased, absolute values shrunken, the "earth loosened from the sun." Frightened and confused they are impatient with complex answers. Their lives are complex enough. They are intolerant of qualifications, conditional truths, the scholarly cautions of historians, philosophers, educators who know the subtle twists and turns of a people and its ideologies

16

which defy simple definitions. They seek gurus, true believers prepared with apodictic truths; *posekim* who can decide our lives and relieve us from the vertigo of multiple choices and the wrestling with what is right or wise or good. They demand the definite articles of faith: "the" truth, "the" essence, "the" authentic. They call for more rigid definitions that exclude the "un-Jewish" and "inauthentic."

They wonder what is wrong with you pluralists in the fourth millennium of Jewish existence still arguing "Who is a Jew?" Is your openness to ideologies a tacit admission of polytheism? Are you open to all in general because you are committed to none in particular? Are you mimicking the celebrated rabbi who says to the plaintiff, "You are right," and to the defendant, "You are right," and then, when criticized by the rebbetzin, who points out the contradictions of his judgments, replies, "You too are right"? I confess to knowing the rabbi. I even know his wife.

THE PLURALISTIC SELF

The deeper challenge of pluralism is not external, how to maintain housekeeping in an ark filled with lions and lambs, hawks and doves, Orthodox and non-Orthodox, religious and secular. The challenge is internal, within the pluralistic self. *Ein bi-chelal ela mah she-bifrat*—there is nothing in the general which is not in the particular. If I can attain the goal of unity in diversity within, it may serve as a clue to appreciate the blessing of a pluralistic society without.

I know myself to be a person of many moods and dispositions. I am alternately optimistic and pessimistic, liberal and conservative, hawkish and dovish. I am moved by J. B. Soloveitchik and Mordecai M. Kaplan, by Hermann Cohen and Martin Buber. Moreover, I admit to finding no small joy and strength in holding on with both hands to the multiple strands which pull against each other. This delight in contrariety enjoys distinguished company. I think of Reb Naftali of Ropschitz, who in a vision described how before his birth angels presented him with a double column of counsel. On one side there appeared a statement from *Ta'anit:* "A scholar should live like a flaming fire of wrath" (4a); on the other side appeared a sentence from *Sanhedrin:* "A scholar should be meek, humble, and forgiving" (88b). On one side of the column a declaration from *Eruvin:* "A man cannot know Torah without sacrificing his concern for his family" (22a); on the other side from *Chullin:* "A man of Torah must have more regard for his family than for himself" (11a and 24b). On one side admonition to be satisfied with a minimum, and from the same tractate, *Ta'anit,* on the other, "He who pledges himself not to drink wine and afflicts the body is called sinner." The two columns of apparently contradictory statements were endless. While Reb Naftali pondered over the list, his birth was announced. He resolved to live his life following the counsel of both columns, to hold both sides in one loving embrace. It is the challenge of the pluralistic self to choose the dialectic tension of both/and over the hard disjunctive of either/or. It calls for wisdom and courage and a spirit of inclusiveness whose roots lie in the soil of monotheism. Sectarianism breathes the spirit of exclusive either/or choice. Polarities are turned into polarization, distinctions into irreconcilable antagonism. In the *Havdalah* ceremony, the wisdom of Jewish monotheism differentiates between Sabbath and weekday, the holy and the neutral, light and darkness, Israel and other peoples. "Between" is not "against." The differentiation points to distinctiveness, not to opposition. The dualities and complementary energies, they need each other for the sake of wholeness. Here is no ceremony celebrating the primordial wars of Manichaean dualism but the organic unity which rejects uniformity along with anarchy.

DENOMINATIONALISM AND IDOLATRY

"Polarity," Abraham Joshua Heschel wrote, "lies at the heart of Judaism." Absolute antithesis is alien to the Hebraic mind. The genius of monotheism lies in its avoidance of both monistic and polytheistic idolatries. Idolatry is not in the worship of many gods nor of evil forces, but in the adoration of a part as if it were the whole. Consider the dialogue recorded in Mishnah *Avodah Zarah* 4:7. The sages, while in Rome, were asked why, if God opposes idolatry, the objects of worship of the pagans were not destroyed. They answered, Were the idolized objects not needed by the world, He would make an end of them. But idolators worship the sun and the moon and the stars and the planets. "Shall God destroy His world because of fools?"

The energies and causes of denominational ideologies are far from evil. They are good and necessary for the world. Only when their partial insights are deified, when they are held as the one and exclusive interpretation of God's will, do they court the seductions of idolatry. The *Zohar* warns, "Woe to the man who identifies God with any attribute." Menachem Mendel of Kotsk added his caution. Even a mitzvah can become idol worship "if it becomes a principle of principles." During the "seder na-anuim" (the shaking of the lulav) of the Sukkot festival, the lulav is directed above and below, north, east, west, and south. But at the mention of the name of God, all pointing ceases, the palm is held motionless. When theologies think to seize hold of God's collar and pronounce "This is God," they point to their own conceit.

THE ETHIC AND WISDOM OF PLURALISM

Do pluralists go about like Will Rogers, insisting that they never met a theology or ideology they didn't like? Do pluralists ever say no? Pluralism is not the surrender of debate or the bleaching of passionate conviction. The House of Hillel argued, debated, and disagreed with the House of Shammai on major issues, but they held on to their religious modesty. Because they were humble, because they studied not only their decisions but those of their adversaries, because they even recorded the ruling of the House of Shammai before their own, their view prevailed (T. *Eruvin* 13b). Pluralism calls forth an ethic of openness, a disposition towards inclusiveness. And beyond its ethic of respectful tolerance, it holds a pragmatic wisdom. Rashi, commenting on the rabbinic judgment concerning the controversies between the Houses of Shammai and Hillel—"Both speak the words of the living God"—explains that there are times when one reason is valid and other times when another reason is valid. "For reasons change in the wake of even only small changes in the situation." How is it possible that what one sage permits another sage prohibits? The Jewish sages of France in the thirteenth century understood the variety of interpretations and rulings, sometimes conflicting, as a blessing. When Moses ascended to receive the Torah, he was shown in every case forty-nine possibilities to "forbid" and forty-nine possibilities to "permit." The intention was that "all these possibilities of interpretations should be entrusted to the sages of Israel of each generation, that the decision be in accordance with their resolution'' (cited by Eliezer Berkovits in his *But Not in Heaven*). There is no contradiction in the disagreement of authorities. Situations change, and what once was permitted may now be prohibited, what was once proscribed may later be allowed. Why was it necessary to record opinions of Shammai and Hillel that do not prevail? "To teach the generations that come after that none should persist in his opinion, for lo, 'the fathers of the world' did not persist in their opinion" (M. *Eduyot* 1:4).

THE PENDULUM

Against the denominational image of Judaism as a single stone cast down from above to which each claims solitary possession, I propose another image for the pluralistic outlook, that of Judaism as a swinging pendulum whose arc describes its breadth and rhythm. As an ideal construct, the pendulum is defined as a material particle suspended by a weightless cord, vibrating without friction. To understand the scope of Judaism and its patterns is to follow its swings, which touch the outer edges of its polarities: mysticism and rationalism, naturalism and supernaturalism, humanism and theism, particularism and universalism, ethnicity and religiosity.

To stop that pendulum, to still its motion, to hold it at one point in order to capture its "essence," is to tamper with the vitality and sweep of our religious civilization. Such fixation is idolatrous. One must be open to the swing of the pendulum. We cannot know beforehand how far the pendulum will travel nor what it will include. "There is no way of knowing a priori," Scholem wrote, "what beliefs are possible or impossible within the framework of Judaism." It is not so simple to call this or that un-Jewish. Who better than Scholem himself can testify to the attempts to fixate the pendulum, to dismiss Kabbalah, Hasidism, Jewish mysticism as aberrations of normative Judaism. Who knows a priori what new traditions may be sanctified and what old traditions be recovered?

The real pendulum of Judaism, unlike its ideal construct, is neither weightless nor frictionless. There is no guarantee that it will of itself swing freely forward and backward. We cannot therefore hop a ride on the pendulum, confident that it will not become locked in arresting dogmas. Beyond the development of our own particular theologies, there is a corrective theology to be practiced in order to keep its dialectic integrity. To keep the pendulum free from fixation is a heritage of the rabbinic counterpoint: *Ifcha mistabera*—just the opposite; *aderaba*—to the contrary; *me-idach gisa*—on the other hand. No two swings of the pendulum are identical. The arc of the pendulum does not describe the pagan circle of eternal recurrence. Because the pendulum swings from one pole to another it is, on its return, altered. Because of the contact with the opposite pole, tomorrow's Jewish liberalism and universalism are not likely to be the same as yesterday's. Mutatis mutandis, the same holds for yesterday's and tomorrow's Jewish conservatism and particularism.

We need each other's trope and dialect, for they enrich and refine our own. Was Judaism enriched by the excommunication of Maimonides, Spinoza, the Baal Shem Tov, Mordecai M. Kaplan? Are we enriched by the exclusion of Jewish mysticism or Yiddish secularism? The homily which points to the name of Adonai in its most concentrated form as spelled with two yuds informs us that if the one yud stands above the other, or is too removed from the other, it does not spell the name of God. We witness daily the increasing distancing of Jews. Students in rabbinic, cantorial, Jewish educational schools have no contact with the faculties of other schools of thought. The laity in our synagogue communities are segregated from each other. Jewish young people are kept apart from each other on denominational lines. Hebrew schools, religious schools, day schools, youth groups, summer camps— sponsored by Jewish religious movements—are denominationally apartheid. The threat of schism and the internal segregation of our young people is real. "In time to come your children might speak unto our children, saying, 'what have ye to do with the Lord God of Israel? . . . ye have no part in the Lord' " (Joshua 22:24).

We who owe our fidelity to our own institutions, movements, ideologies are doubly covenanted. We owe loyalty to our alma mater and to our own school of thought. We own a higher fidelity to the One who embraces the multiplicity of views of our people. Our minimal task is to provide vehicles to keep the pendulum swinging, to keep the polarities from polarization, to keep opposite views in contact with each other. We need retreats so that Jews from different institutional backgrounds and schools of thought may celebrate their Jewishness together, learn to pray together, to study together, to argue together. We need networks of lay and professional Jewish statesmen to seek out and deepen the commonalities between us. Sectarianism is a perilous danger and an idolatrous blasphemy in the lives of the people we are ordained to serve.

On the entering portals of our homes a mezuzah containing two biblical passages from the Book of Deuteronomy is affixed. Rashi affirmed that the proper position of the mezuzah on the doorpost is vertical. Does it not declare "when you rise up"? His grandson, Rabbenu Tam, argued that the proper position is horizontal. Is it not written, "when you lie down"? The rabbinic resolution was to place it slanted, with the upper end pointed inward. It is a resolution typical of the Jewish genius to respect and incorporate conflicting judgments. The mezuzah is a stationary image of the dynamic pendulum of Judaism. "Blessed is He who discerns secrets, for the mind of each is different from the other, as is the face different from the other."

LOVE WITH A BEAR HUG
AROUND MY SOUL

Sometime toward the middle of our heated enounter, he threw his arms around me, protesting his love for my *Yiddisher neshamah,* my Jewish soul whose root is traced to Father Abraham. With a firm armlock around my shoulders, he insisted that theology and observances aside, we were, through a spiritual genealogy, connected. I felt caught. To free myself from his grip would appear a rude rejection—who can spurn another's declaration of love? To return his embrace with my own would be false. I felt neither love nor scorn for this intense, bearded rabbi, ten or fifteen years my junior, whom I had never seen before the lecture.

Resigned to accept his unyielding grip, I sensed within me an ambivalence not unlike that of Jacob when meeting with Esau after having wrestled with the anonymous man beside the Jabbok tributary. When the two brothers met they embraced, and one fell upon the other's neck and kissed him. Commentators on the text, noting the peculiar set of dots over the word "kissed" (Genesis 33:4), suggest that the spelling is ambiguous. Was it a brotherly "kiss" or a long-repressed "bite"?

And this man who sat beside me, this warm, effusive rabbi offering me gratuitous forgiveness for my heresies—did he mean to raise me up or hold me down? The conversation roamed, but the rabbi's bear hug remained the dominant memory. That gesture, that body language took on the character of a metaphor for relations of this sort. Love and suffocation, care and intimidation entwined in one pair of sturdy arms.

23

"Understand, Rabbi," he said, "between us, I mean between all Jews, whatever their beliefs or lack of beliefs, there is a kinship. We met at Sinai, you and I. The Rebbe feels that way. All his judgments are rooted in *ahavat yisrael* (love of Israel). There is nothing that I wouldn't do for a fellow Jew. That's where I spend most of my time and energy—at hospitals. And I don't ask whether they are Orthodox or not. They are Jews. That's all I need to know." It went on this way for quite a while. Though he could not understand my understanding of the evolution of Judaism and the values of Jewishness, he unsolicitedly forgave me and reassured me that my soul was loved.

At one point I grew impatient, turned to him, and said, "You say you love my Jewish soul, and I am moved by that. But you have no respect for my Jewish mind, my way of seeing things, my interpretation of Jewish life and law, nor for those of my Jewish mentors. You speak only of your Rebbe and his opinions, wisdoms, and judgments. I understand your trust, faith, love of him, but what of my teachers, who speak to my heart and mind? You love my Jewish soul but credit it with no integrity. Then you quickly dismiss my choices and motivations as ulterior, regarding them either as 'convenient' or as 'alien.' "

He sighed, held my gesturing hand still. "It's not with me or the Rebbe that you have to quarrel. It's with the Lord, with the traditions. Go argue with the Rambam." And he continued in this vein, and I fell into his sing-song style.

"Not so," I answered. "The Rambam would not support you. Certainly not the Rambam of the *Sefer Mada* or the *Guide of the Perplexed,* which you don't teach. Your interpretations are not confirmed by the opinions of a Menachem Meiri, the Malbim, or Rabbi Mecklenberg. Moreover, Rabbi, *mein neshama iz nisht kein rozhenke* (my mind is not a raisin). I have a fine Jewish training, a Jewish upbringing, and a mind of my own."

He interruped me, "You can't compare yourself to the Rebbe. No one can, absolutely no one."

"It's not a matter of comparison. It's a matter of my Jewish understanding, my conscience, convictions, wrestlings, and those who influence me, without coercion or threat."

"There is only one tradition, one law, one way, one guide."

"Would you admit that the Rebbe could be wrong? Can you

conceive that he may in some things be in error? After all, we are all mortal, fallible beings. Would you follow him no matter what?"

He smiled and in a serious, hushed tone confessed, "I'll tell you the truth. I'd rather follow him when he is wrong than follow you when you are right."

It was not spoken in anger. It sort of slipped out and sensing the possible insult in his remarks, he added quickly, "*Chos v'sholum,* I didn't mean to put you down, but with us it is a matter of *emunah,* of faith."

"But I don't mean for you or anyone to follow me on faith. In fact, I always felt that unlike other traditions, Judaism is free of such personality cults, free from the deification of its leaders. I would be afraid if people followed me because of my word. My challenge is to persuade, not to pronounce."

"And where would our people be today if they did not have faith in Moses and had to be persuaded? *Va-yairu ba'adonai u-ve-mosheh avdo*—They believed in God and in Moses, His servant."

"Yes, yet but first they believed in God, and then in Moses."

We traded biblical and rabbinic quotations, scraps of evidence bolstering our respective positions. The hour growing late, we parted, and once again he hugged me and even kissed me on my cheek.

I thought about our conversation and about my reaction to his loving approach. I love to be loved—who doesn't? But not for my metaphysical *neshamah,* not for my floating soul, a form without content, one I inherited without choice from some distant past. My soul is informed by my mind, choices, moral sensibilities, and by real content. I suspect it is easier to love my abstract soul, but true love includes respect for the Jewish concreteness of experiences and decisions. Not love of condescension or domination, but of respect for the integrity of another's motivation and mind. *Ahavat yisrael* is easier to express toward a metaphysical soul than an embodied self. True love is not an acknowledgment of the mystique of their souls' origination but respect for the diginity of their souls' otherness. Better the preservation of space in our togetherness than a smothering intimacy that obliterates all differentiation.

We parted company and I sat up that night wondering about my ambivalent feelings. What had I expected of this man with his God-sanctioned convictions? What could be expected of any absolutist convinced of his revealed truths? Not to share his beliefs is to join the rank of the heretics. Is this not the nature of the true believer? Can the faith of the true believer entertain the smallest possibility of doubt? Faith must be open or shut.

Yet perhaps that characterization of the true believer was false. I had, after all, been raised in Orthodox circles where such dismissals of other judgments were not so cavalierly brandished. I remembered the precious story told to me when I was younger by a firm believer.

This *apikoros,* the village atheist, boasted that he would soon confront the Rebbe with incontrovertible proofs and demonstrations that God does not exist. The villagers loyal to the Rebbe warned him of the planned onslaught. And as sure as the sun stood still at Gibeon, the *apikoros* at midday entered the Rebbe's home with anticipatory glee. The Rebbe welcomed him, and held him off with one word: *efshar* (perhaps). "Perhaps," the Rebbe repeated. With this, the *apikoros* broke into tears and the two of them embraced.

What kind of an answer was "perhaps" *(efshar)* and especially from a man of faith? It is an expression rarely used these days, especially by those who are blessed with apodictic certainty. Absolutists, from the left or right, fideists or atheists, find "perhaps" a stammering admission of weakness. To know that God is or God is not, to know that this is the only way for all people to believe and to practice, must, for them, be attended with inflexible sureness. To them "maybe" betrays the sound of vulnerable openness or hidden pusillanimity. True believers or unbelievers prefer sweeping terms like "everybody" or "nobody," or "always" or "never." Terms like "some" or "sometimes" or "it depends" or "maybe" are buried beneath the crushing rhethoric of absolutism.

But once in a while, "perhaps" may penetrate the interstices of invincible ignorance and cause one to think again. What did the atheist make of the Rebbe's *efshar?* "Perhaps" the Rebbe was not so closed to doubts, or perhaps, demonstrations and disproofs aside, God could really be. Perhaps there is more doubt in belief and more belief in doubt than either fully understood. Perhaps the time has come to remove the heavy armor of infallible sources and personalities and open oneself to listen to another, even to one's inner self.

Respicere, the Latin root of "respect," means to "look again." Respect means to look again at another's argument and to see what lies beneath it. Once, it was told in the name of Menachem Mendel of Kotzk, a believer came to confess to the Rebbe that he could no longer believe. The Rebbe did not throw him out. Instead, he asked him, "Why, my son, can't you believe?"

"Because I doubt that the world has any rhyme or reason. The righteous suffer, the wicked prosper."

"So—why does that concern you?"

"What do you mean, why does that concern me? If there is no justice in the world, I doubt there is a God governing the world."

"So—what do you care if there is no God in the world?"

"Rebbe, if there is no God in the world, my life has no sense, no meaning at all."

"Do you care so much about the world and His existence?"

"With all my heart and soul, Rebbe."

"If you care so much, are pained so much, if you doubt so much, you believe."

There is a modesty in belief, a skepticism in faith—a "perhaps" which leads to God more surely than the arrogance which finds no room for doubt. So it is told that when some of the disciples of a certain Rebbe had to leave the village, they asked the Rebbe for advice about how to find another Rebbe as authentic as he. Their Rebbe counseled, "When you find one, ask whether he ever doubted or ever had strange thoughts in his prayers. If he answers that he has never doubted and never entertained strange thoughts, know that he is not to be followed." Faith is a peculiar gift, not the last word nor the first. Faith is a process which grows with experience and reflection. It is no enemy of doubt but welcomes it as an ally for deeper understanding.

Faith is a window
to be opened and shut.
Stuck shut, it keeps out fresh air,
Stuck open, it invites the blustery wind.

Stuck shut, it shields the inhabitants but stagnates the air.
Stuck open, it invites congealment.

Faith is a sliding window
    to be opened and shut
        with courage and wisdom.

Since my encounter with my chasidic friend, I have had occasion
to wonder about our separate ways. I wondered about our upbring-
ing and how it may have affected our attitude towards pluralism.
And I wondered as well about our different fears for the future of
Judaism. Let me begin by explaining the natural upbringing of my
Jewish pluralism.

I was raised in a yiddishist Zionist household, influenced by
Orthodox grandparents, trained in a Yiddish shul, Talmud Torah,
Orthodox yeshivah, and Conservative theological seminary. The
Jewish thinkers who have molded my understanding of Judaism
are as varied as Y. L. Peretz, J. B. Soloveitchik, Ahad Ha-am,
Israel Salanter, Martin Buber, and Mordecai M. Kaplan. For me,
pluralism is not an ideology urging toleration towards other approaches to Jewish life outside my own denominational circle.
Pluralism lives in me, an internal dialectic, enabling me to express
a variety of Jewish dispositions, moods, and preferences, at different times, differently accentuated. I am drawn to structure and
spontaneity, "shukling" and quiet meditation, faith and doubt. I
am affiliated and identified as a Conservative Jew, but that definition barely describes the larger ecumenicity of my Jewish self.
Pluralism has enriched my Jewishness, and I would transmit that
advantage to others.

We are not born pluralists anymore than we are born monothe-
ists. Pluralism has to be taught and experienced from within our
institutions and denominational fidelities. Pluralism has to be
taught to others and cultivated within oneself.

Particularly in these angry days it is an imperative of high moral
order to learn how to apply the dictum of "assessing the other
according to his/her merits" (le-chaf zechut) to the other's ideological and institutional attachments. It is important to learn how to
value not only the juridical fact of one's born Jewishness ("A Jew
is a Jew even if he transgresses") but his chosen form of Jewishness
according to its noblest intent. Such appreciation does not entail
our agreement, endorsement, or financial support of our fellow
Jew's commitment. Santayana wrote that "agreement is the sincer-

est form of friendship." I would qualify his adjective. Agreement is merely the easiest form of friendship. Appreciation of the other does not mean agreement, but it does require respect for his decision, and respect means the effort to understand the fears and hopes which surround his beliefs and practices—especially his fears, for fears reveal the vulnerability of others. Fears enable more empathic access to a fellow Jew's formally stated positions. Understanding fears humanizes the theory and practice that frequently appear as hardened obduracy. There is a kinship in fear even when the proposed antidotes set us apart. What do they fear, those "extremists," those "middle-roaders," those "fanatics," those "unbelievers"?

Some fear anomie, the rootlessness of not belonging, and find solace in structure, in rigid adherence to authority and law. Others fear the heavy hand of authoritarianism, the weight that grinds conscience to the dust and are wary of spokesmen who mandate belief and practice in God's name.

Some fear the reduction of Judaism to a metalanguage, a way of speaking and consequently the avoidance of practiced observances. Others fear more the ritual behaviorism that ignores reason and feeling and turns religious sensibility into obedient, mechanical practice.

Some fear the dizzying heights of universalism clutching the air of abstraction, losing their footing on particular soil. Others fear the suffocation of parochialism that transforms a world people into corporate narcissists.

Some fear the obsession with "relevance" that turns eternal truths into the putty of fads. Others fear the veneration of habit, the confusion of antiquity with authenticity.

Some fear the distillation of Judaism into ethical culture alone, while others fear the enforced muteness of the prophetic voice.

Some fear the unmoored idealism which encourages us to live with our heads in heaven, betraying the realistic ground of a people's security, while others worry that the territorial imperative has desensitized our moral sense. Identifying and understanding the fears which tacitly inform all our theories and practices may help us develop a warmer and more natural pluralistic outlook.

Another side to the training of the pluralist sensibility is the willing suspension of faultfinding. With that in mind, I once an-

nounced a series of lecture-sermons on "The Best of Judaism":
the Best of Orthodox Judaism, the Best of Conservative Judaism,
the Best of Reform Judaism, the Best of Reconstructionist
Judaism, the Best of Satmar Judaism, the Best of Lubavitch
Judaism, the Best of Secular Judaism—seven varieties of Jewish
interpretations.

The exercise was designed to overcome invidious comparisons,
and the "gerrymandering" that assigns the best to our own jurisdiction and leaves all the rest to the others. It confronts the avowed
pluralist with a series of questions. Can I preach and teach another
approach to Jewish theology and observances without condescension? Can I suspend all negativities about the other's theory and
practice, and so allow their strengths and affirmations to shine
forth? Can I identify the elements which attract other fellow Jews
to these movements and respond to their needs?

In the course of preparing for these lectures, I experienced the
temptation to find faults in other movements, institutions and
leaders. Somehow their weaknesses were taken as my strength,
their failings as my victories, their flawed projects as justification
for my doing nothing about the problems they sought to address.
With twisted logic, I drew dangerous conclusions. If they were
wrong, I was right; if they faltered, I stood erect. The conclusions
did not follow. Erik Erikson once commented, "You have heard of
the rabbi who felt inhibited when he was asked to make a speech
in heaven. 'I am only good at refutation,' he said." Refutation had
replaced affirmation. Could I make a speech without refutation?

The exercise in pluralism was not designed to kill the critical
sense or to subdue the reservations or objections. I bracketed
these, holding them in abeyance because they tend to eclipse the
brightness of the other side. The task was to humanize our disagreements, clarify our own fidelities and acknowledge the plenti-
tude of our old-new traditions.

The pluralistic exercise celebrated no piety of polytheism—all
the gods are gods. It was not meant to deny conflicting preferences.
But, in the preparation for the series, I sensed the transcendent
unity in Judaism, a confirmation of Chesterson's insight that "heresies are splinters of the whole."

The empathic exercise is not for rabbis alone. Through such
projects, havurot and adult education circles could serve the well-

being of Jewish community and the self-understanding of the individual Jew. No one, I suspect, will be converted from his denominational proclivity to another, though it would be far from calamitous if such a change took place out of conviction. More likely, the attitude towards alternative ways of Jewish believing, thinking, and behaving would elevate one's Jewish commitment.

JUDAISM: FROM EITHER/OR
TO BOTH/AND

INTRODUCTION

Jewish thinkers feel compelled to get at the "essence of Judaism."
What characterizes the distinctiveness of the Jewish belief system?
What is the Jewish position on the Messiah, resurrection, immortality, revelation, redemption? How does Judaism decide such
issues as capital punishment, birth control legislation, pacifism,
nuclear testing? And what, after four thousand years, is the answer
to the question, "Who is a Jew?"

Those thinkers who know the character of Judaism find it difficult to present essences or definitive Jewish positions on these
issues without qualifications. Many of the questioners, however,
have little tolerance for the real universe of ambiguities and ambiv-
alences. They want "yes" or "no" answers without "however"
and "on the other hand" qualifications. It is tempting to surrender
to the call for simple answers, and some yield to the pressure and
pronounce positions in the name of "Torah-true Judaism," the
"authentic tradition," or "normative" Judaism. They claim that
while they articulate mainstream Judaism, the other dissenting
voices are minor rivulets of little consequence or, worse, deviant
paths to apostasy. Closer examination of the course of Jewish
history and thought, however, reveals the windings of a broad river
with multiple branches running into the sea. Another's tributary is
my mainstream and vice versa. Open to the rich diversity of Jewish
ideas, ideals, and practices, we observe that the streams of Jewish
mysticism mingle with the waters of Jewish rationalism, Hasidism

32

and Kabbalah alongside Maimonides and the Haskalah, the analytic temper of the Vilna Gaon joined with the ecstatic passion of the Baal Shem Tov. That which yesterday was excommunicated as an aberration from Judaism is tomorrow celebrated as the vital undercurrent of Jewish faith.

To be faithful to the multidimensional character of Judaism is to make it difficult to respond simplistically, to offer answers with apodictic certainty and finality. To be open to the evolutionary character of the tradition presents an obstacle to those who would settle for doctrinaire denominational definitions. Judaism is an old-new religious civilization reflecting the ideologies, beliefs, and practices of a world people whose career extends across many continents and centuries. It mirrors a variety of responses to the challenges of different environments. Beside the still waters of Spain's Golden Age breathes the calm spirit of rationalism; with the catastrophe of the Inquisition and expulsion, the waters rage with expectations of messianic redemption and the fantasies of mystic salvation. Jewish theologies and philosophies respond to the different moods of a people lonely in the desert, joyous in the vineyards, frightened in the valley, exultant on the plains. Portions of Judaism are consequently this-worldly and otherworldly, ascetic and materialistic, ethnocentric and universalistic.

In this essay we have sought to avoid the hard disjunctions that cast Judaism into forced either/or options. We direct attention to some of the biases which split reason from emotion, law from spirit, ethnicity from religion, nationalism from universalism, ritual from morality. The polemical arguments between liberal and conservative viewpoints, and Jewish and Christian perspectives, have distorted the intriguing dialectical interplay in Jewish thought which allows seemingly contradictory elements to complement each other. We touch lightly upon some of the more celebrated illustrations of prima facie internal conflicts which, seen with a wider lens, are revealed as elements of the civilizational whole of Judaism.

EITHER/OR POLEMICS

Liberal authors characterize Jewish ethics as idealistic, universal, this-worldly, optimistic, rational, anti-ascetic, humanistic.[1] Writers of the Orthodox school depict the same subject matter quite differently. To them it appears otherworldly, particularistic, largely concerned with ritual, law, and obedience to the divine will. With notable exceptions, Christian theologians find Judaism abounding in ceremonialism, legalistic, parochial, formalistic.[2]

These conflicting presentations of Jewish ethics spawn an array of polemics and apologetics. Each polemicist, hiding his own vulnerability, searches for the Achilles heel of the other. The apologist, defending his position through artful theological gerry-mandering, assigns the best portions to his own jurisdiction while projecting the worst onto the lot of his adversary. Such battles have led to convenient but misleading dualisms: law vs. spirit, nationalism vs. universalism, formalism vs. inwardness, material-ism vs. idealism, justice vs. love. Corroborative evidence is carved from the huge and manifold tradition, some citations exaggeratedly pronounced, others chipped away to fall unnoticed by the side. To the uninitiated, Jewish ethics then appears as an unrelieved para-gon of virtue or a monstrous anachronism. He is either amazed by its contemporaneity or repelled by its primitive crudeness.[3]

Upon closer scrutiny, the student will discover that each inter-pretation is capable of producing an array of scriptural and tal-mudic quotations and utterances vindicating either position. As Professor Louis Ginzberg once noted, "The Devil can quote scripture and were he more knowledgeable he would quote the Talmud as well." Supporting quotations are easy to produce. For one thing, there is little apparent concern in the tradition for a systematic treatment of ethics or theology. Yet another factor militating against neatly packaged catechisms of ethics is the long and varied history of an old-new people.[4] It should not be surpris-ing that different levels of civilization and divergent social and economic situations produce a diversity of ethical response. To seize upon one period or one disposition towards ethics as "typi-cal" or "dominant" invariably misrepresents the organic whole.

To appreciate the holistic character of Jewish ethics, it is better to abandon these partisan, single-stranded characterizations which lay exclusive claim to represent the authentic tradition. We have before us two principal sources to draw upon in portraying the nature of Jewish ethics: the maxims and epigrams aphoristically strewn throughout the entire body of the literature; and the ethics, both implied and articulated, in the codes of law and ritual practice.

We cannot produce without distortion an undiversified Jewish system of ethics out of this civilizational complexity. A truer picture will portray a gamut of pluralistic moods and dialectical exchanges reflecting the richness of the Jewish experience.

LIBERAL AND CONSERVATIVE VIEWPOINTS

The Humanistic Bias

Most modern liberal ethicists attempt to demonstrate that Jewish ethics is optimistic, this-worldly, and peculiarly congenial to a naturalistic approach.[5] This version of Jewish ethics is bolstered by selecting such cheerful citations as follows:

Biblical
> Be fruitful, and multiply, and replenish the earth, and subdue it.
> —Genesis 1:28

> And God created man in His own image, in the image of God created He him.
> —Genesis 1:27

> Ye shall therefore keep My statutes and My ordinances which, if a man do, he shall *live* by them.
> —Leviticus 18:5

Rabbinic
> Every man will be held accountable before God for all the permitted things he beheld in life and did not enjoy.
> —Yerushalmi, *Kiddushin,* end

> God's commandments are intended to enhance the value and enjoyment of life, but not to mar it and make it gloomy.
> —*Yoma* 85a

> The spirit of God rests upon man neither in a state of gloom nor in a state of indolence, but solely in the joy of performing a duty.
> —*Shabbat* 30b

> Rabbi Samuel declared: 'He that fasts is called a sinner,' basing this on an interpretation of Numbers 6:11.
> —*Ta'anit* 11a

The liberal, humanistic strain is as unmistakable as it is one-sided. To cite but a few illustrations of what has been omitted by the liberal view:

Biblical

Cursed is the ground for thy sake; in toil shalt thou eat of it all the days of thy life. Thorns also and thistles shall it bring forth to thee. . . . In the sweat of thy face shalt thou eat bread.

—Genesis 3:17–19

. . . for the imagination of man's heart is evil from his youth.

—Genesis 8:21

Rabbinic

Rabbi Jacob said: "This world is like a vestibule before the world-to-come."

—*Ethics of the Fathers* [*Pirke Avot*] 4:21–22

In order to be holy it is necessary to abstain even from things that are permitted.

—*Yevamot* 20a

This is the way of Torah: a morsel of bread with salt must thou eat, and water by measure must thou drink, thou must sleep upon the ground and live a life of anguish the while thou toilest in the Torah.

—*Pirke Avot* 6:4[6]

For two and a-half years, debate between the two rabbinic schools of Shammai and Hillel raged as to the merit of life. A vote was finally taken and it was decided that "it were better for man not to have been created than to be created, but now that he has been created let him investigate his past deeds or, as others say, let him examine his future actions."

—*Eruvin* 13b[7]

Rabbi Eleazer declared: 'He that fasts is called holy,' interpreting Numbers 6:5 for his support.

—*Ta'anit* 11a

Rabbi Judah the Prince said: "He who accepts the pleasures of this world is deprived of the pleasures of the world to come, and vice versa."

—*Avot de-Rabbi Nathan* 1:28, 43a

When confronted by such illustrations contrary to the humanistic mood, liberal theoreticians invoke quantitative and/or qualitative criteria for determining their true weight. Typically, the nineteenth-century Jewish philosopher Moritz Lazarus explained, "But in all the controversies, the party of energetic action and joyous living is represented by the best names and outnumbers by far its antagonists."[8] This optimistic bias sets aside the ascetic traditions of the Rechabites, Essenes and Nazirites, and the talmudic record which cites prominent and compelling rabbinic personalities who not only advocated but practiced a quite severe asceticism. Among the latter are Mar, son of Rabina, who sat in fast the entire year excepting a few festivals (*Pesaḥim* 68b),[9] and Rabbi Judah, the compiler of the Mishnah, who proudly practiced asceticism as evidence of his piety.[10]

The mystic saints in Jewish post-talmudic life who advocated asceticism, and the writings of a number of eminent Jewish theologians and moralists cannot be so readily dismissed. The tenth-century Ibn Paquda includes "renunciation of luxuries and love of the world" as the ninth fundamental principle of the religious "duties of the heart" in his influential work of the same name.[11] Moses Hayyim Luzzatto, the eighteenth-century author of *The Path of the Upright, Messilat Yesharim,* demonstrates that "abstinence is the beginning of saintliness," that man should therefore "avoid contact with worldly affairs as much as possible."[12]

The preceding illustrates how blinded we are to the half-conscious selection of sentiments and heroes we prefer. It was the philosopher Schopenhauer who cavalierly labeled Judaism as optimistic. But much of the optimism is the creation of thinkers who have absorbed the values of the Enlightenment. The age of confidence in human progress which experienced the joy of this-worldly life understandably found little interest in the talmudic heeding that there be "no unrestrained laughter in this world" (*Berachot* 31a). The essays composed and sermons preached in that hopeful era filtered the scriptural and talmudic sea for corroborative texts congenial to the spirit of their own age. Given the absence of structured ethical theory in Judaism and the casual and unsystematic form of ethics in traditional literature, these constructions selected from the classics were readily woven together to form an ethics claiming "major tendencies." By virtue of repetition and the acceptance of this-worldly humanism by the contemporary Jewish audience, these interpretations were presented as the sole authoritative version of the authentic Jewish tradition. We know, however, that in the insulation of the ghetto and in moments of medieval catastrophe, for example, quite contrary versions were acknowledged as authentic.[13]

Ethical Absolutes vs. Contextual Relativism

Conservative interpreters of the tradition tend to stress the absolute character of revealed law. Liberal interpreters of the tradition point to the qualifications which beset the abstract law once it is contextually applied. On closer examination, the tradition appears as a "relative absolutism" wherein the general principles remain constant but are softened by consideration of the particular situations to which they are applied. Jewish ethics allows itself few immutable absolutes. The notable exceptions are the three absolutes which prohibit murder, incest, and idolatry. Whereas ritual ordinances of the highest importance may be transgressed in the interest of the conservation of health and life, the aforementioned cardinal sins are excluded. "We may cure ourselves with all [forbidden] things except idolatry, incest and murder."[14] Yet, in the face of the brutal Hadrianic persecutions, the rabbinic sense of realism attenuated even these absolutes. Consideration of the public or private character of the transgression, distinctions as to who decreed the transgression, the motivation of the transgressor, the number and nature of the public witnessing the prohibited act were introduced to qualify these absolutes.[15] In these ways, the rabbinic exercise of the law encouraged reason and experience to free men from blind obedience to unyielding categorical imperatives.

Religious and Autonomous Ethics

Jewish ethics belongs to the category of religious or theistic ethics. In philosophic literature, this category is contrasted with that of natural or secular ethics. The genesis of and sanction for secular ethics is said to lie in experience, intuition, human reason, and appeal to natural consequences, individual and social, physical and psychological.[16] Secular humanistic ethics prides itself on its autonomous and therefore uncoerced manner of arriving at the ethical decision. Secular morality declares that it does not cringe before the voice thundering from above. It is not bound to the external constraints of the Other's Will. By contrast, theistic ethics legitimizes its moral philosophy by appealing to its Divine Source, by claims of revelatory experiences, or by virtue of the logic which derives ethical principles from those of theology. For its part, secular humanistic ethics dismisses theistic ethics as either arguing in circular fashion or as "pseudo-heteronomous morality" (Von Hartmann), that is, unreflected obedience to an external Divine Imperative. In response, theistic ethics maintains that the secular effort in ethics leads to the conceit of anthropocentrism and unbridled subjectivism.

Is Jewish ethics, then, autonomous or heteronomous, a product of human reason or divine fiat? The answer will not feed into the either/or framework. The hard-and-fast distinctions of heteronomy (subjection to the law of another) and autonomy are largely unknown in Jewish ethics despite the efforts of Moritz Lazarus and others to read the Kantian ethics of autonomy into the rabbinic tradition.[17] While Jewish ethics is traditionally believed to be derived from God's revealed will, its claimed origin does not contradict the free exercise of man's moral reason. The human intellect is a divine gift, and man's autonomous conscience is a manifestation of his divine image. Human moral discoveries may be seen as one side of the coin of revelation. If God's voice is to be distinguished from the ventriloquism of Satan, revelation must be examined by moral reason and adapted into moral law. If fidelity to the covenant is not servile acquiescence to supernatural power, reason and moral sensibility must be elevated to sacred status.

The instance of the universal Noahide laws is instructive. How do the rabbis understand the character of the seven Noahide laws which apply to mankind in general, i.e., the prohibitions against shedding blood, robbery, idolatry, adultery, blasphemy, and eating flesh from live animals, and the injunction to set up courts of justice? Are these laws autonomous, inasmuch as their origin is pre-Sinaitic and no special revelation of these natural principles is explicitly recorded in the Bible, or are they heteronomous, derived from God's will? The rabbis and the medieval Jewish philosophers insisted that these natural laws were derived from the biblical verse in Genesis 2:16 and are thus divinely ordained.[18] Maimonides insists that only those who believe that these seven Noahide laws are revealed by God in the Torah will merit a share in the world-to-come, the desserts of the righteous gentiles of the world. Moritz Lazarus, however, argued that Jewish ethics is autonomous and was determined to show that "reason [as opposed to revelation] was the source of his [Abraham's] ethical instruction."[19] To support his Kantian bias, Lazarus quotes an oft-cited mishnaic passage: "Abraham observed the whole Torah before it was given." Heteronomists quote another *mishnah,* one which maintains that Abraham's practice was divinely ordained, on the basis of the scriptural verse, "because that Abraham obeyed My voice, and kept My charge, My commandments, My statutes and My laws" (Genesis 26:5).[20]

The rabbis appear to be oblivious to the bifurcated realms of nature and the supernatural in the sense that contemporary theologians employ them, just as they did not see autonomous and heteronomous ethics as contraries. Natural law is congenial to divinity because "the earth is the Lord's." Chastity could be learned from the dove, modesty from the cat, not to rob from the ant, propriety from the cock, and "if they had not been written [in Scripture] they should have been written."[21] Man's discoveries in nature are no blasphemy to God but to His glory. The issues which are presented as hard disjunctives, either/or, are reconciled by viewing them as different aspects of the same thing. After all, the reason and ethics of man flow from a being created in the image of God. In the relationship between man and God, nothing divine is untouched by nature, and nothing natural is untouched by the divine. In the realm of ethics, that which God wills is good and that which is good is the will of God.

THE CHRISTIAN-JEWISH POLEMIC

Polemics introduce invidious distinctions. Apologetics return the compliment in kind. Christian theologians, from Paul onward, have for the most part felt the need to loosen Christianity from its antecedent anchorage, to prove its independence and its advancement over the "old" tradition. Ancient Israel is forever portrayed as obsolescent, "concerned with rites and ceremonies, with the maintenance of obsolete, useless and even harmless customs; it has been narrowly nationalistic; it has been socially and intellectually unprogressive";[22] "The principle of love . . . and the principle of moral inwardness" are distinctive Christian contributions.[23] In defense of these harsh critiques, many apologists fall into the very either/or trap set by the polemicists and seek to deny the nationalistic, ritualistic, legalistic character of Jewish ethics. In such a debate, both extremes err. The distortion, common both to those who overrate and to those who berate Judaism, is the assumption that love of people and mankind, law and spirit, ceremony and inwardness, cultus and social consciousness are inherently incompatible. Both defenders and detractors tend to split what is organically whole in Judaism, each taking one or the other part of the disjunction as the essence of Judaism. To worship the part as if it were the whole is to sacrifice at the arena of idolatry. Within Jewish religious civilization, these segregated features strain and struggle but coexist. The following sections touch briefly upon the alleged contradictions within Judaism.

Nation and Humanity

The rabbinic mind sensed no contradiction in holding that Israel stands in special relation to God and holding that "the pious and virtuous of all nations participate in eternal bliss" (*Sifra* on Leviticus 19:18). The prophet who spoke lovingly of God's interest in raising the fallen tabernacle of David could still rebuke the "chosen." "Are ye not as children of the Ethiopians unto Me, O children of Israel?" (Amos 9:7). For the rabbis, the same prophet who conceived of Israel as the Suffering Servant persecuted by the nations could still speak of God's blessing "Egypt, My people, and Assyria, the work of My hands" (Isaiah 19:25). The evident particularism in Judaic literature does not preclude the High Holy Day prayers that God impose His awe upon all mankind and that "all Thy works may revere Thee . . . that they may form a single band to do Thy will with a perfect heart." So, too, rabbinic law ordains that giving charity to the poor, burying the dead, attending funerals, eulogizing the deceased, consoling the bereaved are to be extended to the non-Jew as well as to the Jew.[24] The particularistic rabbinic imagination is capable of spinning a legend of ethics in which God chastizes the ministering angels singing a hymn of praise over the destruction of the Egyptians in the Red Sea: "My children lie drowned in the sea and you would sing hymns of triumph?'' (*Megillah* 10b). To be sure, the danger looms that love of peoplehood may gain the ascendancy and degenerate into zealous ethnocentrism; but the risk is no more real than that universalism may turn into religious imperialism.

Ritual and Ethics

In the relationship between ritual and ethics, something of the polemicist's assumption seeps into the defense walls of the apologists. Theologians on the defense are found interpreting Jewish religion as "essentially . . . the emergence of ethical ideals out of a background of purely ritual and ceremonial observances."[25] The apology thereby accepts the strange logic which sets up ethics in opposition to ritual by placing each in a separate stage, one primitive (ritualistic), the other emergent (ethical). In truth, however, the hard disjunctives separating rite and righteousness, cult and conscience, are not so pronounced in biblical and talmudic literature. Within the breadth of the same biblical chapter, arational and amoral ritual law prohibiting the wearing of wool and linen together is coupled with the moral concern which enjoins the removal of young ones or eggs from the nest in the presence of the mother bird.[26]

The prophets condemn the hypocrisy and mechanism of ritual, but their vision aspires to sacrifice *with* mercy, adoration *with* charity, rite *with* justice, form *with* inwardness. Statute and ordinance of both ethical and ritual significance lay equal claim to divine sanction. The rabbis admonish man to be "heedful of a light precept as of a grave one" (*Pirke Avot* 2:1).

Ritual observance itself was invested with so great a degree of ethical purpose that the two were regarded as inseparable. "For indeed, what difference does it make to God how we slaughter an animal or of what kind of food we partake, except that He desires by such laws and regulations to benefit His creatures, to purify our hearts and to ennoble our characters."[27] Ritual observance is variously taken as a pedagogic means to instruct man in self-control, as obedience to divine law, as hygienic principles, as repudiation of idolatry, etc.[28]

While ritual frequently serves an indispensable function as an active reminder intensifying ethical resolutions, it is dispensable when its observance would violate ethical principle. "Even the entire body of Biblical precepts and rituals are not equal to one ethical principle.''[29] Respect for the personal dignity of a human being supersedes a negative biblical injunction.[30]

The obduracy with which ritual observance is often maintained strongly suggests that there is more here than ritual law for its own sake. Observance or abandonment of ritual is not solely an issue of religious ideology. Many a ritual came to be associated with the supreme virtue of loyalty, and often a history of martyrdom added emotive value to the ritual far beyond the initial intention. The rabbis wisely observed that "every commandment for which the Israelites gave their lives in times of persecution they now observe openly; the others have grown effete among them.''[31] The religious struggle in the Hanukkah story was initiated by ritual struggles whose symbolic meaning was intertwined with the issue of loyalty to one's own people. To have the flesh of swine forced down one's throat was experienced as defilement of one's fidelity to people and covenant. In moments of religious persecution, "even to change one's shoe strap'' may demand martyrdom.[32]

In much the same way, Pauline antinomianism and anticeremonialism may have given additional impetus to the conservation of rituals. The retention of many ceremonial laws, following the destruction of the Temple, was invested with a nation's survival value. The early Christian opposition to dietary laws and circumcision was considered a double-pronged attack upon the efforts to preserve the peoplehood of Judaism and the relevance of the tradition and rabbinic law. Ceremonial laws, more than the more abstract universal laws of ethics, were focused upon because they possessed indigenous national symbolism. Their importance reached unparalleled heights as unifying and stabilizing factors, especially after political sovereignty was lost or, as in the Diaspora, where both territorial and political integrity were absent. The value of Jewish rituals was not only significant as a response to religious imperatives, but as an expression of the ethics of loyalty as well. It became important for the rabbis to insist that Abraham, though living ages before the Sinaitic revelation, had observed all the precepts and regulations of the law,[33] though earlier tradition assured his justification by faith alone.[34] For the Pauline principle, setting up the justification of faith over that of works, sought its sanction from the merit of the pre-Sinaitic religious heroes of the

Bible such as Abraham. "Therefore it is of faith, that it might be
by grace . . . not to that only which is of the law but to that also
which is of the faith of Abraham, who is the father of us all."[35] So
the cleavage between ritual and ethical law was introduced to
polemics over the issue of the justification by faith or by works. In
this manner, ritual works may have been catapulted to a level of
importance nearly eclipsing the sphere of ethics.[36]

Law and Theology

Partly because of this historical pitting of Christian creed and faith
against Jewish deed and act, and partly because of Judaism's
inherent distrust of abstract theory, it is law which identifies the
dominant trait in the Jewish ethic. The Christian antithesis of faith
and works finds its Jewish analogue in the debate over which is
more important in the pursuit of the religious life: the study of the
law or the practice of good deeds.[37] In the talmudic controversy
over which is more important, study or doing, Rabbi Tarfon
emphasizes study while Rabbi Akiva insists upon doing. But then
"they all agreed that study was greater, for it led to doing."[38]

It seems more accurate, then, to speak of Jewish ethics as rooted
in religious law than of its modern formulation as essentially
"theologic."[39] Judaism's religious ethics is not theological in the
sense that Aquinas's systematization of Christian ethics is theological. The problems surrounding evil, atonement, sin, free will in
Judaism developed less as metaphysical or theological issues than
as issues of moral law. The medieval endeavors to theologize
Judaism, to extrapolate a system of belief, were mainly abortive.

The legal character of Jewish ethics does not lessen its implicit
theocentric source. But while the legitimization of halachah, or
law, was viewed as dependent upon the wisdom of a divine ruler
who revealed His will, the theological implications were taken for
granted and not made into dogma. The law was Judaism's applied
theology. The aspirations of the Bible and ideals of the prophets
were there; there was no question of enduring legitimacy. The law
sought to rescue the ethical insights of the prophets from the
mistiness of generalized goodwill and utopian imagination. The
excitement and drama of prophetic denunciation and vision were
translated into prescribed, detailed, concrete, daily activity. Goodness and virtue required more than the good intentions with which

the road to moral laxity is so liberally paved. If ideals were not to go up in the smoke of pious verbiage, fences must be erected to guide the wayward, and transgressors made to sense the reality of this-worldly punishment. "The task of prophecy," declares a talmudic passage, "was taken from the prophets and given to the wise men," to promulgate and enforce regulatory law.[40]

Such guiding principles of ethics as the conservation of health, life, and property and their use for the ennoblement of man and society were concretized into legal precepts. The issue of philanthropy, for example, was not left solely to the whim and caprice of the individual. Laws of tithing and restrictions even as to the generosity of the charity given were articulated. Man should not "squander more than one-fifth of his wealth, lest he himself becomes indebted to society."[41] The levitical formula "to love one's neighbor as oneself" was not allowed to waste away into pious declaration. The rights of adjoining neighbors were spelled out pragmatically in the Talmud. A property owner has a prior claim over any other person to purchase property adjoining his. If the owner, lacking neighborly feeling, ignores his neighbor's rights by selling the property to a third person, the latter may be compelled to turn over the bought property to the adjacent neighbor for the purchasing price.[42] Theological ethics embraced reality through the implementation of law in the daily activities between man and man.

It is undeniable that there are dangers of a law-abiding ethic turning into a monument of inflexible injunctions and prohibitions. The spirit may turn into an empty word and the law may congeal into an impersonal letter. Spontaneity and inwardness in ethical decision may shrivel into a deadening conformity to the book of statutes. Law as instrument can, with imposing power, turn into the end itself; the noble search for God's will may deteriorate to a prosaic casuistry. The Talmud itself cautions, "For those who make a right use of the law, it is a medicine for life; for those who make a wrong use, it is a drug for death."[43]

Many of these dangers have indeed engulfed the consecrated end of Jewish law. The further removed from the sovereignty of natural community, the more stringent grows the conservative impulse, the more timid the initiation of changes and amendments. Dependence upon the past for authentic rendition of the law and reliance upon the talmudic rabbis "greater in number and wisdom than we" increased. The liberating character of classic rabbinic law was threatened.

The Word of God and the Commentary of Man

The Christian characterization of the Jewish law as oppressive, and of the Pharisaic rabbis as narrow-minded legalists, distorted the liberating and democratizing character of the halakhah. One of the consequences of the Pharisaic approach to Bible study was its popularization among the people. The democratization of learning weakened the influence of miracle-men and their charismatic magnetism. The text, not the prophet, was called holy, perfect, divine, and the text was open to all. Neither voices from heaven moving carob trees nor falling walls held still could detract from the law based on verse and chapter, and applied contextually by human intelligence.[44] Interpreters of the text, often locked in conflicting judgments, were equally regarded: "These and these are both the words of the living God."[45]

The law, in the hands of the rabbinic scholars, humanized revelation, allowed it growth, continuity, and change. God's wisdom was not exhausted with the theophany at Sinai. "Things not revealed to Moses were revealed to Akiva."[46] This, the rabbis explained, was due to the omniscience of His word. Divine truth, if given at once, would overwhelm a generation and congeal the hearts of a nation with fear.[47]

With such a concept of progressive revelation, the rabbis could free the people from priestly and patrician bibliolatry.[48] They could transform the pentateuchal *lex talionis* (the so-called eye-for-an-eye law of retaliation) into a complex code entailing monetary compensation in consideration for the pain, unemployment, medical expenditures, and humiliation suffered by the victim. They could, through the subtleties of hermeneutics, so qualify the conditions under which the biblical "stubborn and rebellious son," "idolatrous city," and "leprous house" were to be condemned that they became de facto unenforceable.[49] These laws, it was explained, were made to function for the benefit of jurisprudential theory. The cited biblical instances themselves "never were nor will be." The reason for their preserve was purely theoretical. Their purpose was for "you to study and receive thereby reward."[50] In this manner, halakhah was able to circumvent the

Deuteronomic law (15:1–2) which canceled all debts in the sabbatical year by the imaginative institution of Hillel's *prosbul* that authorizes a rabbinic tribunal to collect the debts. A verse from the Book of Psalms (119:126), "It is time for Thee, Lord, to work; for they have made void Thy law," was audaciously mistranslated to mean that for the sake of God there are times when it is permissible to set aside or amend the commandments of God enjoined in His law.[51]

Both/And

There are scholarly as well as pragmatic reasons to resist a characterization of Jewish ethics neatly tailored to our particular bias. The rabbis, judges, philosophers whose spirit is reflected in Judaism did not consciously sit down to create a uniform and unambiguous code of ethics. The civilizational character of Jewish ethics cannot be simply located. It is better apprehended when viewed as an indispensable part of an organic totality which weaves jurisprudence and theology, legend and philosophy into a religious civilizational fabric. Such a schema exhibits the generalized aim of Jewish ethical life: *kiddush ha-Shem,* the sanctification of God's name, binding heaven with earth, countenancing no rupture in God's universe, transforming the secular into the holy, knitting together the torn fragments of what was originally whole, praying towards the day when His name shall be One. Sanctification uses every means at its command: prayer and charity, piety and social action, body and soul, heart and mind.

The ethics of Judaism clings therefore to both prophet and priest; holds both the love of Israel and that of mankind; believes both in the world-to-come and in the imperatives to labor in this world; remembers the power of human freedom and recalls its frustrating limitations; is both God-centered and aware of the centrality of the self. These conjunctions are not taken by the tradition as paralyzing paradoxes throwing man into despair. They are complementary values, expressions of a healthy tradition, rooted in the twin principles of reality and ideality, in what is and what ought to be. They manifest the dialectic of love and wisdom which reflects the complexity and maturity of life. Mature living and mature religion is not either/or. Polarities need not turn into polarizations, nor dualities into dualisms, nor ideologies into segregating sects.

NOTES

1. See Samuel Schulman's popular essay "Jewish Ethics," reflecting the liberal reform approach to the subject, in *Popular Studies in Judaism*.

2. Notable among these exceptions are G. F. Moore and R. T. Herford.

3. Illustrations of the Kantian formulation of Jewish ethics are conspicuous in Lazarus's *The Ethics of Judaism*, Kaufmann Kohler's *Jewish Theology* ("The Ethics of Judaism and the Kingdom of God") and Emil Hirsch's "Ethics" in the *Jewish Encyclopedia*.

4. Biblical ethics alone includes a period ranging from primitive times to the second century of the common era. Not all of this is of one coherent mood. It contains period ethics of the priestly theocracy with those of the Prophets and Wisdom series. To this must be added the centuries of the talmudic era (ending about 500 C.E.), the philosophic efforts of the Middle Ages, the mysticism of Kabbalah, the romance of Hasidism, the period of Enlightenment, Reform, and the contemporary religious and secular philosophies. For the sake of economy and because works on Jewish ethics usually restrict themselves to the major sources of the Bible and Talmud, we have concentrated on these classic periods.

5. See Van Meter Ames's review of Israel Mattuck's *Jewish Ethics* for such a version. The review may be found in the *Menorah Journal*, Spring–Summer 1955.

6. Israel Mattuck's apology for this dictum seeks to soften its ascetic tone by asserting, "This should probably be interpreted not absolutely but relatively." *Jewish Ethics*, p. 139.

7. C. Montefiore, commenting on this pessimistic note, apologetically assures the reader that "the passage is clearly a record of some famous dialectical discussion, without any true bearing upon the arguer's *real* views about actual life." *A Rabbinic Anthology* (London, 1938), p. 539.

8. M. Lazarus. *The Ethics of Judaism*, vol. 2, p. 120.

9. *Berakhot* 30b, where Rabbi Johanan, Rabbi Ashi, and others assent to this mournful attitude.

10. *Ketubot* 104a.

11. Baḥya Ibn Paquda, *Duties of the Heart*, p. 17.

12. *Messilat Yesharim*, p. 122.

13. Gershom G. Scholem's *Major Trends in Jewish Mysticism*, pp. 244 ff., illustrates the wide influence of these moods in critical times.

14. *Pesaḥim* 25a.

15. *Sanhedrin* 74a–b.

16. Mordecai M. Kaplan, in his introduction to the English translation of *Messilat Yesharim*, pp. xiv–xxx, discusses the basic traits and divergent methods of approach to the problem of human conduct.

17. For a discussion of this issue in Jewish philosophy, see Felix Perles Königsberg's "Die Autonomie der Sittlichkeit in jüdischen Schriften," in *Judaica Festschrift in Honor of Hermann Cohen* (Berlin: Verlag Bruno Cassirer, 1912).

18. *Sanhedrin* 56a, end.

19. Lazarus, *Ethics of Judaism*, vol. 1, p. 118.

20. *Kiddushin* 4:14.

21. *Yoma* 67b.

22. Albert C. Knudson, *The Principles of Christian Ethics* (New York, 1943), p. 285.

23. Ibid., p. 39; see the New Testament critique of Pharisaic morality in such sections as John 7:22–24, Matthew 23:23–26, Acts 15:24–29, Romans 3:28–29.

24. Mishnah *Gittin* 5:8; Tosefta 5:4–5.
25. *Universal Jewish Encyclopedia* (1941), s.v. "Ethics," vol. 4, p. 175.
26. Deuteronomy 22:11, 22:6
27. *Genesis Rabbah* 44.1; *Tanhuma, Shemini* 15b; ed. Buber.
28. See Moses Maimonides, *Guide to the Perplexed,* 3:43–49, for such ethical interpretations of Sabbath, festivals, dietary laws, among others.
29. Jerusalem Talmud, *Peah* 16a, as cited by J. Z. Lauterbach in his essay on the "Ethics of Halakah." He quotes similar talmudic passages, *Sukkot* 30a, *Nazir* 23b, in his notes on p. 271.
30. *Shabbat* 81b.
31. *Sifre Deuteronomy, Re'eh* 90b.
32. *Sanhedrin* 74b.
33. *Yoma* 28b.
34. *Mechilta, Be-Shallach* 6; ed. Weiss, 40b.
35. Romans 4:16.
36. For additional illustrations, see Lauterbach's and Kohler's articles on nomism in the *Jewish Encyclopedia.*
37. See *Pirke Avot* 1:17, 3:12, 3:22, 4:6, for consistent emphasis, giving primary value to works over wisdom and erudition.
38. *Kiddushin* 40b.
39. Lazarus. *Ethics of Judaism,* vol. 1, pp. 109 f. Emil Hirsch. s.v. "Ethics," *Jewish Encyclopedia,* passim. Kohler, *Jewish Theology,* p. 477.
40. *Bava Bathra* 12a.
41. *Ketubot* 50a.
42. See Lauterbach. *The Ethics of the Halakah,* p. 283.
43. *Shabbat* 88b.
44. *Bava Metzia* 59b.
45. *Eruvin* 13b.
46. *Numbers Rabbah* 19:6.
47. *Tanhuma, Devarim* 1a.
48. For illustrations of the democratic "plebeian" character of the Pharisaic reforms through law, read Louis Finkelstein's suggestive chapter, "The Oral Law," in his two-volume *The Pharisees* (Philadelphia: Jewish Publication Society, 1946).
49. Deuteronomy 13:17, 21:18; Leviticus 14:34 ff.
50. *Sanhedrin* 71a. The rabbis' humanitarian employment of law and exegesis allows them to boast that a Sanhedrin (religious supreme court) that executes a person once in seven years is called murderous. Rabbi Eliezer ben Azzariah corrected, "once in seventy years."
51. Mishnah *Berachot* 9:5.

BIBLIOGRAPHY

Moritz Lazarus, *The Ethics of Judaism,* translated by Henrietta Szold (Philadelphia: Jewish Publication Society 1900).

Israel Mattuck, *Jewish Ethics* (London: Hutchinson's University Library, 1953).

Leo Baeck, *The Essence of Judaism* (New York, 1936).

Mordecai M. Kaplan, "The Contribution of Judaism to World Ethics," in *The Jews*, edited by Louis Finkelstein, vol. 1 (New York, 1949).

C. G. Montefiore and H. Loewe, *A Rabbinic Anthology*.

Emil Hirsch, "Ethics," in *The Jewish Encyclopedia*.

J. Z. Lauterbach, "The Ethics of Halakah," in *Rabbinical Essays* (Cincinnati: Hebrew Union College Press, 1951).

M. Mielzinger, "Ethics of the Talmud," in *Judaism at the World's Parliament of Religions*, pp. 107–113.

II
The Holocaust

LETTING GO / HOLDING ON

The Baal Shem Tov was haunted by a strange dream. In the dream the very incarnation of evil appeared in the image of a dark heart seething malevolence. All the cruelties of the world were concentrated in that sinister form. Frightened and repelled, the Baal Shem Tov clenched his fist and pounded furiously upon the evil heart, meaning to kill it. Suddenly, he heard the sobbing of an infant from within it. He stopped, amazed that within such evil, innocence could live.

The dream is rooted in the kabbalistic masterpiece the *Zohar*, which states that when God came to create the world and to reveal what was hidden in the depths, light and darkness were entwined with each other; holy and profane, good and bad impulses cleaved to one another.

What are we who know of this commingling to do? Our task is *havdalah,* the act of differentiation, the disentanglement of good from evil, the search for the sparks of decency buried within the coarse husks, sparks which when gathered together form a torch that can light up the dark corridors. The Baal Shem Tov heard the infant's cry, and in that cry hope was restored.

The Holocaust is the nightmare from which we struggle to awake. It intrudes on our sleep and spills over into our waking moments. *The Holocaust is the dominant psychic reality in our lives.* It lies hidden in our hoarse conversations with our children about mixed marriage, in our arguments over the low fertility rate of Jews, in our debates over support of the State of Israel, in our appeals for Jewish unity, in our fundraising—whatever the Jewish cause. The Holocaust shapes our stance towards the world and our self-understanding. It clings to our skin and penetrates beneath our skin, motivating our agenda and our policies. How could it be otherwise? Who could expect that a people that lost two out of every five of its members—40 percent of its community—should emerge unscathed, unscarred, fully normal?

We are a battered people still working out the shock of abandonment, resentment and disillusionment. Beneath surface tranquility, seething angers and anxieties persist. We are an abused people still working out our grief, still in mourning.

It is not an easy mourning for us, and not easy to transmit its meaning to our children. I know this as a father and a rabbi. Part of me understands that my children must know everything—the charred skeletons, the mass graves, the green and yellow smoke from the chimneys, the diabolic experiments of Mengele. I want them to know it all not only because a feigned ignorance would betray the martyrdom of our family, but because I want my children to understand me: my anxieties, my restlessness, my sensitivities, my paranoia.

Yet another part of me cautions against unwittingly laying a stone upon their hearts, crushing them with melancholy, filling them with a paralyzing cynicism.

How we are to master the trauma, how we are to confront the world, how we are to extract meaning and morale from our nightmare so that we and our children can live with wisdom, courage, and hope—that is the depth agenda for the post-Holocaust generation.

For this internal mastery we need to apply Jewish therapeutic wisdom to our collective loss. How does the Jewish tradition guide us through our personal losses, our private mourning?

When there is a death in the family, the tradition counsels us to "hold on and let go." On the surface contradictory counsel, but upon reflection this bonding and loosening provides a profound key to our healing.

To hold on means to cherish every gesture, kindness, embrace of those we loved. Every recollection has its own afterlife, its own immortality of influence in our lives. *Kaddish, Yahrzeit, Yizkor,* are the ritual bonds to our significant past.

At the same time, we are urged to let go: to rend the garment of the mourners, cut the fringes of the tallit (prayer shawl) of the deceased, lower the casket, return the dust to the earth from which life was drawn. These are the loosening rituals which signify closure. Mourners are like aerialists on a swinging trapeze, letting go of one ring to catch hold of another. Letting go in order to hold on, a dialectic of mourning.

Holding on and letting go means that the *shivah* days of mourning are seven and no more; the *Kaddish* recited eleven months and no more. As our sages observed, "He who mourns more than is necessary does not mourn for the deceased" but for someone else or something else, perhaps himself. At the end of the *shivah,* the mourners are bidden to rise from the low bench, to leave their home and walk around the neighborhood, to reenter the world.

Memory is an ambiguous energy. For the sake of health, it must be used to sustain us, to help us walk "through," not remain "in," the valley of the shadow of death. Life-sustaining memories are selected with the crucial knowledge that those we loved loved us, and, loving us, wish for the restoration of our will to live.

We can do no better in working out our collective mourning. Holding on, we sift through the cremated ashes of our tragic past to salvage some sparks of decency: the courage to resist, the will to live, the talent to choose. But of what are we to let go?

We must let go of those false and dangerous interpretations that extract the wrong lessons for ourselves and our children from the tragedy of the Holocaust. We must let go of the tendency that sees in the Holocaust confirmation of a primitive fissure in the human species, a primordial split between "them" and "us"; between "them," the perennial persecutors, and "us," the eternal victims; between the children of darkness, who carry the genes of Ishmael, Esau, and Amalek, and us, the eternal scapegoats, the hated descendants of Isaac, Jacob, and Israel. This kind of dichotomous thinking uses the catastrophe of the Holocaust to vindicate a schismatic interpretation of Jewish history.

This polarization of humanity is not the wise and reverent exercise of Jewish memory. It is rather the imposition of a deeply divisive metaphysics that visits the mind-set of a Manichaean dualism upon the whole of Jewish history, past, present, and future. It is bound to a belief in the eternal repetition of the hatred of the Jew wherein every anti-Semitic event is seen as a confirmation of an original curse. It is our version of original sin, an anti-

Jewish malediction that is seen to lie in the very blood of our existence. Its maxim is "ever again." Jews were, are, and will be hated by the world. Every and any sign of philo-Semitism is either dismissed as masking baser motivations or simply not registered in Jewish memory. Only the gullible are taken in by the reports of good news. The truly wise know the split nature of human history. As the lyrics of a popular Israeli song in the sixties had it, "The whole world is against us. This is an ancient tale. Well, if the world is against us, to hell with the world."

This sentiment does not properly characterize Jewish history. On the contrary, it endows anti-Semitism with immortality. The eminent Jewish historian, Professor Salo Baron, waged a long intellectual war against what he termed the "lachrymose conception of Jewish history": the one-sided reading of Jewish history as exclusively one of *Leidensgeschichte,* a history of suffering. Its focus on the negative eclipses the positive, creative, cultural, and spiritual activities in Jewish history. I add to his caveat my fear that Jewish history, past and future, is being bent to fit the pessimistic polarization.

It is not difficult to understand the Jewish quarrel with the world, particularly after the Holocaust. Who of us cannot appreciate the rage and disillusionment of a battered people? But for the sake of our collective health, we must be concerned about the disequilibrium of the spirit it leaves in its wake, the imbalance that cripples our morale. That metaphysical view must be let go because its fatalism runs counter to Judaism and is dangerous. It encourages the self-fulfilling prophecy that predicts, "Scratch a gentile, pagan, Christian, or Moslem and find a mortal enemy"; scratch a Jew and find the perennial victim. The Book of Numbers records the power of such self-fulfilling defeatism: "We were in our own sight as grasshoppers, and so were we in their sight."

The metaphysics of fatalism leads to a justification of the growing Jewish isolationism. For if the whole world is contaminated, there is nothing to be done, no one to cultivate, no alliances to be formed. What is left is to withdraw into ourselves. Isolationism of this kind means the abandonment of Jewish statesmanship and a cynical disregard for public opinion.

Some use the split thinking of "them" and "us" to scare Jews into insulated survival. But who would choose to live in the leprous circle of the damned? Moreover, split thinking boomerangs upon us. The dichotomy of "them" and "us" inevitably leads to scandalous divisiveness among "us."

A current anecdote tells of two Lubavitchers who ponder the character of the Jewish condition. One of them explains: "The whole world is divided between 'them' and 'us.' No point speaking of 'them.' Among 'us' the world is divided between Ashkenazim and Sephardim. No use talking of the Sephardim. Among Ashkenazim, the world is divided between Hasidim and Misnagdim. No use talking about the Misnagdim. Among the Hasidim, the world is divided between the Satmar and the Lubavitcher. No use talking about the Satmar. Among the Lubavitcher there are the intellectuals and the *farbrengen* types. No use to talk about the latter. Among the intellectuals, there are you and me. And you know how little you know."

Split thinking may begin with "them" and "us"; it leads to internal polarization, incivility, and the solipsism of Jewish cults.

We owe our children more than a legacy of isolation and basic distrust. We owe them the confidence that marks the great Jewish intuitions: that the human being is created in the divine image; that human beings are potentially good; that the prophetic faith in the possibility of a brighter future enables us to break out of the morose cycle of eternal recurrence.

All well and good. But where in the face of the Holocaust is there any empirical evidence of goodness? Where in the heart of evil is there the small sound of the infant's cry, the glimpse at the remotest trace of benevolence, the slightest record of altruism? There is sacred evidence, hard, authenticated witness to a powerful phenomenon that remains largely unattended, unrecorded, untaught, unused. There are in our midst witnesses to goodness who must be encouraged to come forth and to testify. But to discover goodness, to learn to use it for our recovery, we have to look, we have to want to look. There is no immaculate perception. We have to pay attention to events and persons buried in anonymity or hidden in obscure footnotes.

I have met gentiles, Christian men and women, flesh-and-blood human beings, from all walks of life and from every country that the Nazis occupied, who risked their lives and the lives of their families, and lost their possessions, to hide, protect, feed members of our Jewish family. I have examined the testimonies of survivors who are alive today because of ordinary people who acted in extraordinary fashion to hide Jews sought out by Nazi predators and collaborators, to hide them in closets, attics, barnyards, pigsties, sewers; who lied to authorities, falsified passports, and lost their fortunes. Not saints, these rescuers, but human beings who transcended the environs of prejudice and contempt and shielded Jews out of care, concern, responsibility, love. The experience of these rescuers and the testimony of the survivors—the empirical reality of goodness—have affected my theology, my morale, and my understanding of what must be done to create a healthier society.

I want my children to know the entire story—the killers of the dream, the sadists and torturers of innocence. But I want them equally to know about these significant others. I want them to be exposed, as I have been, to precious persons such as Alex and Mila Roslan, two Polish Christians who hid three Jewish children in their small home throughout the Holocaust years. I want them to hear, as I heard from the lips of Yaakov and David Gilat, the surviving brothers hidden by the Roslans, how the Roslans made themselves "as hiding places from the wind and shelters from the tempest; as rivers of water in dry places; as shadows of a great rock in a weary land" (Isaiah 32). I want them to hear how, when scarlet fever broke out and hit the children, Yurek Roslan, age ten, was taken to a Warsaw hospital where no Jewish person could enter; how Yurek carefully divided the powdered medicine given to him by the physicians so that the Jewish youngsters at home could be treated; how when Yaakov Gilat required surgery, the Roslans hollowed out their sofa and smuggled him into the hospital for an operation; how the family sold their home and repeatedly changed their residence to avoid detection of their "crime." I would remind you that while these activities were going on, the Polish population was warned by the German army that offering a Jew lodging, food, or transportation was punishable by death.

What do the Roslans mean to me as a Jew? What claim do they have upon my memory?

The Roslans were not alone. Should our children not know of the Polish sewer workers who hid seventeen Jews for fourteen months in the rat-infested sewers of Lvov?

—of the village in Holland in which every non-Jewish family concealed at least one Jew?

—of the citizens of Le Chambon sur Lignon who stood up to the Vichy police, the German army, and the Gestapo and saved five thousand Jews from destruction? Philip Hallie, in his *Lest Innocent Blood Be Shed,* describes the arrest of a lone Jew in Le Chambon. When he was put on a bus to be deported to the Nazi camps, the villagers lined up and each of them reached out through the open window to give him a gift: an apple, a candy bar, a newspaper.

—of Demiter Peshev and the Bulgarian Orthodox Church and the Sobranie, the Bulgarian parliament, which steadfastly defied the Nazis and refused to deport fifty thousand Bulgarian Jews? Of Bishop Kiril, who wired King Boris warning that he would mount a campaign of civil disobedience and would himself lie down on the railroad tracks to prevent the trains from deporting Jews to death camps?

—of General Roatta and the Italian army and the Italian diplomats who, in defiance of Nazi orders, rescued tens of thousands of Jews in Croatia and southern France from the clutches of the Nazis who sought their deportation and death?

—Should our children be denied the healing knowledge of the ten thousand Jewish children from Germany, Czechoslovakia, and Austria who arrived in England between 1938 and 1940, rescued by British and Quaker organizations?

—of Paul Gruninger, the Swiss police official; and Aristides de Sousa Mendes, the Portuguese consul; and Sempo Sugihara, the Japanese consul stationed in Cracow—all three of whom defied the Nazis and their respective governments, lost their positions and their fortunes, and were publicly humiliated for their acts of altruism? These three alone accounted for the rescue of 16,500 hunted and persecuted Jews.

Why should our children hear only the curses of the Jew-haters and not the blessings of those who rescued our people? Why are accounts of betrayal and persecution the rightful legacy to leave our children, but not the memories of loyalty and love? Why only the tears of fear and hate and not the tears of love and hope?

There is something tragically wrong that our children know the names of Eichmann, Himmler, and Klaus Barbie but not the names or exploits of the Christian families who hid Anne Frank and her family in an attic for two and a half years. Consult, if you will, the *Encyclopaedia Judaica* in the section dealing with Anne Frank and you will find no mention of the names of the rescuers, what they did, nor what became of them after they were caught. You will find them and their acts dismissed with seven words: "They were kept alive by friendly gentiles."

The anonymity of numberless rescuers, given the moral heroism of their deeds, is a sad state of affairs. With all of the Holocaust centers now in existence, there has been no systematic study of Christian-Jewish relations during World War II, and no active search for these precious spirits of our time. This judgment has been independently expressed by Professor Yehuda Bauer of the Hebrew University, Professor Sybil Milton, formerly of the Leo Baeck Institute, and Dr. Ivo Herzer of the Riverside Research Institute. Why should the name of villainy be immortalized and that of the righteous lie buried in anonymity?

We need Beate Klarsfelds and Simon Wiesenthals to search out the rescuers of our people with the same zeal and energy with which the murderers of our people were and are properly hunted down and brought to justice. Jewish institutions, Jewish historians, Jewish scholars must not allow the history of this phenomenon to be overlooked or to sink to the bottom of some footnotes. And have these rescuers no claim upon us? Should we not know where they are today, how they fare, who protects them, who befriends them?

The reluctance to focus on rescuers is based on a number of understandable concerns. Some suggest that speaking of heroic altruists lessens the tragedy of the Holocaust. I think not. *There are no heroes without villains.* There are no Jeanne Damanns, no Herman Graebes without the Mengeles and Himmlers. The ordeals of the rescuers can illuminate the darkness of the cave which many fear to enter. We may more readily help many face the evil by using the activity of the rescuers to sustain their morale.

Some non-Jews turn away from the Holocaust because they cannot bear the accusation against the Christian world. But I am less interested in forcing on them a collective mea culpa for their forebears, less interested in producing feelings of brooding guilt that frequently prove to be counterproductive, than in presenting them with Christian heroes, models of behavior to be respected,

honored, and emulated. Let them know of the moral heroism of
the priest Bernhard Lichtenberg of St. Hedwig's Cathedral in
Berlin, who insisted on joining the Jews deported to the Jewish
ghetto of Lodz and, punished by the Nazis, died on the way to
Dachau; and of Father Marie-Benoît, known in Rome as Padre
Benedetti and by those he protected as "Father of the Jews," who
turned his monastery into a rescue agency issuing baptismal certificates and passports to Jews. Let them know of the moral courage
of Cardinal Saliège, the archbishop of Toulouse, and pastors Hermann Maas and Heinrich Grüber. Memory is for the sake of the
future. I agree with the historian Yosef Yerushalmi, who, in addressing Christians, concluded, "Not by your ancestors but by
your actions will you be judged."

There are some who resist this concern for the rescuers because
the numbers are too few. How many rescuers were there? Estimates range from fifty thousand to five hundred thousand. Whatever the number, there were too few. There are always too few
moral heroes in history. But let me hasten to add (a) that we do
not know because we have not searched, and (b) that quantity is
no measure of moral quality. We are not dealing with sacks of
potatoes. We are dealing with life-and-death choices that must not
be trivialized by the numbers game. In our Judaic tradition we are
taught that for the sake of thirty-six righteous persons the world is
sustained; for the sake of ten righteous persons Sodom and Go-
morrah would not have been destroyed; and that the saving of one
person is tantamount to saving the entire world. Many worlds were
saved by rescuers. Speaking of numbers, a Dutch Christian rescuer
used the expression "the conspiracy of goodness." "Do you
think," he said, "that I could have hidden that Jewish family
without the knowledge and cooperation of the grocer, the milkman,
the policeman?" If evil has many faces, goodness has many forms.
Goodness must not be whittled down by numbers.

Goodness must not be trivialized. At a recent Holocaust conference someone asked, "Was it so difficult to help a Jew?" To hide
a Jew was a matter of life and death for the protector and his or
her family. On January 29, 1943, the SS executed fifteen Poles in
the village of Wierbicz, members of whose families saved Jews.
One of those fifteen souls was a two-year-old child.

—Ninety-six Polish men were murdered by the Germans in the village of Biala for hiding and feeding Jews.

—In Stary Ciepielow, the SS pushed twenty-three Poles, men, women, children, and infants, into a barn and burned it down with all of them inside for their violation of the edict proscribing protection of the Jews.

—Stephen Korbonski, himself awarded a Yad Vashem medal of honor as a "righteous gentile" who was a leader of the civilian resistance in German-occupied Poland, writes in *The Jews and Poles in World War II* of the twenty-five hundred Poles executed by the Germans for their actions on behalf of Jews.

Cardinal Glemp, in the aftermath of his anti-Semitic remarks regarding the Carmelite convent at Auschwitz, recanted somewhat and spoke of the need to educate Poles as to the meaning of the Holocaust for Jews. Let him tell them of those other Poles who acted out their faith. Let him tell them of another convent, this one in Vilna, where the mother superior of a Benedictine convent and six sisters hid Jews and dressed them in nuns' habits. Among those rescued were writers and leaders of the Jewish resistance in Vilna: Abba Kovner, Abraham Sutzkever, Edik Borak, Arie Wilner. The same nuns later smuggled ammunition, hand grenades, and knives into the ghetto to help the Jewish resistance.

Let him teach responsibility and morality less by inducing guilt and more powerfully by raising to high honor people of example such as Anna Simiate, the Lithuanian librarian at the University of Vilna who smuggled food and books for the beleaguered prisoners of the ghetto, and Mother Maria of Paris, who gave up her identification card to a Jewish woman in Ravensbrueck.

Goodness is a powerful mirror. Goodness challenges us in a way that evil does not. Compared to Eichmann, I am a saint; but compared to the Roslans, how do I measure up? Would I unlock the door? Would I take into my home this sick man, this pregnant woman, this frightened family—would I keep them for days, weeks, months, years, knowing that discovery of my act by the Nazi predators would mean the imprisonment, torture and death of my family? How do I buy food in my impoverished community? How do I call a doctor for someone who doesn't exist, or remove refuse or bury a body without detection, while outside the informer bribed with vodka and cigarettes looks on?

Our people possesses sacred testimony, a double memory of the worst and the best: the memory of indescribable evil, and the memory of the precious human capacity to do good.

Our people possesses valuable information for the character education of a post-Holocaust generation. The behavior and circumstances of these recuers offer the deepest refutation of the Eichmann alibi that there was no alternative to passive complicity with the murderous regimes, and refutation of the Waldheim argument that knowing of atrocities is not committing atrocities. Through their lives we know that there are alternatives to cog-in-the-wheel rationalizations. Through their lives, the rescuers have demonstrated that to know is no cognitive sport, that to know and to do nothing is to be guilty of standing idly before the shedding of innocent blood. Even in hell there were men and women who would not bend to the threats and seductions of the demonic.

We Jews have testimony to offer an embittered, cynical world. The behavior of tens of thousands of rescuers balances the lopsided bias of religious and secular sources that judge human nature to be nothing but nasty, brutish, and short. The philosopher George Santayana writes: "In human nature generous impulses are occasional or reversible; they are spent in childhood, in dreams, in extremities, they are often weak or soured in old age. They form amiable interludes like tearful sentiments in a ruffian, or they are pleasant self-deceptive hypocrisies acted out, like civility to strangers because such is in society the path of least resistance. Strain the situation, however, dig a little beneath the surface and you will find a ferocious persistent, profound selfishness" *(Dominations and Powers)*.

Peel away the thin-layered veneer of civil amenities and there appear the uncosmeticized faces of people who, in Sigmund Freud's judgment, "view their neighbor in order to gratify their aggressiveness, to exploit his capacity for work without recompense, to use him sexually without his consent, to seize his possessions, to humiliate him, to cause him pain, to torture and to kill him."

Against this distorted reading of human nature and the melancholy that inundates us, the mounting evidence of altruism has much to contribute to our spiritual equilibrium. Not only our own morale but the morale of our world must be served. We need, and the future of civilization requires, basic trust; not a naive, uncritical trust but, in the words of Erik Erikson, "a favorable ration of basic trust over basic distrust."

We Jews are morally mandated to search out and recognize goodness. The vital mitzvah for our generation is *hakarat ha-tov*. This recognition requires more than passive acknowledgment. It means to identify the self-effacing righteous people, to befriend these noble and largely anonymous spirits; it means to help them live out their waning lives in dignity. Too many of them find themselves today in dire circumstances, pariahs among their own for acting against popular anti-Semitism. The Roslans had to move to Clearwater, Florida, because they were harassed by former Polish citizens who scoffed at their rescue work, saying, "So what if there were six million and two among their dead?" Those who protected our people with their bodies must themselves be protected from the shame of abandonment and the ignominy of being forgotten. *Hakarat ha-tov* means to study the evidence of their lives so that they enter the teaching curriculum of Jewish and non-Jewish schools, providing a new generation with moral models beyond Rambo and Dirty Harry.

This submerged evidence must become part of our memory and our morale. It can help us work out our grief; free us and our children from the paralysis of cynicism; remind us that we are not alone in facing a genocidal world; remind us that there are friends out there, real friends and potential allies who must be cultivated to restore our human solidarity.

Parenthetically, even in the tragedy of the village of Beita on the West Bank, there were Arab villagers who would not join in stoning Jewish teenagers, and who protected them from the raging mob. This evidence of moral decency must not be ignored. In an atmosphere of dangerous distrust, single events of this sort light up the future, suggesting the possibility of reconciliation. Focusing on the relationship between non-Jewish rescuers and Jewish survivors of the Holocaust may provide a new perspective for the reconciliation of Catholic-Protestant strife in Ireland, and of Moslem-Christian, Buddhist-Islamic, and black-white conflicts. Recognition and study of altruism among those commonly assumed to be enemies opens an untapped vein for harmony. "Who is strong?" the rabbis ask, and answer, "They who are able to make friends of adversaries."

The world needs moral heroes of flesh and blood. Members of threatened societies need models of moral altruism—those who come from the other side, from the enemy side, and who stand for them. Those who have managed to transcend the enmity and contempt within their own circles and stand for the maligned victims of prejudice. The rescuers I have come to know helped me overcome the generalizations that put the others into the role of enemy. I myself came with my healthy share of suspicion and prejudice against Germans and Poles and goyim. But having come to know Graebe, Roslan, Irene Opdyke, Jeanne Damann, hearing them and hearing the testimony of the survivors, I can let go of that morbid view that contaminates my Jewish faith and hope.

The reiterated myth that the whole world wants us dead—always wanted us dead and will always want us dead—is pernicious and false. We are never so alone as when we act on that belief. There are friends out there and potential friends, friends to be cultivated.

Remember the evil, but do not forget the good.

We must not allow goodness to be orphaned. For the sake of these we remember, for the sake of working out our grief, for the sake of our children's vitality, we must apply the therapeutic wisdom of our tradition: let go and hold on; let go in order to hold on.

WHO ARE "THEY" TO ME?

Who are "they" to me,
I, a child of Jewish Polish parents,
whose memories are filled with ancestral
episodes of contempt for my people?

Recollections of their European origins
and of that black blot
that casts so heavy a shadow
over their lives.

Stories of ten decapitated Jewish heads placed upon the S.S.
   desk,
shrunken heads upon which skullcaps are derisively displayed,
"This is your minyan, Jew."
Witnesses who saw green and yellow smoke
out of chimneys fueled by human bodies.

"They" are
the silent spectators who dared to deny
what "they" saw or heard.
"They" are the collaborators,
the betrayers of the rhetoric of grave theology.

Then I concluded
that "they"—all of them—
meant me and mine no good.
"They" are my enemies,

if not overt then hidden foes.
No allies, no friends among "them."

And then, as in a nightmare,
out of the evil heart came
the cry of a sobbing infant.
How could innocence reside in that hellish heart?

And then I heard of others, read of others, met others,
gentiles, Christians, believers, atheists
in every country Nazi tyranny controlled.

Non-Jews, not kith nor kin, not fellow religionists
but those who danced to a different ritual.
Non-Jews from every walk of life
turned themselves into hiding places,
their sewers, stables, attics, basements
into sanctuaries.

Not saints or supermen and superwomen
but persons of flesh and bone like yours or mine,
who risked their security, safety, lives
to hide the hunted.

Others joined the enemy or narrowed their heart
to their parochial group.
But these transcended the boundaries of their faith,
their church,
to enter the leprous circle of the condemned!

They are the heroes from the other side,
whose decency and courage broke through the walls
that denied a common humanity.
They are the healers of our disillusionment,
the brakes upon our generalizations.
They give the lie to cynicism convinced that
beneath the skin of all others is only
my implacable, eternal foe.

They are the ordinary men and women
who did what they did
because human decency and conscience demanded it.
Because, because, because
"and what else could you do?"

They hold up a mirror to my soul.
Would I let them in,
this hunted man
this pregnant woman
this trembling family?
Would I unlock the door?

Would I let them in
for days or weeks or months or years,
would I scrounge for food to feed these strangers
when the offer of a loaf of bread
means imprisonment and death?

Would I get hold of sleeping pills
to silence the cries of the infant
whose sobs might give away the hiding place?

Would I dispose of their excrement, bury their dead
turn my home into whispers
lest the informants lurking about
sell hiders and hidden
for a carton of cigarettes or a bottle of vodka?

Would I falsify identity papers
forge baptismal certificates, visas
lie to the interrogators
seek out allies in a conspiracy of goodness?

They did, and theirs are lessons
that must not be lost to our children:
Know that there is always an alternative to passive complicity.
Know that knowing is no cognitive sport
to hear and see and then feign deafness, blindness, muteness.

Know such knowledge is evil,
a subterfuge for shedding the blood of innocence.

Know that there is goodness
even in hell,
Goodness precious, rare, but that must
be cultivated to resist evil.
Know that goodness must be recognized, searched out,
raised from the dust of amnesia.
Know that the good who protected the persecuted
must themselves be protected by us,
the family of the survivors.

We owe the world a double witness
Of those who slaughtered and of those who saved.
Know the darkness and know the light.
Know the evil and know the good.
Remember the moral heroes for
a generation beyond the Holocaust
enabling our children to hope again, to trust again,
to mend again the tattered fabric of our lives.

Breathe spirit into the smoldering ashes of the cremated past
that the sparks of decency may be fanned
to light the candle of many wicks
to enlighten the future.
Bear witness to goodness that our hearts not fail.

MY GOLDFISH AND
ANTI-SEMITISM

As a youngster, I always wanted to have a dog. By order of the landlord, no one in my apartment house in the Bronx could own a pet. In this case, my parents fully agreed with the landlord. My mother couldn't see herself cleaning up after the dog, and my father claimed that Jews simply don't own dogs. It was years later that I discovered a passage in the Talmud that prohibits raising a *kelev ra,* a vicious dog, in the house. But the little fox terrier I had in mind was far from a vicious animal.

At any rate, a compromise was effected and I received from my parents the gift of a lone goldfish. It was my greatest joy to feed the goldfish, to watch it swim about aimlessly. One day, after Hebrew school, I came home to observe my goldfish swimming lackadaisically, slower than usual and favoring one side. It required no expert in ichthyology to know that the fish was dying. My uncle happened to be in the house at the time and knew just what to do, "Quick, get some salt and put it on the goldfish." With that prescription, I ran to the kitchen closet, grabbed a large, yellow- and red-colored box of kosher coarse salt and poured some of its crystal content on the goldfish, who by this time was floating on his side. Miraculously, the goldfish revived. From that time on, kashruth formed a new rationale, i.e., resurrection. For an hour or so, things went swimmingly. The fish had just righted itself and as suddenly reverted to its status quo ante posture. Once again, I reached for the coarse salt and poured it on the fish, but this time the miracle failed me. The fish died.

I have thought about this incident, so sharply etched in my mind, in the context of anti-Semitism. I remember that whenever Reb Shapiro, our Talmud Torah teacher, was angry at us kids he would drop his chalk and begin his sarcastic tirade, "Sure, boys, go ahead and talk, play games, don't pay me any attention. For this our ancestors died to preserve the holy text? For this they suffered from anti-Semites, so that you should talk and fool around?" Reb Sharpiro's diatribe worked. We all felt properly guilty. We stopped snapping rubber bands and paid him mock attention, but even then, the salt did not work for too long.

I have heard other pedagogues who use anti-Semitism to call Jews to attention, who use the threat and fear of anti-Semitism much the way I used the coarse salt. The belief prevails that pouring salt on the wounds of Jewish fears will revive Jewish consciousness.

It's an old belief, and a passage in the Talmud *Megillah* cites a rabbi who says that the ring which Ahasuerus removed from his finger, empowering Haman to persecute Jews, was more effective in raising Jewish fidelity and promoting Jewish repentance than all of the chastisements of the forty-eight prophets and the eighteen prophetesses. Anti-Semitism, the argument holds, is guaranteed to sting us into regret for our wayward ways. But even if it works, it's not for long. Anti-Semitism won't sustain fidelity and continuity. We are cruelly fooled by symptoms of quick revival. The scare may work once, twice, three times, but sooner or later it proves counterproductive and is resented as manipulative and insincere. I get weekly scare appeals to support dozens of Jewish organizations. Without anti-Semitism would they be forced to file for bankruptcy? Jews can't be scared into life any more than the goldfish could be stung into viability.

What should have been done in the case of the sick fish? Perhaps it would have been better had I been told to properly clean the fishbowl, or to more sparingly feed the fish, or to give it proper light, or to find another venue. In any event, salt was no solution.

People can become habituated to bad news and be discomforted by good news. Over the centuries, a people can inherit a form of catastrophic thinking that dismisses all evidence of philo-Semitism as a facade and accepts only the rhetoric of anti-Semitism as real. People may inadvertently come to depend upon the enemy to keep their sense of oneness, form a kinship held together only by the memory of persecution and fear of repetition. People may without planning find the center of their Jewishness programmed by the killers of the Jewish dream and contribute money, time, and energy only against, never for.

If this is true, it is important to see what may become of us. If genuine tolerance breaks out, who are we to each other without anti-Semitism. When our purported fate as victims is uncovered as specious, what is left of our faith? Are defensive mechanisms our only driving energies? Does our vaunted unity come only from the attacker without? Have we grown accustomed to the vilifiers, and alienated from allies? Will we, like Jonah, curse the gourd because the self-fulfilling prophecy has failed? And how do we appear to our children and our children's children? What has become central in our museums, our memorials, our history lessons, our storytelling, our recollections?

Around the time of the goldfish episode, a popular song made the rounds. The lyrics went, "You've got to accentuate the positive, eliminate the negative, don't mess with Mr. In-Between." The health of Judaism is in its affirmation, not its negation, and most assuredly not in its double negation. To be an anti-anti-Semite does not make you a Jew. It robs you of Jewish song and poetry, Jewish philosophy and Jewish joy. From my goldfish I have learned that a mind-set ruled by anti-Semitism should be taken sparingly, with a grain of salt.

SUFFERING AND EVIL

If a bird's nest chance to be before thee in the way, in any tree or on the ground, with young ones or eggs, and the mother-bird sitting upon the young, or upon the eggs, thou shalt not take the mother-bird with the young; thou shalt in any wise let the mother-bird go, but the young thou mayest take unto thyself, that it may be well with thee and that thou mayest prolong thy days.

—Deuteronomy 22:6

Elisha ben Abuya, observing a child climbing a tree to gather eggs from a nest in obedience of both his father's request and the cited scriptural ordinance, saw the youngster fall from the tree and die. The shock of the death of such an innocent child who dutifully followed the prescriptions of the Torah led this second-century rabbi to the painful conclusion: "There is no judge and no justice." It was such an event, the rabbis speculated, that caused him to turn apostate. Other accounts explaining his loss of faith suggest analogous cases involving the suffering and death of the righteous.[1]

No event sears the soul of the believer more deeply than the discrepancy between an act and its consequence, whether that discrepancy be among the righteous who suffer or the wicked who prosper. And no problem clings more tenaciously to the whole of Jewish literature than the apparent contradiction between the existence of evil and the presence of a wise, powerful, and just God.

Many Jewish solutions to the problem of evil have been put forward. But for reasons that may become apparent, a justification

73

of God's ways or a theodicy is much harder to come by in Judaism than in other theologies.

Unde malum?—"from whence evil"—if there be a God? The Greek philosopher Epicurus formulated the problem as a tight dilemma: "God either wishes to take away evils and is unable; or He is able but unwilling; or He is neither willing nor able."

It would seem that to resolve the dilemma, one or more of the traditional attributes of God—wisdom, power, benevolence—needs to be deleted or seriously curtailed. Traditional theologies of all faiths have been aware of the consequence of reducing God's attributes, and have acted to protect the status of the deity.

In arguments used by traditional theologians, what man calls evil is good in God's eyes. And suffering, pain, and death occasionally end up as the consequences of man's erring belief or behavior, and are therefore just punishments. Invariably and inevitably, the divine image is sustained, and it is man who is diminished. God's omniscience, omnipotence, and benevolence can seemingly be held inviolate only at the expense of man's ignorance, impotence, or malevolence. For this reason, traditional justifications of God's ways tend to read like cases of conflicting interests, clashes of personalities in which God and man are adversaries.

Jewish religious literature incorporates each and every argument employed in these traditional expositions. But there is one significant, indeed revolutionary, difference. This is the cry of resistance never completely stifled, which echoes from the earliest biblical documents down to contemporary writings, and by which the Jew openly resists being shoved downward in the balancing between him and his God. It is the unprecedented struggle in which the Jew asserts nothing less than his moral equality with his Father.

THE MORAL PARTNERSHIP

And Abraham drew near, and said: "Wilt Thou indeed sweep away the righteous with the wicked? Peradventure there are fifty righteous within the city, wilt Thou indeed sweep away and not forgive the place for the fifty righteous that are therein? That be far from Thee to do after this manner, to slay the righteous with the wicked, that so the righteous should be as the wicked; that be far from Thee; shall not the Judge of all the earth do justly?

—Genesis 18:23–25

Right wouldest Thou be, O Lord,
Were I to contend with Thee,

Yet will I reason with Thee;
Wherefore doth the way of the wicked prosper?
Wherefore are all they secure that deal very treacherously?
Thou has planted them, yea, they have taken root;
They grow, yea, they bring forth fruit;
Thou art near in their mouth,
And far from their reins.

—Jeremiah 12:1–2

Awake, why sleepest Thou, O Lord?
Arouse Thyself, cast not off forever.
Wherefore hidest Thou Thy face,
And forgettest our affliction and our oppression?
For our soul is bowed down to the dust;
Our belly cleaveth unto the earth.
Arise for our help.
And redeem us for Thy mercy's sake.

—Psalms 44:24–27

How long, O Lord, shall I cry,
And Thou wilt not hear?
I cry out unto Thee of violence,
And Thou wilt not save.
Why dost Thou show me iniquity,
And beholdest mischief?
And why are spoiling and violence before me?
So that there is strife, and contention ariseth.

—Habakkuk 1:2–3

Thou that art of eyes too pure to behold evil,
And that canst not look on mischief,
Wherefore lookest Thou, when they deal treacherously,
And holdest Thy peace, when the wicked swalloweth up
The man that is more righteous than he?

—Habakkuk 1:13

As God liveth, who hath taken away my right;
And the Almighty, who hath dealt bitterly with me;
All the while my breath is in me,
And the spirit of God is in my nostrils,
Surely my lips shall not speak unrighteousness,
Neither shall my tongue utter deceit;

Far be it from me that I should justify you;
Till I die I will not put away mine integrity from me.
My righteousness I hold fast, and will not let it go;
My heart shall not reproach me so long as I live.

—Job 27:2–6

The vast protest literature in the Bible, of which the above are samples, is echoed throughout Jewish writings, through the Midrash and Talmud, medieval poetry, the parables of the Hasidim, through the intimate conversations with God of Levi Yitzchak of Berditchev to the fierce anger of Yossel Rakover writing his last testament amidst the flames of the Warsaw Ghetto: "I believe in the God of Israel even though He has done everything to destroy my belief in Him. I believe in His laws even though I cannot justify His ways . . . I bow before His majesty, but I will not kiss the rod with which He chastises me."[2]

The religious audacity first articulated in the biblical hero may come as a shock to those whose image of the believer is of one who always submits to the will of God.[3] Traditionally, the man of faith may be depicted as once-born or twice-born; he may be subject to doubt or conflict; but once in the presence of God, kneeling is his posture.

The voice of rebellion in Jewish literature, however, is authentic. It is not considered blasphemous; indeed, it is canonized. The indignation rises from within the religious framework. Expressions of its tensions are therefore not debates but internal conflicts. Out of personal anguish, the sufferer defies but does not deny.

From where stems the moral courage of the Jew, the right to resent? That privilege is based on an unusual arrangement between God and Israel, in which both parties agree to a unique set of terms. The everlasting covenant, entered into by Abraham and his seed with God, unites the two in a moral partnership. Man is to keep the commandments of the Lord, true, but it is also understood that the pact of "righteousness and justice" is undertaken with the Lord.

Both sides are mutually responsible, and a miscarriage calls forth sanctions against either transgressor.[4] This covenant, setting forth the moral responsibilities of both parties, gives Abraham and his descendants heart to dissent even against so awesome a cosignatory as God. So long as man is a partner with God in sustaining the moral universe, protests can be hurled from below as well as from above.

MAN'S MORAL COMPETENCE: RELIGIOUS AUDACITY

Man's status as a moral agent is thus asserted along with his capacity to distinguish good from bad, happiness from adversity, saintliness from sin. Both man and God are released from the amoral decrees of fate, the *moira* of the pagan world.

God is free to change His decrees, to repent of His decisions, to alter the course of events. And man is freed from passive silence: he may now appeal from God to God. "I will flee from Thee to Thyself, and I will shelter myself from Thy wrath in Thy shadow; and to the skirts of Thy mercies I will lay hold until Thou hast had mercy on me. I will not let Thee go until Thou hast blessed me."[5]

The God of Israel can be thus addressed because He is not only the metaphysical God of power and wisdom but also the moral God of justice and mercy. In his anger the religious rebel does not turn away from God but towards Him. God Himself prays, "May it be My will that My mercy may suppress My anger, and that My mercy may prevail over My other attributes."(*Berachot* 7a)

The same defiance is kept alive in the postbiblical tradition. It is not Noah, accepting the decree of the deluge and hiding his impotence in a shelter for himself, who is admired by the rabbis. They praise instead Abraham and Moses, who draw near to God and contend with Him on the grounds of justice. Abraham challenges God's exile of his people, demands confrontation with those who have accused Israel of sin, and successfully silences the Torah from testifying against them. Moses rebukes God for keeping silent before the slaughter of mothers and children.

Rachel dares contrast her compassion and forbearance with God's zealousness so as to move God towards charity.[6] Even Elijah "speaks insolently towards Heaven," accusing God of wronging the sinners; and the Holy One admits His responsibility and error.

In one rabbinic interpretation, Moses is seen as figuratively seizing hold of God's cloak and refusing to let go until "the Lord repented of the evil which He said He would do unto His errant people" (Exodus 32:14).[7] On another occasion Moses "hurls words against the Heavens" and "remits God's vow for Him," for, while the Lord cannot break His word, the righteous may break it on His behalf.[8]

The extraordinary intimacy and audacity allowable within the relationship between Israel and the deity is incomprehensible without a clear perception of their covenant. This unique "contract" explains the Jew's respect for man's moral dignity as well as his more revolutionary faith in God's responsiveness to the call of justice. Moses in prayer attributed to God greatness, might, and awesomeness. But the prophet Jeremiah deleted the attribute of awesomeness from God because "aliens are destroying His temple"; Daniel, observing the captivity of the people, similary reduced the attribute of might from God. The rabbis were perplexed. How could Jeremiah and Daniel abolish the attributes established by Moses? Rabbi Eliezer offered an explanation: "Since they know that the Holy One insists on truth, they would not ascribe false attributes to Him" (*Yoma* 69b).

What is more, in the *Din Torah,* the tribunal or justice to which the Holy One is summoned by man, God cannot lose. For when justice triumphs God is the victor. In His apparent defeat, when the voice of law and righteousness is heeded and the Heavenly Echo is ignored, He rejoices, *Nitzchuni Banai,* "My children have defeated Me" (*Bava Metzia* 59b). In Israel, man does not acquiesce as do the angels, but like Abraham's grandson Jacob-Israel, he girds his loins to wrestle with God and is allowed to prevail (Genesis 33).

Rabbinic tradition holds fast to the basic thrust of biblical literature—the moral impulse. A rich storehouse of speculations concerning God and man is found in the Talmud and other rabbinic writings such as the Midrashim, in their informal, discursive and often conversational commentaries. Of course, the unsystematic and digressive style makes it difficult to cull a well-ordered consistent rabbinic position on given topics. Nevertheless, it is beyond dispute that the rabbis sought a personal God, one directly and primarily involved with man whose purpose for the universe is integrally related to man's salvation. Their major concern was with God's providence, justice, love, and mercy.

THE RATIONALIST INFLUENCE OF MEDIEVAL PHILOSOPHY

It was not until the advent of medieval Jewish thought that a metaphysical view of the universe was introduced, which in turn had great effect on the efforts of Jewish philosophers to justify God's ways. Under the influence of medieval interpretations of Aristotelian philosophy, the goal of theologians like Abraham Ibn Ezra, Abraham Ibn Daud, Gersonides, Hasdai Crescas and Moses Maimonides was to search out God as the principle of explanation of the universe, the very essence of the nature of the world. They paid most attention to God's unity, His incorporeality, His power, eternity and wisdom.

The special challenge of medieval Jewish philosophy was to square the rationalistic philosophy of Aristotle with the claims of biblical revelation and talmudic authority. It sought to harmonize the logical, objective orientation of Greek philosophy with the personal and ethical approach of the biblical-rabbinic tradition. God and man are no longer equal partners in running the universe. Gersonides, intent on retaining human free will, limited God's foreknowledge to the universal laws of nature and excluded His knowledge of particular events. He thus attempted to keep the scales balanced. While man as an individual is free, his freedom is severely limited as a member of the species man. And God's wisdom and providence are restricted to the human species as a whole.

Though Maimonides states that when individual man exercises his intelligence he receives divine providence, this is a far cry from the biblical and rabbinic idea of God's conscious and deliberate extension of His personal mercy. Once again human freedom and divine control need to be accommodated. Crescas moves to protect the absolute sovereignty of God in a system of determinism which virtually eliminates man's free will.

In all these medieval thinkers, God and man are cast as rivals, each contending for natural or supernatural rights as if the attributes of one can only be attained at the cost of the other.

Judah Halevi aptly labeled the difference between metaphysical and moral theology as that between the "God of Abraham and the God of Aristotle." "There is a broad difference indeed between the believer in religion and the philosopher. The believer seeks God for the sake of various benefits, apart from the benefit of knowing Him; the philosopher seeks Him only that he may describe Him accurately, as he would describe the earth."[9]

There is, of course, considerable overlapping between both

approaches in Jewish writings. But it is instructive to note that the
rabbis saw in God the guarantor of the values revealed to and
accepted by man. From this stance, the resolution of the problem
of evil touches the very heart of faith. In metaphysical theology,
however, the problems wrought by evil are secondary to sustaining
the logic of the world order.

THE LOGIC OF EVIL

Medieval Jewish philosophers frequently distinguish between two
kinds of evil which befall man—moral and physical. Moral evil
includes those which people willfully inflict upon each other—
robbery, murder, war, excessive eating, drinking, and passion.[10]
They are taken to be a function of man's free will when exercised
in ignorance. Were man to use his reason to the fullest, he would
maintain the correct course of behavior in harmony with the
ultimate principles of the universe.

Physical evil afflicts man from sources outside himself, such as
earthquake, storm, and disease. Here free will does not seem
involved. A scientific account of the origin of illness appears to
ignore the hand of God in all things. The medieval religious
philosophers have two favored vindications of God's role in the
presence of such physical evil. First is the principle of privation,[11]
the analysis of evil as a negative term and nonexistent.

Evils such as blindness and death are not positive attributes of
life, and God had nothing to do with them in a direct manner. God
creates only positive properties. Blindness is the absence of sight;
deafness, a failure to hear; disease, the absence of health; muteness, the privation of speech. He who blows out the light creates
nothing. Metaphysically, evil, like darkness, is what is not. God,
who makes and forms, is therefore responsible only for what is.

The second oft-invoked metaphysical principle chides the human
being for his egocentrism in believing that the world was created
for his benefit. Many a medieval metaphysician, noting the fullness
of God's universe, invokes the principle of plenitude. Out of God's
infinite being and inexhaustible perfection there flows a chain of
being in which every conceivable diversity and potentiality of kinds
exists. Man's self-centered view of the universe would have it
limited to those things which are serviceable for him. His metaphysical astigmatism, thereby, robs the universe of its pluralism,

the grandeur of its perfection. If lions and snakes and bacteria did
not exist, the universe would be an impoverished structure. Better
that one animal should eat another than that a unique creature be
denied existence.

The twelfth-century Jewish philosopher Abraham Ibn Daud uses
this principle when he argues that without a graded series of being
our world could not have emerged; for all minerals would have
been plants, all plants, animals; all animals, men; all men, angels.
Without imperfection there would be a universe only of God and
angels.[12]

And Maimonides, using another variety of the same principle of
plenitude, shows how metaphysical wisdom can offer its own
solace. Man calls death a destructive evil. Such a misleading error
could be avoided would we but understand: "In accordance with
the divine wisdom genesis can only take place through destruction,
and without destruction of the individual members of the species
the species themselves would not exist permanently."[13]

In general, for these philosophers the issues of morality appear
secondary. They are prepared to concede that there are limitations
in the ordering and preserving of the world. Left alone, the
contrary elements in the sublunar world might destroy each other.
The "higher causes" of the heavenly spheres maintain an equilibrium which may unavoidably bring about some accidental evil to
some element in the universe—to man, as much as to any other
form in the great chain of being. These are the inevitable consequences of running the best of all logically possible worlds. But the
original intent in the creation of the universe is good; and the
physical evils are accidental by-products of divine beneficence and
wisdom.[14]

Both the righteous and the wicked man are viewed as subject to
the general providence which God exerts. But the righteous have
a special stance which they earn in proportion to the exercise of
the divine faculty of reason. The righteous man who actively
employs his intellect has the instrument with which to control even
those harmful events determined by indiscriminate laws of the
universe. Wisdom is the salvation attained by the righteous man.[15]
Interestingly, both Maimonides and Gersonides maintain that while
Job was a great man, he is not to be described as intelligent, wise,
or clever.[16] "It is of great advantage that man should know his

station and not erroneously imagine that the whole universe exists only for him."[17] David Hume, in his *Natural History of Religion,* observes the changing weights placed upon God's attributes as a result of differing ends: "The higher the Deity is exalted in power and knowledge, the lower of course is He depressed in goodness and benevolence."

THE RABBINIC VIEW

For the rabbis, the impersonal, objective explanations of evil offered by the systematic philosophers would be wholly inadequate to explain individual or collective history. Casual laws, like blind fate, are devoid of moral intent; therefore their importance in understanding the world is superficial. If man searches deeply, he discovers that nothing simply happens; tragedy is not the result of a morally capricious or indifferent cause. There is an ultimate explanation of events which lies in a purposeful God. "All is in the hands of heaven, except the fear of heaven."[18]

Most of the rabbis seek explanations of suffering that free God from the possibility of indictment by man. If man suffers, there is good reason. "If a man sees that painful sufferings visit him, let him examine his conduct" (*Berachot* 5a). "There is no death without sin and no suffering without transgression" (*Shabbat* 55b).[19] And if self-examination fails to reveal man's moral failure, let him attribute his suffering to neglect of the study of Torah. Moreover, even if he is a diligent student, he may attribute his pain to God's "chastisements of love."

Many are the modes of punishment for transgression, such as disease, war, accident, sentence by a tribunal; but all can be traced to the just exercise of divine will. When, after the destruction of the Temple, capital punishment could no longer be decreed by the Jewish courts, many rabbis contended that the punishment continues through natural agencies: "He who would have been sentenced to stoning, falls from the roof; he who would have been decapitated is either delivered to the [Roman] government or robbers come upon him; he who would be sentenced to strangulation is either drowned or dies from suffocation" (*Ketubbot* 30a–b). This insistence on the just hand of God behind all events encouraged many rabbis to find ways of erasing apparent moral inconsistencies or injustices in life. Should we discover a righteous man suffering, we need not deny either his goodness or his suffering. We may explain the punishment of the righteous as evidence of the wickedness of his father. Inversely, if an evil man prospers, it may be the merit he inherits from his parents' good deeds.[20]

Other rabbis repudiate the doctrine of reward or punishment as running counter to their sense of justice. They vindicate God by assigning higher meaning to the circumstance. The suffering of the righteous is, in fact, a badge of honor, not a stigma of transgression. "The Holy One brings suffering upon the righteous of the world in order that they may inherit the future world" (*Kiddushin* 40b). "Sickness and death help purge the lesser iniquities of the righteous so that the abounding happiness that is treasured up for them shall be unalloyed."[21]

Saadia Gaon, the tenth-century theologian, explains the case for unpunished evil: God pays off evil men for their petty virtues with trifling this-worldly rewards. Even the devil must be given his due. But this transaction in the outer vestibule of the universe only helps clear the path for the full measure of justice to be exercised against the evil-doers on the nethermost rung of the next world.[22]

Extending their horizons to include both worlds, some of the rabbis thereby can assure ultimate justice. The topsy-turvy moral disorder of this world must not lead us to despair of God's ultimate righteousness. "God does not deprive any being of his full reward." "He who says that God remits only part of a punishment will himself be punished" (*Pesachim* 118a, *Midrash Genesis Rabbah* 9).

While some biblical explanations treat Israel's expulsion from the land as divine punishment for its iniquitous ways, rabbinic theology lifts that disaster to the higher dimension of martyrdom. Israel is exiled for God's sake and suffers because it is witness on His behalf. "For Thy sake are we killed all day long" (Psalms 44:22, Isaiah 43:12). Collective suffering is a badge of courage and religious testimony: "God's rod comes only upon those whose heart is soft like the lily"; the yoke is placed upon "the strong and not the weak"; the potter does not test defective vessels lest with one blow he shatter them. Suffering is the mark of Israel's election.[23]

Taken as a whole, rabbinic theodicy adheres to the basic principle that the world is well conducted by a supernatural moral power.

Suffering is either a disguised blessing or an overt malediction.[24] The face of justice embarrassed in this world may be saved in the tribunal of the other world.

RABBINIC UNEASINESS WITH TRADITIONAL THEODICIES

The biblical view which holds man to be the *shutaf lakadosh baruch hu,* a partner with God, is a magnificent conception, but it generates unique irritants. The partnership between God and man, working together to improve the world and dually accepting responsibility for it, frequently involves conflict over jurisdiction. What if God and man disagree as to who is innocent or what suffering is? If a righteous man suffers grievously is God to be accused or is some way to be found to indict man?

Rabbi Meir, upholding the sovereignty of the divine will, states that God "will be gracious unto whom He will be gracious," and may reward or punish the undeserving. But such an appeal to the inscrutable ways of God did not satisfy everyone. If God alone knows who is truly evil, and if God alone can judge man, then the unique moral structure of Jewish religious civilization collapses. If man is morally incompetent to distinguish the righteous act from the wicked one, he is also legally incompetent. Many rabbis were fearful of such an anarchic situation.

"Should someone whisper to you: But is it not written, 'contend not with evildoers . . . ,' then you may tell him: Only one whose conscience smites him says so" (*Berachot* 7b). A man of good conscience must contend with the wicked and judge them. He cannot bury his head beneath the skirts of God's other-worldly justice. "They that forsake the law, praise the wicked; but such as keep the law contend with them" (Proverbs 28:4).

The rabbinic tendency to take what appears evil and see it as disguised good may quiet the rage of a Job; but it suggests equally a suspension of all human judgment. Involuntarily, such a theodicy is akin to the false prophecy against which Isaiah inveighed: "Woe unto them who say of evil, it is good, and of good, it is evil; that change darkness into light and light into darkness; that change bitter into sweet and sweet into bitter" (Isaiah 5:20).

COMMONSENSE REALISM IN RABBINIC TRADITION

Nurtured in a tradition which provided them experience in making moral judgments and decisions, some rabbis refused to surrender reasonable common sense and this-worldly ways of estimating good and evil. They refused to see in suffering and death anything but affliction, or to transform righteousness from an intrinsic good into sin. They refused to deny that evil can occur without sin.

"Are your sufferings welcome to you?" ask some rabbis. "Neither they [the sufferings] nor their reward," respond their colleagues. With deliberate repetitiveness and dramatic irony, the Talmud reveals how the very rabbis who earlier had preached the doctrine of divine chastisements of love (*yesurim shel ahavah*) to comfort sufferers were unable to accept it when they themselves were stricken.[25] Maimonides too found the doctrine of the afflictions of love offensive both to the intellect and the emotions. God does not cause those He loves to suffer, nor does He test the loyalty of the believers with trials of pain. Such doctrines, he argues, are unscriptural, ignorant and absurd.[26]

Similarly, evidence arguing strongly against the notion of inherited punishment is adduced from the Bible itself. "The fathers shall not be put to death for the children, neither shall the children be put to death for the fathers; every man shall be put to death for his own sin" (Deuteronomy 24:16).[27]

Nor are all the rabbis willing to transform martyrdom into a blessing. When Rabbi Chanina ben Teradyon defied the Roman authorities by reading the Torah in public, Rabbi Yose chastised him for his carelessness. "I talk common sense to you, and you say 'God will have mercy' " (*Avodah Zarah* 18a).

In 135 C.E., during the Hadrianic persecutions, wild and capricious decrees called for such a widespread risk of life that the rabbis were moved to define mandatory martyrdom. At the same time, they discussed criteria for exempting men from such a fate. Distinctions were drawn between decrees which called for private as opposed to publicly coerced transgressions. The source and motivation of the decrees were likewise taken into account before martyrdom was chosen over accommodation.[28]

Death may testify to man's saintliness or heroism, but its evil is neither to be denied nor absolved. Death, counseled Ben Sira (*Exodus Rabbah* 29b), may be preferable to a lingering disease, but it is not thereby transformed into an intrinsic good. If adversity is good, what sense is there to pray and work for its elimination in the messianic era?

Why portray the world of the future in which there will be no need to require blessings over evil tidings, since there will be no evil (*Pesachim* 50a)? How could death be other than evil if God Himself will slaughter the angel of death?[29]

ORIGINAL SIN AND ITS INHERITANCE

Many of the rabbis also refused to accept a verdict against man. Did Moses and Aaron deserve to die, even if they were not perfect? Does God punish twice for the same sin? Therefore, concluded the rabbis, "there is death without sin, and there is suffering without transgression" (*Shabbat* 55b).

While some rabbis accepted the explanation that death is born of Adam's sin and that we all participate in his original sin, others denied its moral implications. The angel of death, the latter argued, was created on the first day, before Adam was even fashioned.[30]

In another Midrash it is stated that Adam himself did not deserve to die for his transgression. He died because God, foreseeing that Hiram and Nebuchadnezzar would declare themselves gods, decreed their death, and thereby rendered all men mortal. Why then were not the innocent such as Adam, exempted from this punishment? The answer: lest the wicked, observing the immortality of the righteous, feign piety and perform insincere repentance for ulterior motives (*Genesis Rabbah* 9:5). These fragments of moral philosophy repudiate the notion of original sin and the claim that death is the just punishment of the evil.[31]

As if to ensure the equality of the heavenly tribunal with the earthly court, there are rabbis who insisted that God Himself does not take advantage of His perception of the secret inner intentions of man's heart. He restricts His own judgments to the public, overt acts of man. "The Holy One combines only intention which bears fruit with deeds [i.e., intentions which are followed by action]; but intention which does not bear fruit, He does not combine with deed" (*Kiddushin* 40a). The human court can take heart from such knowledge of the jurisdictional propriety of the divine court and with confidence judge the publicly observable acts of men.[32]

In summary, rabbinic theodicy, which is predicated upon the divine, moral causation of all events in which man is also a free moral agent, carries with it the warmth and intimacy of a personal God who is the author of justice in the world. But it also bears the sign of strain. The moral dialogue of biblical Judaism can—and often does—emerge as a clash of forces.

Consciously or not, Judaism's justification of God's ways is torn between two ideas that it wishes to maintain equally: *the sovereignty of God* and *the dignity of man*. How well the rabbis recognized this conflict can be seen in their characterization of prophecy. Elijah's prophecy is unsatisfactory in that, while he insists upon defending the honor of God, he ignores the dignity of man. Jonah's prophetic stance seeks to defend the son but ignores the claim of the Father. Jeremiah is the ideal prophet for he insists on the honor of both Father and son—God and man. He achieves this delicate equilibrium by simultaneously chastising and exonerating the ways of God and man (*Mechilta* to Exodus 12:1).

A God endowed with the traits of personality—acting, willing, loving, judging—is both wonderfully approachable and painfully vulnerable. Job's familiarity with God is so close as to enable him to speak of Him as "mine adversary" and to demand that "He set aright a man contending with God as a son of man setteth aright his neighbor" (Job 16:20–21; 31–35). The simile is striking: God and man are both persons, and each has moral claims upon the other.

AFTER AUSCHWITZ: THE CHALLENGE OF ADVERSITY

While easy converse between God and man presents no problems in times of peace and tranquillity, in times of adversity that very intimacy jeopardizes the sovereign perfection of God. The personal God is too close for comfort in moments of despair. If God is to be protected from the Jobian critique, His relationship with man must be formalized. Job must be put in his place and the forthrightness of the earlier dialogue broken off. God, in the epilogue, does indeed appear to Job out of the whirlwind, with all His awesome omnipotence: "Hast thou an arm like God? And canst thou thunder with a voice like Him?" (Job 40:9f.). God is thereby lifted to the heights of inviolability and Job discovers the limitations of dialogue. He now knows that, at best, he can only be a silent partner, and he learns to lay his hand upon his mouth forever.[33]

Similarly, in modern times, Martin Buber's human-divine encounter is severely shaken by the atrocities of the Nazi Holocaust. He is led to ask: "Can one still speak to God after Oswiecim and

Auschwitz? Can one still, as an individual and as a people, enter at all into a dialogue relationship with Him? . . . Dare we recommend to the survivors of Oswiecim, the Jobs of the gas chambers, 'Call to Him, for He is kind, for His mercy endureth forever?' "[34]

The confidence and trust of the original dialogue shrivel into paradox. Buber advises us to await the voice of "our cruel and merciful Lord."[35] We are presented not with a theological diffidence which limits man's knowledge of God's attributes but with the shocking assertion that the moral character of God is unknowable in principle. God is no longer simply "righteous and just" in the manner that Abraham knew Him, in the manner which assured him that God and he shared the same moral universe of discourse. Now Buber speaks of God as "super-good."[36] We have reason to wonder whether our moral language is the same as that which God employs. Stripped of the moral certainty axiomatic in the biblical dialogue, we may well panic. We do not know whether it is God or Moloch who addresses us.[37] After Auschwitz, Buber entertains a God who is the "Absolute Personality,"[38] what he himself calls a "paradox of paradoxes" because an absolute has no personality and is beyond love, desire, and will. And yet without personality there can be no dialogue with the Absolute God. The original innocence of the dialogue fades before the scandal of outrageous injustice. God is said to be "hiding" and man is counseled patience until His unpredictable revelation. What He may say we cannot know for "His coming appearance resembles no earlier one . . ."[39]

The painful truth appears to be that the Nazi atrocity has severed the dialogue. In its place, a mysterious monologue is awaited. After Auschwitz, only one voice speaks, and man is reduced to listener.

A PERSONAL GOD: STUMBLING BLOCK OR ROCK OF COMFORT?

As in Job and Buber, so Jewish theodicy is tossed like a shuttlecock, from a personal to an impersonal God. Yet whether we turn to God as Super-person or Person, toward a good God or one who is supergood, whether the goodness is understood or mysterious, all the traditional explanations invoke a personal God. All events occur through the agency of a deliberate, personal will. Metaphysical and moral theologians may quarrel as to the intent of that will—but all agree that true explanation entails a purposive agent, a personal cause.

The insistence upon a personal God is held to guarantee the objective status of moral values. Feared most are the twin heresies of atheism and pantheism, which are inimical to Judaism. Atheism proposes a rudderless world, wherein God is irrelevant to any proper explanation of history. In pantheism, where God is identified with nature, evils of all kinds are assimilated into the natural system, and nature reigns with an indiscriminate hand. Moral distinctions between good and evil, order and confusion are dismissed as human biases, as functions of man's self-centeredness.[40]

If good and evil are not to be blurred, as they are in pantheism, their separate reality must be maintained. The distinctions drawn between them seem best to be kept intact by finding their sources. Good is most readily personified as flowing from a divine power, but the tendency to personify experience suggests an analogous path to the source of evil: Satanic power. Each seems as real as the other.

Behind every experience to which moral adjectives are assigned, there lies a substantive noun to which it properly belongs. The inclination to forge experiences, events, transactions into things and nouns has an ancient and modern history to which philosophy will readily attest. "Good" and "bad" are transformed into "the good" and "the bad," and further transformed into "God" and "Satan." This metamorphosis generates demons as readily as angels. Little wonder then that the rabbinic tradition felt the need to combat the doctrine of *shtei rishuyot,* two competing divine powers.[41] However, it is no light task to trace good and evil to a common divine matrix so as to avoid the heresy of dualism, while adhering at the same time to the real distinctions between these two aspects of moral behavior. Where distinctions are held to be objective, differences frequently give birth to contending deities.[42]

"WHY?" IS NOT THE SAME AS "WHAT FOR?"

Why does theology bog down when confronted by the challenge to explain evil? Scientific answers will be accepted for questions concerning impersonal events—"Why did the metal expand?" But where personal events are involved, we insist upon a different type of explanation. Birth, sickness, and death demand explanations heavy with personal intent. To answer a question such as "Why was my child blinded?" with a medical report appears to demean the seriousness of the tragedy. The objective answer will be met with another, "But why did it happen to *my* child?" This sort of question is limitless, and each scientific answer only postpones a further one. Only that answer which is compatible with the tacit assumption of the question is acceptable. The question grows out of a mode of thinking wherein serious events can be explained only by conscious, purposively causal agents. Only a universe peopled with motivations, deliberate actions and purposes is regarded as adequate to account for important personal affairs. Hence, we speak of an "act of God" or the "will of God." While such an explanation of adversity may have its initial advantage it frequently leads to resentment against the One Person who, if He were but willing, could have averted the disaster.

It is self-evident that traditional theodicy limits its scope to one kind of theological view: God is a Person who punishes and rewards with sickness and death, with health and long life. Unless we are willing to challenge that underlying assumption, the gnawing problem of evil in God's world remains insoluble.

TOWARD AN ALTERNATIVE THEODICY

Traditional Jewish theology does not equate God with nature, nor does it set God apart from nature. Rather, it allows God to incorporate and transcend nature. A view of God's envelopment of nature is felt necessary to assure belief in His power and control of the universe. In the rabbinic approach, this total embrace of nature implicates God as responsible for all natural events, including disease and nature's disasters. He is involved in every natural catastrophe.[43]

A new approach to the relationship between God and nature sees the latter as belonging to the realm of *chol,* or the nonholy. Nature itself is morally neutral, neither hostile nor friendly to the realm of values. Understood as a system of morally ambivalent energies, it is beyond the judgement of evil or good. "The world pursues its natural course and stolen seed sprouts as luxuriantly as seed honestly acquired" (*Avodah Zarah* 54b). To conceive of God's running nature as we conduct our affairs only leads to the embarrassment of defending God each time lightning strikes or gales devastate the innocent. It leads us to strain for occult moral purposes behind every natural tragedy, and to associate God's activity with havoc and catastrophe.

God is not nature. Physical evils require no justification of His ways, for the ways of nature are not identified with the ways of God. There is no need to search for "deeper" explanations for drought or flood in defense of God.

In this view, nature is the source of potentialities for man's sustenance, health, and security. Nature is not a conscious moral force, but it can be used for conscious moral ends. With natural piety we seize hold of nature. "Is it not our own substance? Are we made of other clay? All our possibilities lie from eternity hidden in its bosom . . . we may address it without superstitious terrors; it is not wicked. It follows its own habits abstractly."[44] And the Jew follows God, not nature. Divinity is not larger than nature, but is discovered *within* nature, in the acts of men who transform the uncommitted powers of nature to consecrated ends.

This position suggests an interesting analogue with that of Gersonides' critique of Maimonides. Maimonides had insisted that God created matter out of nothing, and that were matter co-eternal with God, existing before creation, it would limit God's power and freedom. But Gersonides disagreed. Eternity, he argued, does not constitute divinity. Therefore, let matter be eternal; it does not reduce the majesty of divine creation. Creativity is not in the manufacture of matter, but in the shaping of its raw, chaotic substance into an intelligible universe. As Gersonides was convinced that longevity is no mark of divinity, we are convinced that largeness is equally irrelevant to the character of divinity. In separating God from nature, we do not reduce divinity but clarify its essential meaning.

Physical evil requires no justification. This does not mean that the tragedies wrought by nature are not real. But unfortunate physical accidents which befall man ought not to be converted into events derived from cosmic purpose. If we trace our tragedies to hidden divine causes, we cast a shadow of disillusionment upon an omnipotent personal God who has betrayed us. Such resentment and frustration are needless; because God conceived as Person fails us, we need not repudiate divinity.

GOD CREATES THE WORLD INCOMPLETE

A more positive approach is to see that man and the universe are incomplete. Nature is not law to be followed; it is power to be controlled and organized for moral ends. Endowed with freedom of will man encounters divinity in his effort to overcome sickness, ignorance, and greed. In his transactions with his environment he discovers the attributes of divinity which are essential to his health and moral maturity—love, justice, knowledge, and compassion.

These predicates of divinity are real and effective. But the ideals of peace and love, while they move men to action, are yet to be realized. In what soil can these values be rooted so that their significance is preserved? And what will endow these values with power? The Greeks secured them in a world of ideas, and the Jews in a Person, God. A potentially split world ensues, leading to a strained relation between the secular and the sacred, between person and Person. When man heals and cures, the glory is God's; when man hurts and destroys the blame is his alone. To praise God as a Person distinct from man for the good achieved by human effort and benevolence appears artificial and the assignment of evil to man exclusively appears unjust.

The Nazi Holocaust dramatizes our dilemma. That men who sin are punished is understandable; but that millions of innocents should be destroyed is not. What role does God play here? Is His permissiveness morally justifiable? If the monumental catastrophe belongs to man, what relevance does God have if He washes His hands of the whole matter and sets Himself apart as a spectator?

To save His relevance and to give dimension to our tragedy it is felt that God should be called upon as the controlling Cause of all significant events. But to do so is to rip open the wounds of Job and then to fall back upon the God that hides His face. But the concealed God holds a double-edged sword. In the defense of Adolf Eichmann, his lawyer Dr. Robert Servatius used classic theological overtones when he raised the question: "Do you not believe that irrational factors, transcending human understanding, are responsible for the fate of the Jewish people?" That which is meant to justify God's ways is now used to justify man's. The wicked, as easily as the good, can hide behind the Hiding God.

TIKKUN OLAM: PERFECTING THE WORLD

Depicted as Person, endowed with the traits of personality—willing, desiring, punishing, rewarding—divinity will forever require defense. We call for a different conception of God. We experience divinity not as a Person nor "He who" but as "That which." *That which* cures the sick, loosens the bonds of the fettered, upholds the fallen, supports the poor, we identify as godly.These revelations are not arbitrary, neither being cast earthward from heaven nor capriciously invented. They are discovered, tested, and affirmed in this world through our individual and collective interactions with nature, human and nonhuman. Activities are godly and real without being objects, things, or persons. Evil and good are encountered in the world, not as the effects of contending supernatural powers, but as distinguishable events which frustrate or contribute to our moral maturity.

The moral dualism in the world we experience is the tension between what is and what ought to be—between *chol* (neutral and uncommitted energy) and *kadosh* (energy dedicated to ideal ends). The monotheism of Jewish tradition is expectant. The world is incomplete. "The Lord shall be king over all the earth; on that day the Lord shall be One and His name One" (Zechariah 14:9).

That which works to overcome the tension which ruptures the moral world is divine. Godliness is revealed to us in terms of values we can understand as human beings. Godliness is that feature of the world which penetrates the dumbness of nature and makes it speak the language of moral intent.

In our view, no segregated area exists where divinity may not be found. Moral evil and moral good are not supernaturalized. They are both in the same world, where men may be blameworthy or praiseworthy, but divinity is blameless. For divinity is neither person nor omnipotent will. Divinity, by our meaning, designates those energies and activities which sustain and elevate our lives. Such an understanding of divinity requires no justification in the presence of evil.

NOTES

1. *Kiddushin* 39b. From *Chullin* 142a, the rabbis opine that this turning away came when he saw the tongue of the scholar R. Judah Nachtum in the mouth of a

dog, or that he saw Chutzpith the interpreter dragged along by swine during the Hadrianic persecution and then commented in sorrowful disillusionment, "The mouth that uttered pearls licks the dust." Thereupon he went forth and sinned.

2. Zvi Kolitz, "Yossel Rackover Speaks to God," *The Bridge* (New York: Pantheon, 1958), vol. 3.

3. See, for example, the reactions of Barry Ulanov and Elisabeth Orsten to the "blasphemy" of the Jobian stances in two separate essays published in *The Bridge*, vol. 3.

4. Genesis 17:10 ff.

5. Ibn Gabirol, *The Royal Crown*.

6. *Lamentations Rabbah*, introductory proems.

7. *Berachot* 32a. The Moses legend is based on the text in Exodus 32:9–14, in particular on the verse in which God exclaims to Moses, "Now, therefore, let Me alone that My wrath may wax hot against them."

8. See *Berachot* 32a; also *Ta'anit* 23a, and *Mo'ed Katan* 16b, where David is given the power to annul God's decree.

9. *Kuzari* 4:13.

10. Maimonides, *Guide for the Perplexed* 3:2.

11. This argument is used most effectively by Saadia, Abraham Ibn Daud, and Maimonides. The intent of this argument is to keep God uninfected by contact with the physical basis of evil. The logic of separating God from matter has taken on a variety of forms, including the doctrines of demiurges, emanations, angelic intelligences which serve as middlemen or buffers between God and matter.

12. See Isaac Husik, *A History of Mediaeval Jewish Philosophy*, pp. 229 ff.

13. Maimonides, *Guide* 3:12.

14. The view of Christian Science and some Hindus that suffering, illness, and death are illusory and unreal is foreign to Jewish belief.

15. See Gersonides, *Commentary on Job* 41–42.

16. Maimonides, *Guide* 3:22; Gersonides, *Commentary on Job* 1.

17. Maimonides, *Guide* 3:12.

18. *Megillah* 25a; also *Berachot* 33. In *Bava Metzia* 107 we read, "All is in the hands of heaven except cold and heat."

19. R. Isaac declared, "Let one always pray for mercy not to fall sick, for if he falls sick, he is told, 'Show thy merits and be quit of this disease' " (*Shabbat* 32a). See also *Mechilta* 95b.

20. *Berachot* 7a, where R. Jonathan, in the name of R. Yose, argues that this explanation was the secret wisdom God revealed to Moses.

21. From the traditional confession made on the deathbed (*Viddui Shechiv Mera*). A variety of justifications for the "chastisements of love" are summarized by the fifteenth-century theologian Joseph Albo. See his *Sefer Ha-Ikkarim*, vol. 4, pt. 1, pp. 117 f.

22. See Saadia's *Book of Doctrines and Beliefs* in *Three Jewish Philosophers* (Philadelphia: Jewish Publication Society, 1960), p. 135. Also *Nedarim* 41a and *Lamentations Rabbah* 5:1, where Akiva sees reason for rejoicing in the Temple's destruction: "If they that offend Him fare so well, how much better they fare who obey Him."

23. *Song of Songs Rabbah* II, 16:2; *Genesis Rabbah* 32:3, 54:1.

24. *Sifre* 73b, *Ta'anit* 82.

25. *Berachot* 5b. Note that R. Chiyyah and R. Yochanan, who have previously been cited in this passage as having advocated the doctrine of "afflictions of love," reject it in their suffering.

26. *Guide* 3:17, 24.

27. More explicit is the formulation of Ezekiel 18. See also *Numbers Rabbah* 19:33, where Moses is credited with "instructing" God against visiting the sins of the fathers upon the children.

28. *Sanhedrin* 74a–b. See Maimonides, *Mishneh Torah, Hilchot Yesodei ha-Torah* 5:4. "He who sacrifices his life for religious precepts when not required by the law to do so is guilty of a deadly sin." See also *Ketubbot* 3b.

29. From the last chorus of the Passover song *Chad Gadya*.

30. *Midrash Tanchuma, Vayeshev,* sec. 4.

31. The mystic theorists of the old Kabbalah and Zohar sometimes identified evil as existing in a metaphysical domain. Evil is here viewed as independent of man, "woven into the texture of the world or rather the existence of God"; see Gershom Scholem, *Major Trends in Jewish Mysticism,* p. 36.

32. See *Sotah* 37b and *Sanhedrin* 43b, where not the "secret things" but those overt acts of sin are to be judged and punished by the community.

33. In his *Answer to Job,* C. G. Jung analyzes the Job story as a conflict between an amoral, unconscious power and a moral, conscious finite son.

34. "The Dialogue Between Heaven and Earth," in *Four Existentialist Theologians,* ed. Will Herberg (New York: Anchor Books, 1958), p. 203.

35. Ibid.

36. Martin Buber, *Eclipse of God,* pp. 60–61.

37. Ibid., pp. 118 f.

38. Ibid., p. 60.

39. Ibid., p. 61.

40. Baruch Spinoza, *Ethics,* Appendix to pt. I.

41. *Berachot* 33b, *Chagigah* 15a.

42. K. Kohler, *Jewish Theology,* pp. 195 f. The author deals with the personification of angels, messiahs, and Satan.

43. Albo, *Ikkarim,* bk. IV, pt. 1, p. 66.

44. George Santayana, *Reason in Religion,* p. 133.

III
Family and Synagogue

FIDDLER ON A HOT TIN ROOF: PORTRAIT OF THE MISHPACHAH

A woman whose husband had abandoned her went to a rebbe to find out whether he would return. Since the rebbe was busy elsewhere, she spoke to the shammes (sexton), who wrote a *kvitl*, a note describing her problem. The shammes disappeared and showed the *kvitl* to the rebbe. After the rebbe wrote his response, the shammes returned and told the woman, "The rebbe says that your husband will return. But I assure you he will not return." She replied angrily, "Who are you to tell me that he will not return when the rebbe says he is going to return?" The shammes answered, "The rebbe sees only the *kvitl*. I see the face."

The evidence sustaining our analysis is not derived from the *kvitl*, from statistical and sociological accounts of anomie and alienation. The data are derived from reading the joyless face of the abandoned woman. The well-dressed, externally successful are mostly too proud to admit to the crumbling character of their families. They put on a wonderful face. Everything is fine. The family is thriving. But beneath the appearance of well-being, the family is hemorrhaging. The *kvitl* of statistics is frightening enough. In a seventy-year period from 1870 to 1940, the population of America increased twofold; marriages increased threefold; and divorces increased twenty-fold. The statistics of the eighties are no more comforting. The sexton was right. He/she will not return. However persuasive the theological and ideological arguments in

99

praise of Jewish love and marriage may be, the trend of family disintegration in our society mocks the noblest ideals. In its wake a cynical wag proposes that marriage is the major cause of divorce.

No statistics are required to be reminded of the tragedies about us. She who was married less than a dozen years comes to the rabbi facing her imminent divorce. What concerned her were her two daughters, the eldest of whom, hearing of the pending divorce, threatened to do away with her life. She had asked her mother, "Tell daddy I promise I won't be bad anymore," so convinced was she of her responsibility for the terrible separation. The younger daughter grows sycophantically attached to the mother, hanging onto her skirts, afraid that she too will be abandoned. She lives under the threat of the undelivered punch. "The altar sheds tears over him who divorces. The Lord hates sending away" (T. *Gittin* 90b).

Two parents, stammering their embarrassment, came to see their rabbi because their twelve-year-old daughter had run away a second time. The police reported that 2,723 young children in his community ran away last year, children from the ages of eleven to seventeen. We are witness to a mounting tragedy. Here are manifestations of no isolated psychological disorder, but evidence of a widespread sociocultural pathology. Something is eating away at the core of the Jewish family. No matter how hard the rabbis preach about the home being a *mikdash me'at*—a sanctuary in miniature, it is losing its sanctifying powers.

Some sociologists and psychologists predict the eventual dissolution of the family. Others, like R. D. Laing and David Cooper, virtually advocate the death of the family. Alvin Toffler of *Future Shock* fame gathered the prognostications of futurologists who prepare us to accept the marital trajectory of sequential polygamy, the game of marital musical chairs. A psychological "art of disrelating" is advocated. Readers are informed that ties to family, friends and associates must be painlessly severed if they are to enjoy the upwardly mobile spiral that is indispensable for the modern dynamics of success.

The dying of the family is a universal threat. For Judaism it is a particular threat because its religious civilization is rooted less in dogma or doctrine than in a people who sees itself as an extended world family. Jews may not share the same theology or ritual practice, but they know themselves to be of the same mishpachah. Therein lies one of the major insights of the Book of Genesis, which concludes by tracing our ancestry to father Jacob. Jews own a common fate and a common faith that grow out of their familial status. For the Jew, the dying of family drains the vitality of his faith. The Jewish home has long served as the portable sanctuary of our people. All the tales of migration and settlement and resettlement, from Joseph and the brethren and Jacob in Egypt, to our parents' experience from the old country to this country, and in our times, Soviet Jews from behind the iron curtain and Ethiopian Jews returned to the Jewish homeland, weave sustaining legends of the solidarity and the interdependence of the Jewish communal family.

In the past, the mishpachah functioned as the great shock absorber of the resentments, insecurities, and threats to Jewish life. In the past, researchers such as Srole and Langer in their study of mental health in the metropolis commented on "the impairment limiting mechanism" of the Jewish family which protects its members from psychoses. They wrote of "the homeostatic support of family" evident in the virtual immunity of the Jew to the afflictions of suicide and alcoholism. But the contemporary Jewish family seems unable to withstand the corrosive acids of modernity. It will not do to romanticize its past and indulge in false nostalgia.

THE SHTETL FAMILY

Fiddler on the Roof nostalgia rests on the lean myth of the glorious past. It is not simply that *Fiddler* does not tell it like it was. Not only can Jews not go home again, but most Jews don't want to go home again. To salvage the Jewish family calls for restructuring the roles of the members of the family and struggling against the mass culture that threatens the power and idealism of the Jewish family.

Fiddler on the Roof is not the Jewish world. Its characters are the dramatis personae of a mythic shtetl mishpachah. Papa sings, "Who has the right as master of the house to have the final word at home?" Mama reprises, "Who must know the way to make a proper home, a quiet home, a kosher home?" The son recalls, "At three I started Hebrew school, at ten I learned a trade. I hear they picked a bride for me: I hope she's pretty.'' The daughter declares, ''Who does mama teach to mend and tend and fix, preparing me to marry whoever papa picks?'' But those songs are not all in the family today.

THE PAPA

Today's papa is not the master of the house, nor does he want to be master of the house. We hear his complaints. He has been sucked into the vortex of career, profession, or business. By his own account he has ''a tiger by the tail.'' Papa feels driven by some ubiquitous force that makes him expand in order to stay alive, because if not his murderous competitors will ''eat him up alive.'' The demands upon the middle-class father are limitless. There are no price and wage controls on his aspirations because there is no accepted ceiling on his standard of living. There is no Shaddai in papa's life, no God who declares ''dai'' (enough). The criterion of success is insatiable and the expectation level is borderless. Success's demands are omnivorous. They devour every moment of his life. The cocktail party, the country club, the golf club are not simply his private joys. He consumes liquor in order to consummate deals. Herbert Marcuse characterized papa's condition as the ''introjection of totalitarianism'' into his daily business and leisure time. Papa is not Tevye, and certainly not Hayim Topol. There is little song or dance in him. He does not speak with God. He is too spent for poetry, too drained for that intense dialogue. The world of ritual, the world of choreography, the world of wine and candles and spice box is entirely alien to him because it is a nonutilitarian, nonprofitmaking domain. His life has been taken over by the values and ideals of the marketplace. Papa is no ogre. He simply knows no other way to express his fidelity, his Jewish loyalty, except to buy. And so he buys tickets, scholarships, raffles, bonds, memberships; he buys his belonging, his believing and his behaving. He is defined by the quip about the ''alimony Jew,'' a Jew willing to support Judaism but refusing to live with it.

What can reasonably be expected from this figure of middleclass masculinity. To be masculine in the middle class means to be independent, industrious, competitive, manipulative. Can it be expected that upon seeing the mezuzah on his doorpost, he will suddenly be transformed into a playful, warm, cooperative, poetic husband and father? The home and the job make contradictory claims upon him. With all his gifts for compartmentalization, he cannot leave his business or career back in the office. Papa's domestic persona can not be conveniently turned on and off. He remains torn between the demands of father and husband and the drivenness of an upwardly mobile middle-class male. His split consciousness barely prepares him to be master of the house. In truth he does not want the final word at home. He may play the game of "pater familias," barking out some orders, but nobody is listening. To be listened to you have to invest time and patience, and papa has neither time nor patience. So like the comic he mutters half-seriously that he gets no respect at home.

Papa, increasingly invisible and incomprehensible at home, tries to compensate. He is forever buying father surrogates: baby sitter, scoutmaster, youth director, camp counselor, piano teacher, karate expert and the great electronic pacifier, TV in living technicolor. He would rent the rabbi as father to his children. In Leonard Fein's study, *Reform Is a Verb,* the investigators sought to determine what the congregant regards as the outstanding quality of a good rabbi. The respondents did not speak of the rabbi's erudition or ability to preach or piety, but primarily of his capacity to relate to young people. Papa wants a hired papa for his children. The child senses that he is condemned to living with an ersatz papa. Arnold Green, the social psychologist, maintains that the middle-class child knows that he is unwanted and senses that he is an economic and psychic drain upon the family. Part of the scenario of the dying of the family is the missing father.

THE MAMA

If papa is too absent, mama is too present. If papa is too passive, mama is too aggressive. How has the Jewish mama become the domineering, protective, semihysterical bearer of children, chicken soup and the extra sweater? How is it that she, freer now than ever before, gifted with more labor-saving devices, more leisure and affluence than ever before, has become so subject to brooding depressions?

Consider the built-in contradictions of the middle-class female in the last two or three decades. For fifteen years, from kindergarten through college, she is exposed to the same intellectual experience to which the boys are exposed. She is exposed to mathematics, chemistry, physics, philosopy, and art. With matrimony, it all fades away. She is expected to surrender her talents, her dreams, her unfulfilled potentiality because she is married. Every once in a while it may gnaw at her. What could she have been before she settled for Marjorie Morningstar?

Now that she is married, she is expected to find her contentedness through someone else. At the end of the day, when her husband comes home, she is to be dressed cheerfully, answering the door chimes, skirt swirling, greeting her Prince Charming who comes with a message from the outer world. But the Prince is too tired. He wants only a cigar and slippers.

Unmarried, she is a failure; married she has at best fulfilled mama's expectation. Mama says, "My son the doctor," but "My daughter the doctor's wife." Her glory years will be in pregnancy or when the children are two or three years old, because then she is needed. When the children grow older and enter the school years, she becomes the great family teamster. The perennial chauffeur, she is ever driving for the growth of others. When the children turn adolescent, a new crisis sets in. The adolescent child wants autonomy while mama needs purpose. The adolescent cries, "Please, mother, I'd rather do it myself." The mother is petrified because she is psychologically unemployed. She feels herself a mutilated self. When the children outgrow her, she turns once again to the husband. But his world is strictly off limits. It is like living with an atomic scientist working on a secret project at Los Alamos. He will tell her nothing and she knows nothing. At funerals rabbis discover what it means for two people to live together without knowing anything of each other.

In the sixties and seventies, mama's critical years were from age thirty-nine to fifty-nine. If one can speak of postpartum depression, one may speak of postparental depression. Without child care, what could she do? She could enter into what Veblen called the "occupation of ceremonial futility." She could wash, dust, mop, cook, and make beds. But that was hardly a job for a nice Jewish girl with a B.A. The TV commercials have their fingers on the pulse of America. The commercials know the boredom and the frustration of the homemaker who is delighted with any break from her pseudo-occupation. Colonel Sanders liberated her from the home. But where should she go? The tragic elements of the middle-aged, middle-class woman were analyzed by Pauline Barth, professor of sociology and psychiatry at the University of Illinois Medical Center. She claimed that the Jewish woman more than any other ethnic group shared the highest degree of depression. You cannot expose a girl to her intellectual, aesthetic and idealistic potentialities and then condemn her to a life of vicarious existence.

Mama had to live for everybody except herself. What was her success? Her success was the success of others. And so she became a nagging, demanding, driving woman. She became Minority Whip of the House. In the last few decades the middle-class papa and mama grew less and less happy with their roles. The change was in the wind. The centrifugal pull was away from the home.

THE SON

The son is caught in the trap of the nuclear family. The extended family has shriveled down to two parental gods. There is no zaydeh, bubba, cousin, uncle, or aunt around. He is caught by the family's need to move up the ladder; but if you move up, you have to move out. Upward vertical mobility requires outward horizontal mobility. The extended family has become excessive baggage. Americans move a lot. Toffler tells us that the average American moves fourteen times in his lifetime. Forty million Americans change their home addresses at least once a year. And so the son is left stranded with nobody but two gods who alone hold love or neglect in their hands.

With papa away most of the time, mama becomes the sole companion of the single child, exercising her control. But the control is not that of other ethnic families from abroad. There is no beating, no smacking of the Jewish child. In its place is something more intimidating. No physical punishment is as powerful as the implicit threat of the withdrawal of love, the dread of "disappointing" the parental gods. A popular Jewish joke asks, "How do you say 'disappointed' in Yiddish?" Why did they choose that word for translation except for its ubiquity and power in upbringing the child. You need not know how to translate "disappointed." The look that terrorizes suffices.

The son is born into a competitive meritocracy. Everything is measured and tested. Everything is compared from birth to death; weight, height, intake, silver star, gold star, IQ, SAT, 3.5, 3.8, 4.0. From that innocent remark, "Let my son play something for you," to the bribery of a dollar for every A you bring home, the relentless pressure to perform, achieve, to excel persists. The child of the middle class has become precisely what Marshall Sklare called "a naches-producing machine."

David Reisman writes of the anguish of students who, because they cannot be brilliant, deliberately or unconsciously fail so as to be relieved of the pressure. They will oversleep the examination, or not find time to prepare for it because they have found an excuse. Had they only prepared they of course would have been brilliant, outstanding. There is an unspoken conspiracy between parents and children in the matter of academic failure. The parents will trace the failure to indolence—better the charge that the child is "lazy" than not smart. Not to be smart reflects on the parents' intellectual endowment. Parents live through their children's reputations. In a brilliant conspiracy, the child will admit to laziness because lack of brilliance is intolerable. He will argue that the failing was due to indolence, not incompetence. If at first you don't succeed, say you have not tried. So oddly enough the parental pressure to achieve boomerangs and the tragedy of the academic failure is compounded. Term papers and research papers are bought and sold on the academic black market. What would you not do to avoid being a disappointment to your mother and your father?

There is pathos here. What if the son is not brilliant, if he cannot make 3.4 or 3.5, or 3.8 or 4.0, if he is not academically gifted? Is quantitative measurement of his school achievement the criterion of his worth? What of his kindness, spontaneity, unselfishness, gentility? It is rare to hear parents boast, "My child is kind," unless the child is an academic failure. Praise for his good character is the loser's compensation. But a severe price is paid for the performance of our children. Success drivenness is no small factor in the increased dropping-out of Jewish young people from college, or the appeal of cults. They are elements in the revolt against the exaggerated pressures upon the young to perform. They explain youth's "affective revolution," which prefers feeling to performance, feeling to achievement, feeling to winning. For many, anti-intellectualism is not against books and ideas but an opposition to academic and vocational pressures that are oblivious to the idealism and sensibilities of the young.

THE DAUGHTER

If the son who is not smart is doomed in the pressure-filled environment of the upwardly mobile, pity the daughter who is not pretty or popular. What does the daughter absorb from the atmosphere of the suburban matriarchy that we have described? Is the mother a proper model of what a wife and mother should be? Are the portraits by Philip Roth and Bruce J. Friedman correct? Has the middle-class Jewish girl become Brenda Patimkin? In suburbia, Jewish girls are called JAPs, Jewish-American Princesses. It means a girl who is spoiled, narcissistic, a demanding replica of her mother. Is this a true characterization? Is she a correlate of the pressurized son? Professor Werner Cahnman, writing on the issue of intermarriage, reports that young Jewish men "feel oppressed by the expectations of the relentless pressure of obligations to which they will be subjected in the families of prospective Jewish spouses." He finds that they have a preference for gentile girls because with them they do not feel the great pressure to achieve in the marketplace and to remain docile at home. Professor Cahnman sounds a warning that Jewish girls should learn to compete more efficiently. In conversation with young people, Jewish boys complain that Jewish girls are materialistic and demanding, and Jewish girls in turn complain that Jewish boys lack poetry.

A SECOND LOOK AT THE FAMILY

The family is an interdependent unit. The family is so linked together that if there is a stress upon one member of the family it places a strain upon the others. Let us return to the supermother. Children of my generation may remember a popular Yiddish song that made young people cringe. The lyrics of "Mein Yiddishe Momme" filled us with unspoken guilt. "How few were her pleasures. She never cared for fashion styles. Her jewels and treasures, she found them in her baby's smile. Oh, I know that I owe what I am today to that dear little lady so old and gray, to that wonderful Yiddisha momme, momme mine." We loved our mothers too much to deny her pleasures. Who asked Mama for such awful altruism? That martyr role turned into an anxiety-producing love. To say no to mama became the great betrayal.

In a study of the East European shtetl, *Life Is with People,* by Zborowski and Herzog, a Jewish folktale is retold that sent terror into the hearts of its listeners. A young man begs his mother for her heart in order to please his betrothed. She cuts out her heart and gives it to the young man, who eagerly runs with it to his betrothed. He stumbles and the heart falls to the ground and is heard to cry out, "Did you hurt yourself, my son?" Here is a mother legend with revenge.

Who would perpetuate that sick altruism upon wife or daughter? Healthy altruism grows out of self-esteem or else it turns into a perverted form of egoism that endangers us all. The Jewish woman should be freed from that confining role for her own sake and for the sake of her family. Those women who cannot find vicarious fulfillment in the joys of others must be liberated from the household and the obsessional supervision of their children. Contrary to the argument that they will soon wear the pants in the family if "allowed" to express their potentialities outside the home, many women have become aggressive at home precisely because it is the only outlet for their competence.

To restructure the role of supermother is a task not to be lightly undertaken. Love requires compassion, *cum passio,* which means "with suffering." Love costs. When a wife or mother goes to school or engages in organizational commitments, children and husband must not expect dinner on the table on time. The menu may not be as varied as before. The chores of the home will have to be shared with the husband and with the children. The family calendar will have to consider her life.

The father too must be liberated. If we are to regain the father, the pressures to have him achieve must be reduced even if it means a lower standard of living for the family. Wife and children play important roles in changing the single criterion of "the great provider" as confirmation of papa's success. The upper middle class is living psychically above its needs. The preservation of the values of mishpachah cannot afford the luxury of trading the family for material prosperity. What good are the stolen moments of vacations when they are bought by draining Papa's psychic energy? The cultural mythology that defines the woman as dependent, gossipy, and panicky, as well as the culturally perverse definition of masculinity, must be overcome if the family of modernity is to regain its health.

The son must be emancipated from the grinding pressure to get into a prestigious university, to earn a Phi Beta Kappa key, to "make it." We have to protect his affective life, honor his character, respect his sensibilities, become aware of his spiritual needs.

Basic cultural factors lie at the root of the changing Jewish family and its future. Critical is the creeping axiological revision of the meaning assigned to "goodness." What do we mean today by attributing "goodness" to parents or children? In our times, "goodness" has lost its moral connotation and has been supplemented by amoral success. To be a good son or a good daughter or a good husband or a good wife has less to do with the traditional virtues of character—kindness, empathy, sensitivity—and more with economic, social, professional success. To be a good husband is to be a good provider, to be a good wife is to run a good home, to be a good son is to bring home good marks, to be a good daughter is to be popular. What is at stake is a profound struggle of values. Middle-classism and Judaism have unconsciously been identified and are popularly viewed as two sides of the same coin. The equation is false and dangerous. Aspects of their incompatability cannot, without distorting the authentic character of Judaism, remain ignored.

MIDDLE–CLASSISM AND JUDAISM

Jews in America are overwhelmingly middle class. And while there are compatibilities between middle-class values and those of Judaism, Jews have reached a point where the value conflicts between the two cannot be dismissed. No one can deny the advantages and the positive values of the middle class. Jews have done exceedingly well with the emergence of the middle class in the eighteenth century. A people peculiarly gifted with creative assimilation, Jews rose out of the "ascribed status" in which persons were measured by the social class or religion to which they belonged, into the "functional status" wherein the important question is what have you achieved. In less than three generations, Jews managed to deproletarianize themselves. But while some of the values and

ideals of the middle class overlap and may find support in the
Judaic value system, there are serious consequences in falsely
equating middle-classism with Judaism.

Intellectuality, worldliness and individualism are three middle-
class values said to be found in Judaism. Certainly Judaism encourages belief in the rational mastery of the world, in the conviction that the world can be transformed by knowledge and effort.
Jews inherited a tradition of meliorism that would not succumb to
paralyzing fatalism.

But the distinctive character of Jewish intellectuality lies in its
attachment to moral purpose. Moral teleology informs Jewish
rationality. When a Jew offered thanks to God for gracing him with
knowledge and understanding, it was not for the knowledge to
become smart, to gain degrees, or to accumulate wealth or fame.
Jewish intellectuality was directed towards *ma'asim tovim*, the
practice of good deeds. The rabbis compared learning that ex-
ceeded good deeds to trees with many branches and few roots.
The Talmud warned that "he who occupies himself with study
alone is as one who has no God." Once the moral end of intelligence is decapitated, its remainder is a calculative intelligence.
Many children are repelled by manipulative intelligence, by the
pressing energy to achieve which they wrongly associate with
Jewish intellectuality. They rebel against investing so much energy
for amoral ends. It was truer in the sixties, but the resentment
retains pockets of disillusionment in our decade. They are less
impressed with status, homes, cars, and vacations than the children of the depression years. Theirs is less an anti-intellectualism
than a hunger for superordinate causes to justify the kind of self-
sacrifice imposed on them. Moreover, they are a post-Holocaust
generation who have seen how readily intellectuality may be pros-
tituted for the most banal of ends. Hitler's doctors and professors
have taught them the amorality of knowledge and titles. Many
young people have become more concerned with the motivation
and purpose of intellectuality than their parents' generation. The
distinction between middle-class smartness, calculative intelligence and Jewish moral intellectuality must not be blurred.

The same need for distinction applies to the worldliness of
Judaism. Jews celebrate life and the goodness of life. They have
heard cited the statement in the Talmud Yerushalmi that we will

have to account for all the permissible good things in this world that we did not enjoy. A midrashic parable compares the denial of the joys of this world to an invited guest who sits at the banquet table touching nothing. For men and women not to eat and drink is to shame the host. The invited guests in God's world insult their divine host by their asceticism. But again, Jewish worldliness is connected to moral purpose. That the earth is given to man means that man is responsible for its preservation and repair. This kind of responsible worldliness is of a different order from that of exploitative materialism and hedonism. Prophetic this-worldliness is radically different from the consumptive styles of the middle class. Jewish this-worldliness is not the culinary orgies at Bar Mitzvahs and weddings.

The same applies to the values of individualism. From Abraham at Sodom throughout our history the dissent of the wronged against the oppressive authority is repeatedly illustrated and proclaimed. But religious audacity against those who trample the divine image is a far cry from an individualism that ends in self-centered privatism.

Much of the stress and strain in family life is exacerbated by the perversion of Judaic values. Judaism recognizes the moral ambiguity of individualism, industry and intellectuality. The tradition urges the community to be cautious of Balaam's ambivalent benediction. According to some rabbinic commentaries, the maledictions of Balaam turned into benedictions and ironically his benedictions turned into curses. The blessing of affluence, unless wisely and morally used, may be turned into a curse. The power of worldliness, intellectuality and individualism wields a double-edged sword. We need Judaic stability so that the values of Jewish family life are not swept away in the maelstrom of an overly competitive, depersonalizing middle-class culture. To preserve the ideals of the Jewish family requires a reappraisal of the roles superimposed upon its members. It needs an appreciation of the values of Judaism which have been twisted out of shape. It requires collective courage and intelligence to live against the grain of middle-classism. As difficult as all this may be, history is on our side. In eras of violence, Jews did not shed blood. In environments of illiteracy, Jews read and wrote. Amidst drunkenness, Jews remained sober without vows of abstinence. Surrounded by murder and suicide, Jews cherished the sanctity of life. In a society riddled with mindless materialism, purposeless pressure, joyless hedonism, and devastating loneliness, Jews can restructure the family to oppose the shallow ethos of mass culture.

But it cannot be done alone. No family is an island. If anything, familism, the retreat of individuals into the insularity of their individual families, may prove counterproductive. Narrow familism is another form of incestuous narcissism. The traditional Jewish family did not live against the grain of mass society by isolating itself from the community. It will not save itself today without the cooperation and planning of the community.

In our times the Jewish family is underinstitutionalized. It needs Jewish institutions to offer wisdom and therapy, to provide innovative vehicles to help the family bind itself in dramatically new circumstances. The havurah and the rabbinic paraprofessionals are two such instruments for family empowerment. Reviving the moribund Jewish family must be placed high on the Jewish domestic agenda. This will be discussed in the following chapters as an illustration of the power of the Jewish community to serve the Jewish family in a renewed therapeutic role.

JEWISH PARENTS AND THE PRESSURES ON THE UPWARDLY MOBILE CHILD

One of the dominant concerns of the young in our society is the fear of failure: academic failure, vocational failure, failure in popularity, marital failure. Fear of failure has supplanted the traditional fears of *yirat shamayim* and *yirat chet,* the fear of heaven and the fear of sin. Failure is the secular sin that replaces moral and religious transgression. It begins early, in the children's inability to live up to the fantasies of their parents, who often themselves live in fear of failing their parents' ambitions for them. This fear gives no rest to the hurried child and harried adult. It produces an anxiety that robs them of the enjoyment of their accomplishments.

The relentless demand to achieve, perform and succeed, so characteristic of the ethos of the perpetually upwardly mobile middle class, has so successfully swallowed up the ideals of the Jewish ethic that they seem synonymous. The motivating ethic of middle-classism has been so assimilated by the Jewish child and parent of the middle class that its ways are identified as the authentic traits of Jewishness. A new equation is established. Judaism is middle-classism. Inadvertently Jewish institutions perpetuate this deformity of the Jewish ethic. It begins at home, within the family and is reinforced by the surrounding institutions.

The child is enveloped by measurement, the weight of meritocracy hangs heavy over him filled with endless rewards and punishments. From cradle to grave, from the silver and gold stars to 3.8

and 4.0 averages, from the scores on the SAT to the GRE, the child is judged by the extrinsic marks of success. Years ago the sociologist Andrew Greeley noted that certain communities operate nurseries that will accept only college material. The result of such pediatric exclusivity leads ambitious parents to engage professionals to train toddlers so that they will pass the admission test into elite nurseries. Consider the shame of having a nursery school dropout. As we approach the beginning of the next millennium, Operation Headstart may offer prenatal courses.

At home and in school, sin is failure and virtue is success. And the semantic change in the meaning of vice and virtue portends an axiological revolution. ''Robert is a good boy'' has come to mean one and only one thing. Robert knows and does whatever is required to bring home A's. Rarely do parents refer to Robert's gentility, kindness, idealism, piety, altruism as manifestations of his goodness. Goodness now assumes an amoral connotation. Goodness is assessed by the acquisition of the tokens of academic success, the major criterion that judges Robert's worth. The revolution of values means that goodness no longer points to moral character but to the external marks of grade achievement. The moral connotation of goodness is substituted and sabotaged.

Towards what kind of goodness is our Jewish education directed? There is a collusion between home and school. The parental judgment of the child's worth in terms of the extrinsic tokens of academic success is corroborated by the judgment of the Jewish schools. In this, Jewish schools are no different from secular schools or Jewish homes. It is not piety or moral character that is valued. For all the disparity between the goals of the Jewish school and the home, there is marked agreement as far as the criteria of ''goodness'' are concerned. The Jewish school, wittingly or not, becomes an appendage of middle-classism, and the teacher stands ''in loco parentis,'' which some translate ''crazy like parents,'' an extension of the middle-class parent. Who is praised and who is rewarded in our Jewish schools? The moral ambience of the religious school is not different from that of the middle-class home. Are the relationships between students in the environment of a Jewish school different from those between students in the secular school? Do we celebrate the child for his devotion to Jewish causes, or his compassion, or his altruism?

Celebration is reserved solely for his performance achievements. Who is the "successful" Bar/Bat Mitzvah? He who has a smooth voice, a good ear, and faithfully echoes the Haftarah as he has heard it from his teacher's taped "trope." Who is concerned about his feelings, how he experiences his Jewishness at this critical passage of his life? Who cares what he believes or how he behaves or even what he really knows? The extrinsic marks of his success are in the chanting without fluff, in the job well done, the smooth performance. Is this kind of performance what is meant by Jewish intellectuality?

From infancy the child is trained to repay his parents for their sacrifice and love in one and only one way: the report card. He has been weaned on the myths of the "Yiddishe kop" and tales of Jewish Nobel Prize winners. There is only one way to deserve their love and respect. The child knows the dread of disappointing his parents. A grade of C or D is a mark of betrayal, a sign of ingratitude. For the Jewish parent will accept no excuse for academic unsuccess. "If he only applied himself. If he weren't so lazy, he could get any grade he wanted." The complaint of indolence sounds as if the failing mark were deliberately intended by the child, more evidence of the child's moral failure than his academic limitations. To bring home a failing mark is to be judged a failure, and to fail is to sense oneself unworthy of love. It is difficult for parents who place such an inordinate stress on grades to convince the child to feel other than a failure.

There is a stereotypic parental response to the criticism of their relentless pressure. "All we ask is that Robert try his best." And that appears to be so reasonable a request. On examination however, trying your best provides a built-in formula for failure. "Good–better–best." The best is enemy of the good. For all its sweet logic, trying your best conceals an impossible goal. Whoever tries his "best"? Who cannot do better? Can I not study more, read more, write more? When can I declare in any undertaking that I have tried my best?

Realistically "the best" is unattainable. But it is a sure prescription for a drivenness that can only lead to self-disillusionment. Is it any wonder that "anhedonia," the inability to take joy in any accomplishment, is so common a psychological diagnosis in an insatiable community?

The best is truly the enemy of the good. For if I cannot be the best it may be smarter to surrender the race from the start. If at first you don't succeed, better say you never tried. To be accused of indolence is surely less serious than to be dismissed as an academic failure. Paradoxically, the nagging parental urgings to try your very best may encourage the child to opt for early resignation.

Parental pressures on the young may help explain the attractiveness of the cults, especially for youngsters who have felt the heavy hand of conditional love, i.e., "I love you if and *when* you do well in school." It is hard for young people not to be tempted by a cult community that accepts them unconditionally, without regard to high academic status. The cultic talk of "original sin" for some even serves to relieve the fear of failure. If we all sin, if we all fail, and can be saved only through the intervention of a savior, the pressures to succeed are mitigated. Cults, the pressurized children claim, speak not of test and best but of hug and love.

In the voices of young people who cannot make the dean's list one can detect an echo of Esau's cry, "Have you, dear parents, no blessing for me? Without the academic honor roll, am I so loveless in your eyes?" However reprehensible their manipulations may be, the cults appear to offer Robert another benediction, one not tied to grades. By comparison the Jewish home is heavy with the joyless pressures of the middle-class family, whose bribes of love and material rewards revolve around the virtues of competitiveness and aggressiveness. As in the preparation of the Bar/Bat Mitzvah, the area of devotion, prayer, and Torah is reduced to public performance, feats of verbal fluency or memory, not inner conviction and feeling. The inner life of the child is reduced to public reading, and the ultimate spiritual accomplishment is to be capable of standing before the congregation and leading the service.

What among many of our youth may appear as an anti-intellectual preference for feeling over thinking is as much a protest against the perversion of Jewish intellectuality, which was classically motivated by moral ends. Traditionally, Jews pray daily to be granted wisdom and discernment, to learn in order to teach and to fulfill the moral imperatives of the tradition. In Judaism wisdom is a holy pursuit because the end of wisdom is to repair the world, not to "make it." The acquisition of Jewish wisdom is to cultivate the heart, not to fatten the purse. But middle-classism has severed means from ends, the drive from the moral goal. It has rationalized the isolation of intense initiative from spiritual telos. The result is the driving ambition that makes Sammy run for gains that in truth offer him less and less fulfillment. The Jewish child is left without the uplift of high purpose that justifies the sacrifice.

A popular song begins and ends with the haunting refrain, "Is that all there is?" Is that all there is after the obsessive striving for grades, the idolatrous concentration of energy to get into prestigious institutions, and the eventual killing in the stock market? Does the bottom line mark our depth?

It is one thing to struggle against the deliberate assimilation of individual Jews to the ideologies of un-Jewish cults. More serious is the unconscious assimilation of Judaism to contradictory value systems. Here it is not Jews but Judaism that is being converted. Here Jews are raised to subconsciously believe that the mass media stereotypes of sharp, avaricious go-getters are in fact "Jewish." The Jewish child of the middle class is raised to somehow identify the calculative, manipulative intelligence with the moral wisdom sought by Judaism; to identify middle-class privatism with Jewish respect for individual worth; to identify middle-class aggressiveness with Jewish emphasis upon human freedom. That identification is played out in the media of mass culture.

Responsible Jewish educators must raise to consciousness the axiological disparities between Judaism and middle-classism. They must provide, in the Jewish environment of schools and synagogues, centers and federations, and in Jewish homes, a culture relieved of the mindless compulsion to succeed, an ambience in which character, prosocial behavior, and idealism are exalted, and where the spirit of the child and adult are acknowledged as praiseworthy.

Judaism must regain its own measure of ethical merit, restore the moral connotation of goodness, recapture its own spiritual criteria of success. There are pockets of significant growing dissatisfaction with the embourgeoisement of American life. They are to be found among the *ba'alei teshuvah,* the religious and secular returners to Judaism. There are signs of yearning for a nobler, kinder spiritual life. Jewishness and Judaism, unfettered by the pressures of middle-classism, are challenged to offer the hard crust of idealism to youth who hunger.

BETWEEN SESAME AND WALL STREETS: AN APPEAL TO THE BAR AND BAT MITZVAH

Historians of culture have observed that the first markets were sacred markets, the first banks were temples, and the first to issue money were priests. The attraction of gold and silver was due to their symbolic identification with the sun and the moon gods. That "the value ratio of gold to silver remained stable throughout classical antiquity and into the Middle Ages and even modern times at 1:13½" is explained by the astrological ratio of the cycles of the sun and moon, their divine counterparts (cited by Norman Brown in *Life Against Death*).

In the fall, *Forbes Magazine* publishes a listing of the four hundred richest Americans. But who is rich? George Bernard Shaw said, "A man with a toothache thinks everyone rich whose teeth are sound." A poor man thinks a rich man is one who makes a million dollars. But to be included in the Forbes listing requires a minimum of $150 million—a fact which leaves me out this year. While I'm not on the list, I enjoy reading the names. I'm looking for family. And incredibly, out of four hundred at least one hundred are Jews. (Since we are mishpachah, I derive no small naches from their success. I am like the poor Jew who identifies himself with Rothschild and dreams, "If I were Rothschild, I'd be richer than Rothschild, because I would do a little teaching on the

119

side.'') But it remains truly amazing. A group less than 3 percent of the population comprises 25 percent of the richest Americans. Beyond the millionaires are the billionaires. Of fourteen American billionaires, at least four are Jewish. While the wealth of Canada is not included in *Forbes,* the three most prominent families there are Jewish—Bronfman, Belzberg, and Reichmann.

Some Jews are embarrassed by such revelations and are jittery because of what "they," the anti-Semites, will say. So Jewish defense agencies point with pride at the number of Jews who are poor, and apologetically point out that Jews are not at the real power basis of society: steel, oil, banks, insurance companies, major industrial corporations.

I'm not so worried, because I know that anti-Semites don't need excuses to hate Jews. If Jews are regarded as rich they are accused of manipulating the world; if Jews are seen as poor they are condemned as parasites on society. As we have learned from history, a real anti-Semite is someone who hates Jews more than is absolutely necessary. A real anti-Semite can believe that Jesus never existed and still believe that the Jews killed him.

I refuse to find excuses for Jewish success. I am no more embarrassed by Jewish upward mobility than I am by the dispro-portionate number of Jewish Nobel Prize winners, writers, scien-tists, chess-players and violinists.

Professor Edward Shapiro, a historian teaching at Seton Hall University, has pointed out that while most of the gentiles on the *Forbes* list made their money by inheriting it, the Jewish names earned theirs the old-fashioned way, i.e., they earned it. They earned it the American way, from rags to riches in accord with the American legend of Horatio Alger and Lee Iacocca. In aristocratic societies, status was a matter of birth; in democratic societies, status is determined by hard work and Yankee ingenuity.

Poverty is an embarrassment for society, but why be embar-rassed by wealth? The Jewish Bible is not the New Testament. Judaism has never proclaimed with the Gospel of Matthew that "it is easier for a camel to go through the eye of a needle than for a rich man to enter the Kingdom of God." Judaism has never regarded poverty as a desirable condition, and has never proposed a vow of poverty similar to the one assumed by monks and nuns. Poverty is degrading. As Shalom Aleichem put it, "When a poor

man eats chicken, one of them is sick." Judaism has never espoused the pinched-nose puritanism that H. L. Mencken described
as "the haunting fear that someone, somewhere may be happy."
To the contrary, we declare, "Serve the Lord with joy." R. Dimi
in the Talmud (Yerushalmi *Nedarim* 9.1) sarcastically criticizes
those who assume vows of self-denial, "Are not the prohibitions
of the Torah sufficient for you that you must look for additional
prohibitions?"

Every Sabbath eve and in the prayer for the new month, Jews
pray for *parnasah,* a life of sustenance, and for *osher ve-kavod,* a
life of wealth and honor. Judaism is a preponderantly this-worldly,
optimistic tradition encouraging human initiative and energy, and
the enjoyment of all the permissible treasures of this world.

I respect wealth and do not deride it nor those who earn it. Far
from being embarrassed by prosperity, I am deeply embarrassed
by the desecration of wealth, disrespect for money, and the misuse
of its power. Money is not the root of evil anymore than wine is
the cause of intoxication. The Judaic struggle against idolatry is
not directed against the trees, stones, mountains that are worshiped, nor against the gold and silver out of which the calf was
shaped. Its struggle is against the idolatry that blindly worships
means as ends and that adores a part of the world as if it were the
whole of the universe. It is not the coin per se that is evil, but the
coin pressed against the eye that blocks out the whole world. With
the confusion of ends and means, life is trivialized. The idolatrous
pursuit of "more" ends in the miseries so often testified to in the
revelations of the rich and the famous.

The exposure of corruption in New York politics, of fraud,
bribery, tax evasion, and the number of Jewish names associated
with it—Lindenauer, Lipschutz, Manes, Simon, Friedman, Ehrlich, Kaplan—along with the Wall Street scandals and the names
Levine, Siegal, and Boesky, embarrasses me. Not because of *la-
mah yomru ha-goyim,* "what will the gentiles say," but because I
wonder, What will our children and grandchildren say?

I hear enough of the Jewish half-knowing acceptance of the
stereotype of the Jew as hard, overaggressive, driven by ruthless
competitiveness, shrewdness, and greed. I fear the internalization
of the Jewish caricature. That introjection is dangerous on at least
two counts.

First, because it adds fuel to the fires of self-hate, a disgust with the manipulativeness of Sammy Glick and Duddy Kravetz which in some minds become associated with the nature of Judaism itself. The false myth is found in Karl Marx, who in his self-hating diatribes wrote, "What is the cult of Jews? Bargaining. What is their worldly God? Money."

Secondly, because there are those who appear to believe that the mindless materialism of our society is in fact vindicated by Judaism. There are those who, hearing what is said about Jewish this-worldliness, twist it into a justification for greed and the insatiable lust for more. Judenthum is converted into Yuppiedom.

The perversion of Judaism is a more serious apostasy than the conversion of Jews. For if individual Jews assimilate to another faith, we may correct them with the ethics and theology of Judaism; but if normative Judaism itself is converted into hypermaterialism, what are we defending, and with what? Against the thrust of cults, mixed marriage, assimilation, we can struggle, provide arguments, change the environment, but when the very foundation of Judaism is subverted, when Judaism itself becomes deethicized, we are left defenseless.

The stereotype of the Jew as hustler is repeated and reinforced on talk shows, in movie caricatures, and from the mouths of Jewish comedians. This false identification of Judaism with the lust for money is a tragic equation.

While opposing the asceticism and self-denial of other traditions, Judaism unambiguously repudiates the obsessive drivenness for possession, the conspicuous and wasteful consumption of the world, and the sharp practices which raise knees and elbows over heart and mind. Those who have "made it" are challenged not by physical destruction or material bankruptcy but by our spiritual capacity to cope with abundance. They must resist the surreptitious placing of the glatt kosher label on the lifestyle of the extravagant and ostentatious.

Precisely because our tradition has its eye on this world and how it is lived, the Talmud imagines a series of questions to be answered at the end of our lives. The leading question is *Nosata ve-notata be-emunah*—"Did you deal honestly in your business?" Precisely because ours is a this-worldly tradition, our biblical and rabbinic ethic stresses the importance of moral behavior between an employer and employee, seller and buyer, professional and client. The Jewish Bible is not about abstract formulations of the nature of God or salvation but about concrete dealings in the marketplace. "You shall not falsify measures of length, weight, or capacity. You shall have an honest balance and honest weights" (Leviticus 19:35). You shall not deceive anyone through "stealth of mind." You shall not rationalize your overcharging or disinformation by claiming *caveat emptor*—let the buyer beware. Against that ethos Judaism declares, *caveat venditor*—let the seller beware. To be a good Jew is to be careful not to place a stumbling block before the blind or curse the deaf. To be a good Jew is not alone to observe what goes into your mouth but to watch what goes into your business dealings. Rabbi Israel Salanter explained that if one finds a *bluts-trop*, a blood speck in a fertilized egg, it is not fit for consumption. He added that if there is a speck of blood on your silver dollar, i.e., if your money is gained unjustly, shall it be fit for use?

Jewish ethics is predicated upon a fundamental belief about the ownership of possessions. "The earth is the Lord's and all that is in it." Bless the earth, work its soil, but remember that your possessions are derived from God, and consequently all energy, power and good must be used in a Godly fashion—to heal, not to hurt; to profit, not to steal; to raise up, not to grind down the faces of the poor.

Let there be no misunderstanding. Greed, avarice, mendacity, are not temptations affecting Jews alone. Lying, cheating, white-collar crime, and corporate fraud are universal phenomena, trans-denominational tragedies in our society. We read repeatedly of scores of indictments and arrests of non-Jewish violators. But that "everyone does it," that our society has gone berserk in its obsessive pursuit of wealth and power, does not alleviate our particularistic hurts and fears or justify our silence. It is a universal problem, but we are addressing our people, a talented, choosing people who chose to "love justice, love mercy, and walk modestly with God."

Furthermore, the issue we are dealing with about politics and Wall Street is not restricted to millionaires and billionaires. It concerns the struggles we all face raising our children in a society that is so relentlessly seduced by material things. The malaise runs deeper than the patent condemnation of overreaching, sharp practices, and greed. It involves the Jewish character and the stewardship of our estate.

Consider the Bar/Bat Mitzvah as a metaphor for the dilemmas spawned by wealth. Last year the *New York Times* covered a Jewish event in several columns. It had nothing to do with financial corruption or political scandal. A real estate tycoon, a member of a New York Synagogue, hired the *QE II,* the *Queen Elizabeth,* for an overnight cruise with six hundred guests to celebrate his son Jason's Bar Mitzvah. The *Times* reported it as the first floating Bar Mitzvah. The spokesman for the Cunard Lines itemized the expenses, which added up to a half-million dollars.

It began dockside on Sunday at 4:00 P.M., with a string quartet and helicopters touching down on the sports deck of the ship to drop off latecomers. The vessel sailed forty-six miles into the Atlantic with its load of guests, who stayed in three hundred choice cabins. It had everything, a crew of one thousand, a Golden Door spa, beauty parlor and massage service, movie theater, sports facilities and the Peter Duchin orchestra.

The *Times* reporter included in the piece a conversation aboard the ship between a child of ten and his father. The boy asked if he could have a Bar Mitzvah like Jason's. The father said, "Well, we'll see." All the meals served aboard the *QE 2* were strictly kosher, including the fillet of beef Wellington with truffle sauce. The menu, a mouth-watering cuisine, was detailed in the *Times.* The rabbi from the Synagogue was present to officiate at morning services with tallit and tefillin.

Tallit, tefillin, kashrut, and all—yet it felt wrong. But what was wrong here? Papa earned it. He worked for every penny. Nothing was stolen and he could well afford it. Why then the discomfort, or did the embarrassment conceal a basket of sour grapes? Why did I hear the echo of my father's voice: "*Es past nicht*"—it doesn't fit, it is inappropriate.

I could not get my mind off Jason and his parents, who undoubtedly love him and would do anything to make him happy. Inadvertently Jason has been poorly instructed for life. His parents have money—and that's no sin. Wealth is a power, and that's no sin. But to so misuse money and power is blasphemous.

Money can save lives from sickness and death. Money can save minds and bodies. Money can build hospitals and synagogues, research centers and graduate schools, seminaries and yeshivot. Money can clothe the naked, feed the hungry, raise up those cast down. Money is not yours or mine to burn or to scatter to the wind. Power derives from God, who is the Lord of all the earth from which we borrow. God is the Lord of the land, the proper landlord. It is not for us who gain prosperity to destroy God's wealth, scorch the earth, flood the fields, rape the mines. The world is not given to waste.

It is no casual matter that the Bible repeatedly prohibits labor on the Sabbath and the festivals, and commands that we withdraw from working the land during the Sabbatical year and at the Jubilee. We are not to plow the soil, thresh the wheat, harness the animal, squeeze the earth at these sacred times. In the same breath, that the prophet Isaiah calls on us to bestow our bread on the hungry and relieve the afflicted soul, he urges us to "refrain from pursuing thy business on My holy day" and to call the Sabbath a delight. The prohibitions against working on the holy days are to remind us that we are not the owners, masters or creators of the world's resources. We rest to remind ourselves that what we have and enjoy is God's gift to be shared with His children: the orphan, widow, sick and poor. Wealth is not to be frittered away. It has conscience against it. There are homeless people in the world we inhabit, hungry men and women and children, shattered lives.

The desecration of wealth has the conscience of the Jewish prophet against it. Woe to those who "lie upon beds of ivory . . . and drink wine in bowls . . . but are not grieved for the affliction of Joseph." "Woe to those who sell the innocent for silver and the needy for a pair of shoes . . . who trample the head of the poor and turn aside the way of the afflicted."

As tragic as the waste and despoiling of the poor and weak is the injustice to Jason, who is robbed of that elevating passion for justice, mercy and compassion. Jason and the children of entitlement do not need to be defensive about wealth. They do need to find meaning in their labors and purpose in their affluence. Jason and the children of affluence are poorly defended. They are bombarded by the culture and ethos of *Dallas, Dynasty, Knot's Landing, Falcon Crest,* and the strident, screaming, empty ambitions of Robin Leach's beautiful people—tanned, tawny, pampered, promiscuous, vacuous souls—so repulsively vain, so self-indulgent, so childishly narcissistic, with "champagne desires and caviar dreams." It ends in despair. "Is that all there is?" Well, if that's all there is, let's keep dancing. Let's bring out the booze, the drugs and the games.

For their sanity and sobriety, Jason and his generation must be exposed to authentic Jewish sensibilities, to the Jewish lifestyle that raises "walking with God in modesty" to an elegant art. Jason and his cohorts must be taught talmudic passages like *Mo'ed Katan* 27a–b. It begins by telling us:

> In former times, the faces of the corpses of the poor were covered to hide the marks of poverty: only the faces of the rich corpses were uncovered.
>
> In former times, the poor used a bed made of reeds to carry the deceased, while the deceased of the rich were carried on stately, ornamental beds.
>
> In former times, the food brought to the house of mourners was carried in silver and gold baskets for the rich mourners, while for the poor mourners the food was placed in baskets of willow twigs. In former times, the poor mourners drank wine out of cheap colored glass, but the rich drank out of white crystal glass.

After describing the conspicuous consumption of the earlier era, the text goes on to tell us how and why more modest practices were adopted by the wealthy. The rabbis of the Talmud, encouraged by the actions of the affluent Rabban Gamliel, changed their ways. Observing that the disparity between rich and poor was causing shame to the poor, they adopted rules of modesty in order to preserve "the honor of the poor." Henceforth all deceased, rich or poor, were to be dressed in plain white linen shrouds; all deceased were to be carried in modest caskets; all mourners were to drink and eat out of simple vessels. Jewish noblesse oblige called forth the responsibility, compassion and wisdom of the affluent.

Jewish moral culture knows how to own wealth and not be owned by it, to master wealth and not be enslaved to it. When Alexander of Macedon ordered a Torah written in gold, it was buried in the earth by the rabbis. A Torah written in gold? When the high priest entered the Holy of Holies on the Day of Atonement, he shed his vestments of silver and gold and dressed in linen. Atonement dressed in gold and silver? When the shofar was covered with silver and gold, it was discarded as invalid. Cry to God with precious metals?

The behavior of those who are members of congregations has a profound impact on our community. The peer pressure upon parents and children to have a Bar/Bat Mitzvah as lavish as those they have been invited to is strong. It seems to lead to an upward spiraling with more and more lavish and extravagant accoutrements—from tassled, silver- and gold-mirrored invitations to Bar and Bat Mitzvah themes and florists and bands louder and larger and hors d'oeuvres and midnight snacks catered with longer and more expensive menus.

After all our concerns about wealth and power, it may seem a trivial matter to draw attention to the Bar/Bat Mitzvah extravaganza. But it's important because it comes at a critical time in the lives of parents and children, an impressionable moment in which parents, not professionals, are moral educators and decision makers. The Bar/Bat Mitzvah rite of passage is a moment when a youngster is inducted into adulthood and shown the meaning of maturity.

We hear quite often that the child informs his parents that since all his friends have had this Bar Mitzvah bash, "everybody does it," he must have it. Here the parental response has nothing to do with whether they can afford it. How shall parents respond to the cry "but everybody does it"? The child must be given to understand that "everybody" is not a good reason. Living in a copy-cat world, "everybody does it," justifies drug abuse, alcohol abuse, sexual promiscuity, cheating on exams, falsifying insurance claims, bribery, corruption, shredding documents. Children must learn how to say no not only to drugs but to the inebriation of "more." They must become reacquainted with the biblical name of Shaddai—whose name means "Enough." If we do not cultivate self-restraint, modesty, the sense of propriety in them, they will grow into voracious adults, spoiled children dressed in long gowns and tuxedos. If they follow "everybody," they and we will add to the desacralization of our society, in which the value of art, theater, music, literature, culture is viciously reduced to the bottom line. Following "everybody," youth's choice of profession and vocation is measured solely by its cash value. Talent, ambition, culture are increasingly measured by box-office salability.

Parents, who know themselves as models for their children, must appreciate the implications of their submission to the youngster's cry of "everybody does it." Parents must observe the dangers of following this anonymous "everybody" whom we pursue like lemmings in the North Sea. "Everybody" are the people crazed by the urging to be "numero uno" in all things, from Little League to Ivy League. Is there no room in this world for number 2 or 3 or 4? Do we prepare ourselves and our children for the possibility of "downward mobility," or will the stock market of life forever be bullish? "Everybody" means that the worth of Jason and his peers will be defined by their W-2 forms. It calls for family wisdom, courage and Jewish sensitivity to insist that "everybody does it" is precisely why we don't. Parents create memories in children and a spirit not found in books. Leo Baeck wrote, "And a spirit is characterized not only by what it does but, no less, by what it permits."

Danny Siegel reports that lately when he speaks to youngsters and asks whether they would like to tithe and share their Bar Mitzvah gifts with the underprivileged he receives from some a clear no. They argue, "I worked hard for my Bar Mitzvah. I've earned the money. My parents promised." Here is the totalitarianism of the materialistic spirit, the profit motive triumphant. That is not a child speaking, and the implications of the response are not restricted to the Bar Mitzvah illustration. The refusal to tithe is part of a money culture that will not do anything without profit. It is a consequence of conditioning the child to study, to be good, to help out through the allurement of bribery. But if everything we do is motivated by profit, our faith and civilization are bankrupted. What greater contribution to the character and health of our children and our society can we make than our transmitted conviction that some things are never to be bought or sold.

The appeal to place limits on the excesses of Bar/Bat Mitzvah celebration is made not only to the parents but to the young people who are to be inducted into the tradition. The youngsters are *benai mitzvah,* children subject to moral imperatives. They are *benai de'ah*—children of discernment, knowing right from wrong. They are, according to Jewish law, responsible for commercial contracts. They are eligible to pray and read the Torah on behalf of the congregation. Their vows are valid. They are not "kids." According to the rabbis, conscience (the *yetzer tov*) is cultivated by the thirteenth year. Our youngsters are not blind or deaf, and they must not be mute. They have a say in the way their coming of age celebration is expressed. They must know that there are people less fortunate than they are—developmentally disabled, homeless people, frightened people, abandoned by society. They must be shown that there are people without the means to pursue their education and administrations forever cutting down on welfare programs, training programs, food programs.

Their help is needed to create another ambience for our rejoicing. They must be enlisted to struggle against those who conspire to have them keep up with the Cohens, to resist the flaunting of wealth, to oppose those who would turn their Bar/Bat Mitzvah into orgies out of *Duddy Kravitz, Marjorie Morningstar,* and *Goodbye, Columbus,* to fight against those who regard modesty for the sake of charity as "cheap." They must be instructed that showing off is "cheap," gaudiness is "cheap," and wastefulness is "cheap." What is not "cheap" but large-spirited is to provide blankets for the unsheltered, food for the hungry, scholarship to Jewish camps for those who can't afford it, tithing to Mazon, concern for Jews entrapped in Soviet Jewry and Ethiopia.

The Bar/Bat Mitzvah rite of passage can open up a world of meaning to the youngster. Meaning in their studying, in their choice of vocation or profession, in their talent for living. They must be taught through precept and conduct that being a Jew is to be enlarged, that their horizons are expanded beyond the shriveling shopping malls. They must be taught to respect themselves as children of prophets who gave the world, Western and Eastern civilizations, the idea of a God who cares for the weak and is angry with the callous and cries with the dispossessed. They are children of a community who in the eighteenth century supported one out of every three Jews in Germany, Italy, and England. They must be taught the moral vocabulary of our tradition: *zedakah, rahmanuth, gemilut chasadim, hachnasath kallah, tamhui, linat hatzedek, moshav zekenim, beith yetomim*—the Jewish semantics of meaningful living charity, compassion, loving-kindness, dowering the bride, soup kitchens, homes for the aged, the orphans, the poor.

The Bar and Bat Mitzvah has in our times become a major event in the life-cycle of Jews. It can become a sacred event, a significant transition from childhood to mature Jewish adulthood.

RAISED IN AN ADDICTIVE CULTURE

Reb Nachman of Bratslav told of a king who received a disturbing report about the new harvest. Whoever ate of the new crop would be driven mad. He gathered his counselors and told them: "Since no other food is available, we must eat in order to live. There is nothing else that we can do. But at least let a few of us keep in mind that we are mad."

It is not among the few that addiction has taken hold. Addiction is not restricted to the poor or the uneducated or the black or the young or the disenfranchised. It is found as well among the affluent and the influential, the white and the mature, women and men. It is not isolated in the ghetto or barrio. Less than 3 percent of the addicted are found on Skid Row. Marijuana, cocaine, heroin, lysergic acid diethylamide, PCP and angel dust are all equal opportunity employers.

The steady drumbeat of the statistics grows louder and more persistent each day. Three thousand teenagers try cocaine for the first time every day in our country. In the last six years the average age of users has dropped from between eighteen and twenty-five to eleven and twelve. At least 100,000 elementary school children report getting drunk on a weekly basis, according to the American Council for Drug Education.

Addiction is ecumenical. One out of ten Americans is addicted to some substance or other. The same figure applies to Jews. Professor Ben Zion Twerski of the Forbes Metropolitan Health Center in Pittsburgh writes, "not only do Jewish alcoholics exist, they may have a greater susceptibility to cross-addiction," i.e., simultaneous abuse of alcohol and other drugs. Years ago a major study by Dr. Samuel Pearlman already indicated that Jewish collegians were overrepresented in the drug culture: "Almost regardless of the drug considered, Jews are heavier users than Catholic and Protestant students."

Addiction is nondenominational. Mitchel Wallick, the executive director of Jewish Alcoholics and Chemically Dependent Persons, headquartered in New York, observes that of the 160 people participating in the last sponsored retreat, 40 percent were practicing Orthodox and ultra-Orthodox Jews. Tallit and tefillin are not talismans warding off addictive behavior.

In the year 1989 alone, 245 of the 1,099 bills introduced in the House of Representatives dealt with some aspect of drugs. Measures are contemplated to commit the military to land, air, and sea surveillance of drug traffickers, presidential candidates call for multinational strike forces to attack drug-production facilities, death sentences are proposed for kingpin drug pushers, the appointment of a Drug Czar is advocated.

And all the while recidivism rises. The surgeon general informs us that 80 percent of those who give up smoking relapse by the end of the year; the same rate as heroin users who try to give up the habit. Four thousand heroin addicts die each year, and eighty times as many people in this country die as a result of using tobacco products, i.e., 320,000 deaths.

Addiction in its multiple guises, the compulsion to gamble, to drink, to smoke, to take drugs, to overeat, is overwhelming. Something deeper and wider than individual idiosyncratic behavior is involved. As Yeats wrote,

Things fall apart; the center cannot hold;
Mere anarchy is loosed upon the world,
The blood-dimmed tide is loosed, and everywhere
The ceremony of innocence is drowned;
The best lack all conviction, while the worst
are full of passionate intensity.

What kind of people are we? What kind of culture do we breathe into the nostrils of our children and our children's children? Why do they hurt themselves, oblivious to the consequences? Why do they drink themselves blind, bludgeon their consciousness, rip up their flesh with needles and ingest poisons into their systems? Why, when denied access to the substances, do they rob and steal and kill to support their habits?

My grandmother, no mean psychologist, would have said: *"nisht fun kein naches"* ("not from any joy"). These men, women, and children are in pain. They feel poor—and no trust or will or bank deposit can overcome their sense of impoverishment. They feel bored—and no cruise or vacation can overcome the nausea. They feel empty—and no amount of food can fill the vacuum. They feel worthless—and no number of titles and awards can raise their stature. They feel anxious, awkward, nervous—and no amount of liquor or drugs will overcome their self-doubts.

Why are they so many, and why do they come from all walks of life? Why are they so easily hurt, so quickly discouraged, so readily bored with living? They are raised in an enveloping hedonistic culture that prepares the soil for addiction. It is a mass culture rooted in an unstated theology, a popular system of belief more pervasive and more influential among more people than any of the established religions. And like every religion, it is a belief system that teaches what is real and what is phony, what gives meaning and what turns us off to life. Its presuppositions are summed up in its two imperatives: (1) Pursue pleasure. (2) Avoid pain.

Hedonism is a meaning system not boldly and publicly articulated but nonetheless widely and privately held. Hedonism presents itself as offering the unvarnished truth. Conventional preachments call for sacrifice, commitment, pain, and struggle to achieve salvation. Hedonism is neither moralistic nor hypocritical. It whispers to our confidential selves that all the appeals to self-denial, altruism, idealism, commitment, martyrdom are deceiving; that they would have us believe that salvation is something rare, something hard, something to be received at some other time or some other place. But the naked truth of hedonism tells it straightforwardly: what we really want is pleasure here and now, what we desire is pleasure and the avoidance of all pain, and it is accessible.

Hedonistic wisdom promises liberation from a world of imperatives, duties, obligations. Flow with natural desires. Put aside your Bibles and your prayerbooks. Live your life without sadness or sorrow or martyrdom or disappointment or defeat. Admit to your innermost private thoughts that hedonism is the desire and the end of salvation.

The hedonistic confession registers a simple, sincere honesty. Who doesn't want pleasure? And who would not avoid pain? The pleasures of love and family and friendship; the pleasures of fortune and fame; the pleasures of creativity and aesthetics. Hedonism cuts to the bone of reality and trims aside the moralism and demands of traditional faiths.

But it is seductively misleading and, for all its claims to "tell it like it is," dangerously naive. Hedonism is the stuff that feeds the addictive personality. For a second thought makes it clear that nothing we want in our lives, nothing we regard as valuable, nothing of worth and significance can be gotten without pain, struggle, sacrifice, suffering.

What do we want and what is valuable in our lives? And what can be gained without suffering? Do we want to love and be loved? And without pain? He came to me, this man with his doubts, and asked in all seriousness, "How do I know if I love her?" I answer, "Are you willing to sacrifice for her sake, to suffer with her? If you answer yes, it is a sign of love, but if you answer no, it means that there is no love." To love and be loved requires compatibility and compassion, two etymologically related terms derived from the Latin *com* + *pati,* "to bear, to suffer together." Whoever loves a spouse, a child, a parent, a friend opens himself up to wounds. Vulnerability is the price love pays for its wonders. To love and be loved by a child—is there ever a moment that we stop worrying about our children as long as we live? To love and be loved by parents, those whose names we call out in the black night when we are feverish and alone, parents who someday will call out our name, reversing their parental roles with us, does it not demand responsiveness, suffering, and reciprocity? No one can hurt us more than those we love.

And so with friendship. Can we have a friend or be a friend without offering some sacrifice of self? Where is friendship more truly tested than when deprivation and sacrifice are called for. Who will hear the confession of our errors and not condemn; who will contain your fears, who will add their blood to our own? Is there anything we want, anything that brings us joy that is immune to struggle?

And so with creativity. Can we write an essay, compose a song, paint a picture, play an instrument, run a race without pain?

Hedonism misrepresents real living. Against the illusion of hedonism, Judaism presents us with an unflinching reality principle. Cast out of the Garden of Eden into the real world, God addresses Eve, "Chavah," the principle of life: "With pain and travail shalt thou bring forth children." No birth without sacrifice. In your blood, Eve, you give life to the world. And to Adam, God spoke reality, "In the sweat of thy face shalt thou eat bread till thou return into the ground, for out of the earth wast thou taken; for dust art thou and unto dust shalt thou return."

The myth opens the innocent eyes of Adam and Eve to the real world, east of Eden. Pain is the companion of birth. Pain is the companion of growth. The whole of life is nothing but the process of giving birth to oneself. To live and to love, to create and to work, one must be willing to suffer. One must be willing to rip thorns and thistles from the earth's growth and wrestle with God's angels and rise up limping lame. To give birth to another or to give birth to your own self is to endure anguish. Life is filled with births and deaths, with attachments and separations.

So hedonism couples two ideas, the pursuit of pleasure and the avoidance of pain, that turn out to be discordant, contradictory. Judaic wisdom knows that spiritual, cultural, aesthetic, creative pleasures cannot be achieved without pain. Now when hedonism is caught in the lie, it holds out a heavier dose of enticements. If the pleasures we seek are too painful to accomplish, if it requires too great an effort to master a talent or to transform the perverseness of society, if the desire of our hearts is too high or too heavy to achieve, then drop them for pleasures that come without pain. If love requires commitment, if struggling against hunger, battle against prejudice, idealism is filled with blood, sweat and tears, then let go of the ideals. Relax, play it cool, don't let things bug you. Take the shortcut, grab hold of easy, quick, immediate sensations. Eat and drink, suck the juices of easy joy. Feed the body. There is pleasure enough in good food, good wine, good sex. If the self aspires to higher things, redefine your self. I am stomach, I am erotic zone, I am sensations. The boundaries of my self need only be as broad as the elasticity of my skin. There is no stretching for the stars, only for the beer and pretzels.

Not so terrible, peanuts and television. Except, of course, for the boredom the life game of trivial pursuits yields; except for the nausea in self-indulgence; except for the prison of emptiness into which the escape has led. Fearful of getting hurt, our pain threshold is increasingly lowered. The smallest irritation, a traffic jam, long lines at the theater, unreserved seats are intolerable. We grow anxious before every challenge, we fear any disappointment, any defeat. From infancy we are raised to fear pain, to instantly stop the headache. And we have found the cure, the technological panacea. Open up the sacred chest. Open the medicine cabinet, the *aron kodesh* of our homes and behold a pharmacopoeia of potions and pills promising salvation. Twenty billion dollars a year spent on sleeping pills, stomach settlers, headache tablets, analgesics. Dexamils, Halcion, Restoril, Valium—amphetamines and barbiturates, stimulants and sedatives: "Cause us, O Lord, to lie down in peace, and raise us up again unto life." Thy miracles are daily with us "evening, morn and noon."

Marx claimed that religion is the opiate of the people. The inverse is more accurate. Opiate is the religion of the people. Our materialistic faith is in "better living through chemistry."

We are a hedonistic culture that prepares the way for chemical holidays, that vests its hopes in the magic of technology. Stress, strain, conflict need not be engaged by mind, heart, and will. Salvation is but a swallow away. We pressure our physicians for the prescriptions of instant relief. Ingestion, intravenous incorporation is quicker than meditation or philosophy or psychology or religion. One pill, one shot, one snort can anesthetize the spirit, bludgeon awareness, turn the miserable monster in us mellow, indifferent to evils and sufferings, ours and theirs, at home and abroad. Quick, now and before it wears off, more. "Every delay appears to be a deceit, every wait an experience of impotence, every hope a danger, every plan a catastrophe" (Erik Erikson). As we pressure the pharmacist for soporifics, we pressure our religious institutions and leaders to write quick prescriptions, easy answers, ritual routines that will help us escape from the pains of life. Prescriptions and proscriptions faithfully followed by rote will avoid the exertions of thinking, the wrestlings of conscience, the struggles to wrest convictions out of ambiguities.

In the movie *Arthur,* the intoxicated man is depicted as amiable, affable, cheerful, carefree. We envy him his hedonic stupefaction. "He feels no pain." The drugged are mellow. In his *Doors of Perception,* Aldous Huxley, the philosophic mystic, describes the holy indifference of the one under the influence of mescaline. Here too is a holy indifference to the world, a vaunted paralysis of the will. "The mescalin taker sees no reason for doing anything in particular and finds most of the causes for which, at ordinary times, he was prepared to act and suffer, profoundly uninteresting. He can't be bothered with them, for the good reason that he has better things to think about."

The addict comes in many forms. In the gambler, compulsive overeater, alcoholic, sexaholic, drugaholic, workaholic, cultaholic there is an underlying desire to escape reality, to escape its ambiguities, conflicts and cruelties. By pouring oneself into one activity or one obsession we hope to block out the world.

A word about the workaholic, the most acceptable addict in our culture. The surgeon general doesn't dare place a warning label on the obsessive work ethic, "Dangerous to your mental, moral, physical, and spiritual health and to your family." Still, the person who has this addiction to something vaguely called "career" who is drawn by some endless compulsion called "upward mobility" is no less an escapist than the substance abuser. He is as compulsively dependent as the others. He is drunk with mirthless sobriety. He is intoxicated with the cold efficiency of the computer. If only his employees could be so efficient and impersonal. He seeks escape from the affective world of personal relationships. He mocks at community service, at everything that cannot be summed up with the bottom line. He has not time nor room for poetry nor philosophy nor religion nor family nor friends. The workaholic has no time and no interest in the commitments of causes, the struggle for ideals or idealism or personal service. He will pay someone else to meditate for him, to parent for him, or to engage the world for him. Annoyed, he will cheerlessly write out a check to avoid the pain of involvement. Only let him alone to feed his accounts.

Hedonism is the religion of our mass culture. Hedonism is an idolatry. The addict is an idolater who has found his small gods and has blocked out the larger God. He has chosen his compulsions and denied his freedom. Frightened of life, he has unconsciously decided not to live. Afraid of pain, he has deadened his sensibilities. Fearful of independence and the responsibilities and pains it entails, he has become dependent on something or someone other than his self.

Hedonism lies to us. It insists that all we want out of life is the presence of pleasure and the absence of pain. But it is untrue. Who would allow a frontal lobotomy to be performed on himself even though an incision severing the nerve fibers to the brain would deaden all pains, all fears, all concerns? Who of us would allow the implantation of electrodes connected to the pleasure centers of the brains, bombarding us with ceaseless pleasures, requiring from us no struggle, a life of immediate and constant gratification until we die by exhaustion?

We would not choose to be chained to a pleasure machine devoid of pain because a life without aspiration, ideals, or purpose is euthanasia. To live is to know that you are mandated, that there is something significant that you must do, something purposive that offers meaning to your life, and therefore something deserving of your suffering. To be alive is to know that you are a child of imperatives. Micah summed it up, "It hath been told thee, O man, what is good and what is required of you: to do justice, to love mercy, and to walk humbly with thy God." None of these imperatives can be realized without struggle, pain, and sacrifice. Therein lies human dignity, self-respect, and meaning. No one chooses suffering for its own sake. We choose life and love and peace and justice. But no one can truthfully choose these ennobling ideals without embracing struggle. Therefore wisdom counsels, "See to it that what you live for is worthy of your sacrifice. Only the dead have no imperatives, no mitzvot." As the Talmud puts it, "When a person dies, he is freed from Torah and mitzvot, from study and deeds of kindness" (*Shabbat* 30a). The dead are beyond pain and beyond life.

We Jews do not seek pain. There is no masochism in our tradition. But we know that to feel no pain is to court disaster. There are children born with familial dysautonomia, the inability to feel pain. Such children will burn themselves, break bones, contract fevers, destroy themselves. Not to feel pain is far more dangerous than to feel pain. "Only a brain that is functioning pathologically is characterized by the attempt to avoid tension unconditionally," Kurt Goldstein wrote. Spiritual anesthesia is the loss of moral sensibility which Stekel characterized as "the cocaine of the soul."

We live in a culture founded on a dangerously false understanding of reality that prepares the ground for addiction. Its lure is a painless life, but its price is death. Recall the humor in the story of little Harold who, despite all the coaxing of his parents, would not utter a single word in his infancy. At age four, the child was served his bowl of porridge. "God, it's hot," Harold screamed. His parents were overjoyed. "You spoke, Harold. Why now?" Harold answered, "Because everything was just perfect up till now."

It is part and parcel of the hedonistic culture to avoid pain, and this has affected the education of our children. When parents will not allow children to visit the sick relative in the hospital or attend the funeral of their grandmother lest they see human beings cry or mourn their loss, they rob them of their humanity, and prepare them for the perpetual search for painkillers. Their character is spoiled by parental overprotection that reduces life to the avoidance of unpleasantness and the pursuit of proximate pleasure.

Hedonism declares, "Choose pleasure." Judaism calls on us to "choose life." The two are not synonymous. We must not deprive ourselves or our children of the right to struggle, the capacity to suffer, the courage to endure pain, the mandate to afflict our souls. To be Jewish is to be prepared to struggle, to combat those who step on the throats of the innocent, to free the prisoners of Zion behind the Iron Curtain, to love and care for each other. To be Jewish is to bear with dignity the scars and blemishes that give meaning to our lives. Hedonism has nothing to live for, only a life to avoid. In heroin heroism is denied. The addict lives with the fantasy of substance magic and the superstitions that avoid engaging life. "Whether or not it is bad luck to meet a black cat depends on whether you are man or mouse." To choose life entails courage and hope. Hedonism, the mother of addiction, spawns cynicism, nihilism, the despair of "no meaning." There is more lasting joy in Jacob wrestling with the angel than in the "happy hour," guzzling another round and ordering, "Make mine light." The addictive culture is a preparation for a living death. The Judaic culture is a preparation for living life.

It is not enough to tell them, "Just say no." They will not say no to drugs without going back on their word until they learn to say yes to life. And to say yes to life is to say yes to pain and struggle and sacrifice, without which no ideal can be touched. God is called "the life of the universe." Alive He does not sit above the clouds in holy indifference. Alive God too feels and suffers and is afflicted in our afflictions. "For a long time I have kept silence, I have kept still and restrained Myself; now I will cry out like a woman in travail, I will gasp and pain" (Isaiah 42:14). As God lives, we are alive. As God lives and struggles, so must we who would live.

"He who learns must suffer. And even in our sleep, pain that cannot forget falls drop by drop upon the heart, and in our own despair, against our will, comes wisdom to us by the awful grace of God" (Aeschylus).

COUNTERING THE ATTRACTION OF CULTS: AN ARGUMENT FOR RABBINIC AND LAY COLLEGIALITY

I know that I am perplexed, that my fears are irrational, incoherent. At times I am given over to panic; I am afraid of death. At other times, I am horrified by the thought of becoming, God forbid, incapacitated during my life-time. . . . I don't know what to fear, what not to fear; I am utterly confused and ignorant.

—"Redemption, Prayer, Talmud Torah" *Tradition,* Spring 1978

Can a sick person afflicted with a fatal disease tell a "thou" who happens to be a very dear and close friend, the tale of a horror-stricken mind confronted with the dreadful prospect of death? Can a parent explain to a rebellious child, who rejects everything the parent stands for, his deep-seated love for him?

In the majestic community, in which surface-personalities meet and commitment never exceeds the bounds of the utilitarian, we may find collegiality, neighborliness, civility, or courtesy—but not friendship. . . .

—"The Lonely Man of Faith" *Tradition,* Summer 1965

I am lonely. Let me emphasize, however, that by stating "I am lonely" I do not intend to convey to you the impression that I am alone. I, thank God, do enjoy the love and friendship of many. I meet people, talk, preach, argue, reason; I am surrounded by comrades and acquaintances. And yet, companionship and friendship do not alleviate the passional experience of loneliness which drains me constantly. I am alone because at times I feel rejected and thrust away by everybody, not excluding my most intimate friends, and the words of the Psalmist, "my father and my mother have forsaken me" quite often ring in my ears.

—"The Lonely Man of Faith" *Tradition,* Summer 1965

Who writes these lines? Who is it that so craves personal expression? Who seeks attention to the anxieties of the lonely self? Is it someone far removed from the Jewish community, a stranger to the poetry and wisdom of our tradition? These words come from the writings of *Ish ha-halachah,* Joseph Baer Soloveitchik—a personality deeply immersed in the Jewish community and grounded in the embodiment of halachah.

Soloveitchik's cry is not unique among modern and contemporary Jewish thinkers. We hear echoes in the later writings of Hermann Cohen, more fully in the words of Martin Buber, Abraham Joshua Heschel and Franz Rosenzweig. The author of *The Star of Redemption* is not consoled by the vacant smile of philosophy and theology which teaches him that death is merely the loss of the body. "What does philosophy care that the fear of death knows nothing of this division into body and soul; that it bellows 'I' 'I' 'I' and refuses . . . this relegating of fear to a mere body."

What is missing in Jewish life to satisfy the longing of the soul? Is halachah not enough? Is Jewish ritual not enough?

Is Jewish philosophy not enough? If these learned, pious, Jewish leaders cry out their discontent with the community of Jewish *Gesellschaft,* if they seek attention for the shivering self, what may be said of the fears of the individual Jew they serve? And what may be said of the loneliness of those who lead others into community?

The existential torments of Jewish thinkers are more profoundly articulated but not less deeply felt by ordinary Jews. The individuals we serve make up the real personal histories out of which sociologists and psychologists construct the concepts of anomie, alienation, and anhedonia. They are part of the statistics of rising divorce rates, rising suicides among college students, rising delinquency rates.

It is not enough to talk theology or halachah or mitzvot or

peoplehood to them. Not because these people are too foolish or irreverent; but because other, personal things press heavy on their hearts and minds and call for attention.

Inattention to suprapersonal preachments is not a mark of people's insensitivity. When you walk in a forest amidst flowers and trees and a sharp pebble cuts into your foot, you are apt to lose your aesthetic sensibilities. People are beset by the tensions between parents and children, the disharmonies of marriage, the dying of parents, the limits of career, the emptiness of their lives in the midst of the plenitude of their possessions. These are not "bad Jews," but the classic rabbinic categories which divide relationships between man and God, and man and man, do not touch their personal anguish. Shabbat, kashrut, tefillin, liturgy, observances *bein adam la-makom;* Soviet Jewry, Israel, social action, duties *bein adam le-chavero* offer them no "Guide to the Depressed." What of the interior life, *bein adam le-atzmo*—between man and himself.

The youngster who has spent months now fighting with his confused parents comes to your study to explain why he has joined Scientology. He is filled with newfound importance, with a sense of personal idealism, but is mystified by his parents' opposition. He needs something more from Judaism.

The frantic woman whose husband has just left her hands me a scribbled note written by her nine-year-old daughter and addressed to her father: "Please, daddy, come back. I promise I will be good." She needs something more from Judaism.

A Jew is defined by what hurts him. Our people are hurt. Around them swirls a revolution of values and expectations. The old sanctities of God, Torah and Israel have lost relevant application to their personal lives. Contemporary rabbis are caught in the vise. They cannot offer the same answers if only because Jews are not asking the same questions.

"Do not tell me what I am to do for Judaism; what I am to do for the sake of the synagogue, or for Zion's sake, or for the sake of mitzvot. Tell me what Judaism can do for me. Tell me what the synagogue can do for me. Tell me what the Jewish community can do for me. Tell me what mitzvot can do for me. For me—not as a dues-paying member; not as an element in the collective set of a people; but for me—in my existential loneliness, in my despair and boredom; in my inability to celebrate, to feel, to laugh or to cry." Their voices give new meaning to Akiva's statement: *Kol tzarah she-hi shel yachid, tzarah, ve-chol tzarah she-einah shel yachid, einah tzarah,* every distress of the individual is a genuine distress, but every distress of the community at large is not such a distress (*Deuteronomy Rabbah* 2:22). A revolution. The pendulum has swung wildly away from the traditional pole of "we and there and then" to the modern pole of "me and here and now." The troubled have no heart for history, eschatology, or community. "Pay attention to our personal lives. We are falling apart."

THE PUBLIC AGENDA

What can rabbis say to them? We have been raised to speak the language of *reshut ha-rabbim,* the discourse of the public domain. We were not prepared either by our home background or our seminary training to handle these cries out of *reshut ha-yachid,* from the private domain. In our most imaginative moments, we cannot conjure up an image of *zaydeh* complaining to his rabbi that he lacked spontaneity and craves self-fulfillment. *Zaydeh* and we were raised in the liturgy of community.

So, in one form or another, rabbis convey the message: "Dear friend, I understand your personal needs, your anxieties, your quest for personal meaning and intimate meeting. But here in the synagogue we are concerned with other things—with prayer and ritual observance, with study and the celebration of weddings and Bar Mitzvahs. For what you want, you must go elsewhere."

And that is precisely where they are going. They are searching out a whole variety of encounter groups, growth centers, human potentiality movements, Scientology, transcendental meditation, Arica, Synanon, Daytop, Gestalt, Actualizations, and Est.

It is tempting to dismiss all of this as a regional phenomenon restricted to the wild and woolly west. Surely California is unreal, a state of mind on the outer reaches of culture. But in fact it is far from an idiosyncratic phenomenon limited to a particular geography. Carl Rogers characterizes the phenomenon of group encounter as "the most rapidly growing social invention of the century." And there are enough Jews among the leaders and followers of these group movements for us to take them seriously. Statistics aside, I am constantly surprised by how many Jews are drawn to these experiences and by the high caliber of the participants.

The attraction of so many Jews to encounter groups represents a major ideological and pragmatic challenge to the synagogue and to the ethos of Judaism. At the heart of these movements is more than another form of therapeutic relief. They signal the emergence of new secular religions, religions of remission and release.

Secular religions with their own doctrines of human nature and salvation, rituals of confession and therapeutic sacraments, gospels of self-fulfillment, charismatic leaders and supportive communities.

Scholars such as Huston Smith, Robert Bellah, John Sealy and Kurt Back have observed that these secular, psychological, and social therapeutic enterprises contain all the marks of religion. They articulate a new faith form in which "theological supernaturalism" is supplanted by "psychological supernaturalism," and "prophetic faith" is eclipsed by "ontological faith" (Tillich), the celebration of what is. Today many of these causal enterprises appear to be in a transitional stage, moving from therapeutic meetings to societies advocating an alternative way of life; in short, a religion.

NEW SECULAR RELIGIONS

The challenge to the synagogue from the emerging psycho-religious movement may prove more serious than the conversionary efforts of Christianity we are accustomed to.

First, because the secular religions claim no triumphant design to convert us, the stigma of apostasy is not attached to the new believers.

Second, because most Jews are so secularized that joining such secular religions causes no cultural shock. The "God-terms" of the humanistic secular religions sound a familiar ring to Jews: *awareness, creativity, freedom, care, concern, change, I-Thou relationship, responsibility.*

And third, because there may be some comforting legitimation for encountered Jews who enjoy tracing the Jewish antecedents of so many thinkers, originators, and organizers of these movements: Erich Fromm and Abraham Maslow, Fritz Perls and Werner Erhard—and a host of others.

Right or wrong, Jews are disproportionately represented in these activities.

Right or wrong, they feel themselves disaffected from Jewish communal life.

Right or wrong, they hunger for something the synagogue fails to offer them.

Right of wrong, they are drawn away from us, and we are conscience-bound to understand why and to consider whether and how they can be won back.

The new psycho-religious enterprises are more respectable, more expensive, more secularized than the counterculture youth experiments which have been with us for quite some time. But there are significant similarities. Beatniks, hippies, the psychedelic revolution, the attraction to cultism from Meher Baba to the Unification Church—despite the varieties of style and motivations—present a harmony in despair along with the secular religions: a profound discontent with an increasingly impersonal, pressuring society and a yearning for spirituality.

Maase avot siman le-vanim, the parents reveal their children; *banim siman le-avot,* the children reveal their parents. Significantly, both phenomena have emerged outside the institutions of the establishment; outside the academy and outside the synagogue and church.

The root metaphor held in common is "the wearing of masks." Masks superimposed upon them from infancy; a facade of roles, obligations, duties meant to please others: *naches*-producing machines for others: parents, teachers, employers, institutions.

A tyranny of shoulds muzzles their personal desires; and should they rebel they will be met with a chorus of accusations: bad son, bad daughter, bad husband, bad wife, bad Jew. For all external appearances they are successful, accomplished, contented souls. But they feel suffocated beneath the iron mask, their inner voice muffled. Under the burden of surplus repression, the buried self twists and turns, knows itself to be dancing the unlived lives of others.

Here the new secular religions enter to encourage "the cracking of the masks," the liberation from false facade. From massages to primal screams, from shedding of clothes to breaking in and out of humanly formed circles—the promise is release;

the hope is in new revelations out of the inner core of the self;

the miracle is in the resurrection of deadened affect;

the major sacrament is in the self-confession of repressed aspirations.

A relative of mine—talented, prosperous, educated—attends Synanon and describes the savage verbal assaults upon him. Why does he allow himself to be so attacked? Because the torpor of his daily existence is so oppressive that he welcomes the abrasive intrusions. It is a parody of the shaving lotion commercial: the brisk slap is gratefully acknowledged: "Thanks, I needed that."

The passion for aliveness, the need for expressivity in a muted and deafened society, the desire to unburden oneself of the anxieties which haunt them, the promise of a community which pays attention to the self swallowed in the anonymity of the conventional assembly moves them to search for more intimate community.

This is no brief for the encounter movement. We all know the failures of many of these groups. The collaborative studies of Lieberman, Yalom and Miles, published in their *Encounter Groups: First Facts* (New York: Basic Books, 1973), reveal the shallowness, the exaggerated and unsubstantiated claims, as well as the outright danger posed by many of the therapy and encounter circles they studied.

We know the hucksterism and commercial exploitation of many of the entrepreneurs of encounter.

We know that much that lies behind the salvation of self-assertiveness is rationalized narcissism; that the ethos which declares that each of us has his own space and each of us does his own thing ends up as *middat sedom,* the characteristic of Sodom, "mine is mine and thine is thine"; the code words "I am responsible for myself and you are responsible for yourself" translate themselves into detachedness; "don't lean upon me, don't come to me with your hurts."

We know how often "spontaneity" is confused with impulsivity; how what passes for "feeling" has nothing to do with the feeling of compassion and commitment but is more akin to the adolescent's whining, "because I feel like it."

We know how readily the self as sacred center spawns a society of "panthers roaming round separate cages," snatching at the world with red claws.

We know the tragic irony of the preoccupation with the self; the

overconcentration upon the health of the self which ends in hypo-
chondria. Viktor Frankl has warned about the consequences of
such hyperreflectivity upon the self. Said the fox to the centipede:
"In what succession do you move your legs?" And the centipede
grew paralyzed, immobilized by hyperreflectivity.

We know the false promises of instant community formed out of
brief encounters with intimate strangers.

But the success or failure of these groups does not concern me.
What concerns me is the hunger of our people, which the Jewish
religious community does not seem to be able to satisfy. Criticism
is important; but it is not enough. Their failures are not our
successes.

Theirs, we say, is a commitmentless communion. And ours?

Theirs is a skin-deep culture of contacts. And ours?

Have we a more compassionate community to offer them?

Is there within the synagogue, the temple "family," a place
where the need for emotional honesty can be expressed?

Is there a group for those who would unburden themselves of
the normal crises we all face; to find support and relief in confession and sharing their concerns with others?

Can they tell of "peak experiences" in synagogue encounters—
at membership meetings, at minyanim, at board meetings, at
services? Can they tell of hugging and embracing the other as a
friend?

Do we offer them, out of the Jewish tradition, some personal
wisdom which can help them cope with their agonizing problems.
Does our rich ritual life inform their personal lives?

Does halachic wisdom enter the crucial private lives of our
people?

Or do we simply dismiss all this as secular affairs; individual,
private concerns. *Chukkat ha-goy*—imitation of the gentile world.
What has all this to do with halachah? With the keeping of the
Sabbath and dietary laws? With the public agenda of our collective
lives? With the texts the rabbinic seminarians have studied? Is it
Jewish?

That is what Rabbah argued. When his father, Rav Huna,
wondered why his son did not attend the lectures of Rav Chisda,
Rabbah replied that he was not interested because Chisda lectured
about anatomy and hygiene, *millei de-alma,* secular things.

To which Rav Huna responded, "Rav Chisda deals with matters of health and you call them secular matters? All the more reason for your attending his lectures!" (T. *Shabbat* 82a).

SPLITTING THE JEW FROM THE MAN

Heschel warned against such narrowness. "The Torah speaks in the language of men. But the sages have overlooked *the man in the Jew*. They gained no insight into his difficulties and failed to understand his dilemma. Every generation has its own problems. Every man is burdened with anxieties. But the sages remained silent; they did not guide the perplexed and showed no regard for the new problems that arose."

These are not the words of some unknowing, unfeeling outside critic of the tradition, but the descendant and teacher of rabbis.

The "man in the Jew": Have we, in our desire to search out the Jewishly unique, ignored the humanity of the Jew?

Have we, in our wish to preserve the particularity of Judaism, identified it exclusively—as Moses Mendelssohn did—with *geoffenbarte Gesetze*, revealed legislation, the ceremonial acts of ritual observance and relegated the personal to the secular, universal order?

Have we, as Heschel charged, reduced the grandeur and pertinence of Judaism to "Is it permissible or forbidden, is it kosher or not?" And is that what is meant by declaring that Judaism is a way of life?

The synagogue must respond to "the man in the Jew," not by muttering the psychobabble of the popularizers of encounter and not by imitating the facile theology of the new secular religions; but not by ignoring the cry for attention of the man and woman in the Jew. "He who says Torah is one thing and the affairs of the world are another is as if he denies God" (*Midrash Pinchas,* chap. 4).

How are we to begin? We have been called "people of the book," but it will not happen by books alone. There is no dearth of texts in Jewish life; there is a dearth of persons.

THE JEWISH FEAR OF JEWISHNESS

Jews need Jews to be Jewish. Jews are hungry for the warmth and sympathetic intelligence of other Jews. Most Jews within the synagogue and outside the synagogue are not comfortable with Sanctuary Judaism. I speak not of the Jews of the "daily minyan" but of the overwhelming majority of our Jewish constituency: the affiliated, the unaffiliated, the disaffiliated. They are fearful of their ignorance and of their doubts about being Jewish. They have questions of all sorts—questions so elemental that they are embarrassed to raise them publicly. They are fearful of the institution.

Some remember the humiliation of being called for an aliyah and then stumbling and muttering the benedictions, and rejoicing when the *ba'al keri'ah* drowned out the stammering with a loud "amen."

Some remember hearing the rabbi speak about the beauty of the Shabbat and are ashamed to ask which comes first, the *Kiddush* or the *Motzi* or the lighting of the candles.

Some remember hearing about the *berit milah* and are confused about the mystery and complexity of the rite that entails surgery and blood, *mohel, sandek, kvater* and *kvaterim*.

They wonder what the fuss is all about; what difference— philosophical, moral, psychological—could it make whether it is the eighth day or the third day, or whether it is a *mohel* or a doctor who performs the surgery.

Some wonder what great principle attends the *kohen*'s questioning the father *mai ba'it tefei* at the *pidyon ha-ben* and the father's declaration that he prefers his firstborn son to the five silver coins on the plate. They titter at the ceremony and now it is I who am embarrassed.

The "nice" ones do it for the sake of grandparents or for the sake of the children. The others simply skip over it. But both the nice ones and the others are not personally convinced that there is personal wisdom in these acts. The "nice" ones join but then remain hidden behind the skirts of the community, affiliate only to melt into the anonymity of the congregational crowd, pretend that belonging is enough, attend a few services or public lectures to assuage their guilt and mark their public identity. Others cover the embarrassment of their ignorance or doubt by attacks on the vulgarities of institutional religion and the high cost of affiliation. In any event, both remain unreached, ignored and ignorant.

Their fears and fantasies about the synagogue and Judaism will keep them from the rabbi. Who can touch them? Who will reach out to them person to person? Who will talk with them? Who will befriend them?

Neither books nor scholars in residence nor adult education classes can touch these frightened Jews who represent the major constituency of our Jewish community.

Nor can the rabbi himself, however conscientious, meet their needs. For what they crave is intimate, personal, nonthreatening supportive relationships with Jewish persons. And speaking for myself, I know I have neither the energy nor the time to personally satisfy their real need.

Is there no one upon whom we can call to help us fill the vacuum of Jewish feeling and spirituality? Have we no allies to help us personalize and humanize the tradition: to relate personally to the married couples so attended to on the day of the wedding and so neglected after the honeymoon is over; to relate personally to the newly affiliated families who would be ready to create a Jewish ambience in their homes; to counsel personally with expectant parents confounded by half-superstitious rumors they pick up about the naming of the child and the ceremonies of *berit* and *pidyon;* to help the proselyte in our midst, so uncertain of his or her way in the synagogue and in Jewish life; to assist in the forming of a havurah and enriching its life? Or is this all to fall upon the rabbi's shoulders, and then, because no single person can attend to so much, is it to gnaw away at his conscience?

THE JUDAIC PARAPROFESSIONAL

We are not so helpless or alone. There are Jews within our synagogues who want to do more with their lives than attend public lectures or sit at endless meetings or usher. There are Jews who can understand the challenge to Jewish life and would respond to a call to serve Jewish life; would respond to a serious program based upon classic Jewish purpose; *Le-haskil lishmoa u-le-lamed, lishmor ve-la'asot*—to understand, to listen, to learn in order to teach, to observe and fulfill in love all the teachings of Thy Torah.

I propose for consideration a program which each of us can undertake individually or in partnership with other colleagues— for the training of Judaic paraprofessionals.

A program, under our rabbinic supervision, for the training of laymen and women willing to tithe their talents and energy for the purpose of entering the lives of fellow Jews who can only be reached personally by their peers.

A Judaic paraprofessional program to help us transmit, on a personal level, the Jewish art of celebration, Jewish *chochmah* for their personal lives and for the lives of their families.

Consider the emergence in the last few decades of paraprofessionals of all kinds. Paramedical, paralegal, paraprofessional psychological counselors, lay people, trained so as to extend the influence of the professionals in the community and to help the professionals use their energy and talents more effectively. Why not pararabbinics? Is the rabbinic vocation less demanding, less complex, less worthwhile than these others? Does Judaism need no help? Do rabbis need no help?

There is much untapped energy and idealism in our laity. For the sake of Judaism and our sacred tasks, the laity cannot be allowed to remain as passive critics, spectators, and audience outside the circle of commitment. They must be brought into our confidence, to share the gravity of our calling and to help us. We cannot afford to continue the distance which grows between us. Rabbis need allies. We need collegiality with our laity.

I do not present this proposal to you on theory alone. Some five years ago, I witnessed in my own congregation the formation of a paraprofessional counseling service, made up of synagogue laity, and trained for two years by psychiatrists and social workers. Thirty-four of them, supervised by professionals—psychiatrists, psychologists, family counselors—who all volunteer their services, and serve the congregation and community within the walls of the synagogue. Their altruism, their desire to learn in order to help, has gained new credibility for the synagogue as a community that cares about the man and the woman in the Jew.

LIFE PASSAGES

Based on this model and on this experience, we initiated a pararabbinic program drawn from the congregation.

The participants have committed themselves to a two-year program of study and to three additional years of service to the congregation. For the first year of study we chose the *rites of passage,* for two major reasons.

1. Because there are few moments in the life of a Jew and in his

family when the observance of Jewish mitzvot has so much wisdom to offer him personally.

2. Because we have seen in our rabbinic career the tragic waste of opportunities to transmit Jewish values to our people. Inadvertently but undeniably we have stood by to see mechanical routinization lay its dead hand upon the rites of passage. We have allowed the rite to become isolated from the living passage so that what remains of my rabbinic role has to do with answering questions about technique: where, how, when.

We have provided no occasion or time to explain the new states, the new turning points which such rites of passage celebrate.

It is not for naught that the *berit* is known to many Jews as a circumcision, a surgical procedure, not as the child's covenant with God.

We have insisted that those divorced by the civil authorities go to the Beth Din because there the religious community expresses its spiritual and moral sensitivity and wisdom. Does the Beth Din—the rabbinic council—deal with the emotions and ethics of separation, the responsibility towards the separated partners, towards the children and their education, towards the rebuilding of life—or is its justification satisfied with the punctilious writing of the twelve lines and the proper presentation of the scribe and witnesses? And do we thereby convince Jews that a *get* is qualitatively different from a civil divorce?

Illustrations can be quickly multiplied of the neglect and perversion of Jewish spirituality when the rite is reified and the passage unobserved. The rites have nothing to do with the passage. Jews are not being instructed how to cultivate the Jewish virtues which attend each stage in the development of the Jewish human being. But life passages without rite passages are blind. Rite passages without life passages are empty.

CONTEMPORARY PSYCHOLOGISTS

When we read the literature of contemporary psychologists, e.g., Erik Erikson, Daniel Levinson, Roger Gould, many of us are jealous for Judaism. For it is they, the "secularists," who in dealing with the life-cycle, wrestle with the spiritual and moral "virtues" of the growing self. It is they who discuss the need for basic trust, the balanced self, fidelity and ideological commitment, generativity and altruistic concern. It is they who deal with the passages, turnings, crises of the journey. It is they who are physicians of the soul, and I who have become a master of customs and ceremonies. It is we who are relegated to the role of ritual functionary along with the caterer, florist, photographer, and leader of the band.

It is not fair to us or to Judaism or to the Jewish community. And it has been going on for a very long time, despite the grandiosity attached to the notion of *mara de-athra,* the master authority of the community. Can we pay attention to rites without concern for the spiritual struggles of the passage, external gestures without interior affect? Am I part of the problem Isaiah described as *mitzvat anashim melumadah* (Isaiah 29:13)?

We are overwhelmed and outnumbered. The attribute of omnipresence belongs to God alone. I need, rabbis need allies in the sacred task of creating Jews. We need Jewish persons to relate personally and sympathetically to other Jews. We need Jews who can listen to other Jews and who can help them anticipate the kinds of concerns they will confront at the critical junctures of their lives. The ritual can be redeemed from perfunctory enactment when it is preceded and followed by living contact with Jews who care.

This will not be accomplished by noble urgings, but it can be achieved by personal engagement; not by abstract rationale but by concrete doing. For people believe what they do more than they do what they believe; people feel what they do more than they do what they feel.

Judaism is doing. So let Jewish consciousness be raised and internalized through personal encounters between para-rabbinic counselors and expectant parents weeks before the ritual choreography of *berit* and *pidyon;* through Jews who are trained to explain the moral and spiritual presuppositions articulated through the rites; through personal meetings with the families about to celebrate Bar and Bat Mitzvah, which will deal not only with the logistics of the event but with some of the constant concerns of parents and adolescents in their transitional stages; through personal sessions with engaged couples to discuss the etiquette of the wedding and the theology and morality of consecrated love;

through personal involvement in assisting the mourner in arrangements for the funeral and attention to the grieving period.

The synagogue today is challenged by the secular religions to create a community of personal concern centered around the mitzvot of every Jew's life-passage.

In an age of loneliness, the synagogue has a golden opportunity to make of Jewish rites of passage the celebratory outcome of Jewish activity.

Jewish activity in which Jews as Jews help Jews through the normal crises which attend the stages of personal and family growth. The man in the Jew and the Jew in the man needs a compassionate ear, a responsive spirit, an informed intelligence in which to confide.

Not all of these ends can be accomplished at once; nor should they fall upon all the para-rabbinics. In the course of their training, para-rabbinic students will discover special areas which are particularly meaningful to them and with which they feel more comfortable. The rabbi has not vanished from the scene. He remains the supervisor, the personal resource center of the para-rabbinics. He will enter situations where the issues warrant and according to the capacity of his energies. But he must be relieved of the pretense of ubiquity—for it ends with exhaustion, despair, and self-accusation. Rather than scatter his energies to the public winds, he will serve the Jewish community better by devoting his talents to training these men and women as partners in the elevation of Jewish life.

SEX AND THE SINGLE GOD

Intergenerational controversies about sexuality usually center around "concrete" issues calling for "concrete" answers. The parental triple threat of detection, infection, and conception is countered by the single technical triumph of the omnipotent Pill. Rabbis are frequently asked to adjudicate, not to discuss the issues philosophically, but to render decisions on such concrete issues as "living together." All parties expect "concrete" answers to "concrete" questions: yes or no, permitted or proscribed. "To sleep with or not to sleep with"—that is the question. Only after the biological facts and sociological statistics have been trotted out in support of both sides and a silent impasse is reached does it become apparent that the shoe pinches elsewhere. The referred pain must be traced to deeper sources. How we treat our bodies sexually, what meanings we ascribe to the most intimate of interpersonal relationships, and what expectations we demand of those relationships cannot be relegated to the arena of fact and physiology. In the matter of sexuality, fact and value are as intertwined as body and soul. The body language of sexuality expresses the intuitions of our spiritual sensibilities. Sexuality and theology are not such strange bedfellows.

RESPECTABLE SILENCE ON SEXUALITY

We do not normally discuss sexuality in the synagogue because we somehow feel it inappropriate. Matters of sex are aired outside the sanctuary, given over to psychologists and sociologists, not to those who deal with spiritual matters. But sexual silence in the sacred centers of our living is both unwise and un-Jewish. We are

156

not the children of Paul or Augustine or Luther. On the most awesome of all our days we read out loud about sodomy, transvestism and adultery. On Yom Kippur afternoon we read the eighteenth chapter of Leviticus. The rabbis were remarkably astute in picking that section for a holy day when Jews are said to act like the angels, neither eating nor drinking. Perhaps they chose it to remind us that we are not ethereal souls but that we all have bodies. *Ha-guf shelach ve-ha-neshamah shelach,* the body is Thine and the soul is Thine. We are rooted in a biblical and rabbinic tradition which deals explicitly and frankly with the most intimate sexual relations. In Judaism there is no shame in the body and no sacred precinct in which discussion of its role is out of place.

It is unwise not to speak about the Jewish view of sexuality because silence creates a vacuum. And if it is not filled with Jewish wisdom, it is likely to be occupied by alien interpretations. Even the "religious" view of sexuality presented under the hyphenation of the "Judeo-Christian tradition" misrepresents the Jewish view. Many of the sexual attitudes of Christianity are contrary to ours, and the generic blanket "Western religion" only weighs us down with burdens not our own. For example, a Jew should have little quarrel with Freud, Marcuse, or Norman Brown where they are critical of the religious repression of the sexual instincts and its denial of the joy of sensuality. Judaism is no stranger to the affirmation and celebration of body and soul. Yet Kinsey, in his *Sexual Behavior of the Human Male,* argues that the duplicity of the contemporary standards on sexual morality is the product of an original Judeo-Christian code reflecting "the pervading asceticism of Hebrew philosophy." I trust that Kinsey knew more about sexuality than he knew about Hebrew philosophy. If there is anything that clearly differentiates the classic perceptions of Christianity and Judaism it is their respective attitudes towards sexuality and the status of the body.

The *locus classicus* in the New Testament's treatment of the body and marriage is found in the sixth and seventh chapters of the First Epistle to the Corinthians. There we find articulated the Pauline idea of celibacy and of virginity. "It is good for a man not to touch a woman. . . . I say, therefore, to the unmarried and widows, it is good for them if they abide even as I. But if they cannot contain, let them marry, for it is better to marry than to burn." Based on such New Testament scriptural statements, the church fathers and figures like Augustine viewed marriage as "the hospital for the sick" (Luther). Augustine saw marriage as "medicine for immorality." Tertullian, one of Christianity's great theologians of the third century, opposed digamy, the remarriage of widows and widowers. Addressing those who had experienced "the fortunate decease of a mate," he urged the survivors to take advantage of the opportunity to break their carnal desires and not remarry. The same position is found in Jerome and Origen. Popes Paul and John Paul II restated the decree of mandatory celibacy for priests and single deacons, and prohibited the remarriage of married deacons once they had become widowers.

Why is the flesh of passion to be crucified according to classical Christianity? Why is the spiritual man, according to Matthew, to make himself "a eunuch for the sake of heaven"? In the same seventh chapter of I Corinthians Paul declares, "For I would have you without carefulness. He that is unmarried careth for all things that belongeth to the Lord, how he may please the Lord, but he that is married careth for all things which are of the world, how he may please his wife." Paul argues that when a man marries his interests are divided, and Paul sees this conflict of interest as basic. Will you serve God or man? Will you serve your Savior or your family? Will your interest be in the salvation which comes from another world or through transforming this world? In much of Christian teaching the world appears bifurcated. There is a split between the body and the soul, the sensate and the spiritual, the inner and the outer, the human and the divine, law and the spirit. Salvation is not of this world nor through this world nor in this world. This world is to be overcome and transcended. The Christian ideal of celibacy reflects man's decision to withdraw from Eve, or Chavah, the matrix of life and reproductivity, so as better to serve God alone. The consecrated celibate comes to God unencumbered by concerns and responsibilities for the human family. Only singly is he or she able to fully serve the Single Other.

KIERKEGAARD AND BUBER

This ideal in Christian theology was expressed by the spiritual father of Christian existentialism, Soren Kierkegaard, who, after betrothing his beloved, Regina Olson, gave her up out of exclusive fidelity to his God. Martin Buber's response to the great Danish theologian articulates the Jewish understanding of marriage. Buber insists that God wants us to come to Him by the Reginas He has created, not by the denunciation of them. Not by the subtraction of the human other but by his addition is the religious equation formed. God and human are not rivals. If the classic Christian ideal is celibacy, the classic Jewish ideal is marriage.

For a Jew the task calls him to be connected with the world. Marriage is the way we enter the world of care and responsibility. God and the human other are not adversaries. The human being is the co-creator with God in the repair of the world. To marry, to have a child, is a religious act reflecting the seriousness of the commitment to transform the world. To have a child is to have a blood and flesh connection with the future. Alone, childless, we may cavalierly declare, *Après moi le déluge*. But knowing that it is our children who may be caught in catastrophe we think more soberly of the chaos to come. Through our husbands and wives, through our children and our children's children, we have an investment in the future. Marriage, in Judaism, is far more than a privatistic concern for you and me, here and now; it announces a cosmic concern for the future of civilization. In marriage the Jewish passion for unity is celebrated. For in the consecration of love the segregation of self from the human and divine other is transcended.

THE JEWISH VIEW OF THE YETZER

The opposition to a polarized view of the world is demonstrated in Judaism's approach to the *yetzer* of man. By *yetzer* is meant the seething cauldron of drives, desires, wants, and needs within us. To a Jew, libidinal energy—sexuality included—is an ambivalent power and is far from being condemned as irredeemably evil. Nowhere in the Jewish tradition will we find the counsel offered in the Gospel of Matthew: "To pluck out one's eye before the shapely form of a woman whom you desire. He who looketh at a woman to lust after her, hath committed adultery with her already in his heart." Nowhere in Jewish sacred literature do we find that an act like Origen's self-castration for the sake of escaping the temptation of lust is deemed praiseworthy.

The tractate *Yoma* (69b) relates an intriguing legend of the *yetzer*.

For three days and nights the rabbis fasted, seeking to capture the *yetzer ha-ra*, the evil inclination, which appeared to them in the form of a fiery lion from the Holy of Holies. When they at last captured and imprisoned the *yetzer ha-ra*, they were warned that in destroying it they would destroy the world. They decided therefore to imprison the evil impulse for three days. "And for three days they searched throughout the entire land and could not find a freshly laid egg."

Without the energy of libido, civilization is exhausted. Therefore the *yetzer* in the human is not to be extirpated, but is to be harnessed to consecrated ends. The strong person, according to the wisdom of the sages, is one who can control his libido, not one who denies it or seeks its suffocation. Even in the eras of pogroms and persecution, when ascetic practices were not uncommon among Jewish mystics, sexual asceticism was not countenanced. One of the distinguishing marks differentiating Jewish mysticism from non-Jewish mysticism, Gershom Scholem informs us, is the absence of sexual self-abnegation in the former.

THE MANY MOTIVATIONS OF CONSECRATED LOVE

What in Judaism are the motivations for marriage? It is primarily the mitzvah to see that the world does not die. The corroborating text repeatedly used by rabbinic commentators to sustain this stance comes from Isaiah 45:18, "He created it not a waste, He formed it to be inhabited." The Hebrew term for "bachelor" is *ravak*, which means literally "emptiness," for the willful bachelor empties and thereby wastes the world. Folk tradition dramatized the point by denying the bachelor the prayer shawl, which made him something of a marked man.

But procreation is far from the sole end of marriage. A statement from the tractate *Yevamot* (61b) reads, "Though a man may have many children (and has thus fulfilled the mitzvah of procreation), he is not to remain unmarried, because it is not good for a man to be alone." To be alone is a dreaded curse among our people. Pleasure cries out to be shared. In Judaism, the ideal love of a man for a woman and a woman for a man has to do with the body as well as the spirit. The notion of a marriage of platonic love is alien. The tradition contains no marriage arrangement such as the "syneisaktism" of the church, in which, ideally, a man and a woman vow to live together as a brother lives with his sister. In the Jewish tradition, love is concerned with the whole being of the other, and that whole being of the other is physical, psychological, economic, moral and religious. We must love the other with all our heart, with all our soul, with all our might and with all our body. For a man or a woman to contract marriage vowing sexual abstinence would violate the character of the marriage covenant. Such a vow would cause *tzarah de-gufah*, pain of the body. The Nazarite may observe his ascetic vows, may not eat meat or drink wine, may grow his hair long. But sexual abstinence is of another order. For it inflicts suffering upon the other. Even in the male-dominated society of ancient times, the tradition declared that *simchat ishto*, the rejoicing of his wife, is the moral duty of the husband.

In a thirteenth-century treatise, *Menorat ha-Ma'or*, written by Israel Ibn Nakawa and popularly attributed to Nachmanides, we find a chapter dealing with the sanctity of sexuality in the relations between husband and wife. In the "Epistle of Holiness" addressed to the husband, the author writes: "Engage her first in conversation that puts her mind at ease and gladdens her. Thus, your mind and intent will be in harmony with hers. Speak words which arouse her to passion, union, love and desire. Never may you force her, for such a union the Divine Presence cannot abide. Quarrel not with her . . . win her over with words of graciousness and seductiveness." To those who had fallen under the influence of Aristotle, such as Maimonides, and deprecated the sense of touch, our author served admonition: "Let a man not consider sexual union as something ugly or repulsive, for thus we blaspheme God. Hands which write a sacred Torah are exalted and praiseworthy; hands which steal are ugly." And so it is with the sexual organs of the body. All energies are ambivalent. There is nothing that is intrinsically contaminating or intrinsically holy except the use to which that energy is put.

The non-Jewish contemporaries of Al-Nakawa and Nachmanides, Peter Lombard and Pope Innocent III, insisted that the holy spirit absent itself from the room where a married couple have sexual relations, even if their union is only for the sake of procreation, for such action shames God. There thus grew up a church tradition that on Friday one is to abstain sexually in memory of the death of the Savior, on Saturday abstention is in honor of the

Virgin Mary, on Sunday in memory of the resurrection. For in this tradition holiness and sexuality are contradictory. By contrast the Jewish view, expressed in the tractate *Sotah* (17a), asserts that "when a husband and wife unite in holiness, there the divine presence abides." The Shabbat is the celebration of the world. What more appropriate time to rejoice with one's wife than on the day set to remember freedom and creation.

THE NEW CHALLENGE TO JEWISH SEXUAL MORALITY

The pendulum has swung the other way. It is clear that today people are struggling far less with the sexual inhibitions of the Victorian era. The old Victorian morality proposed the ideal of loving without falling into sex. A new sexual morality counsels sexuality without falling in love. For one, love is separated from sexuality, for the other sexuality is separated from love. But in common, both positions are dualistic. Judaism contends with the dualism of the new morality as it does with the dualism of the old Victorian and Christian morality: against loveless sex outside of marriage and sexless love in marriage. Both divisions oppose the Jewish ideal of organic wholeness. The new sexual morality derives much of its validity from its protest against the false prudery of our culture, the pseudo-idealization of woman, and the hypocrisy of double standards wherein premarital relations are evidence of the male's virility and virginity the proof of the female's fidelity.

In its bluntest form the new morality is spelled out by the publisher of *Playboy* magazine, Hugh Hefner. Hefner's magazine and his many imitators are significant elements of our mass culture. It sells over three million copies a month and is read primarily by college students and young people from the age of eighteen to thirty. Hugh Hefner puts it on the line. "Sex is a function of the body, a drive which man shares with the animals, like eating, drinking and sleeping, it is a physical demand that must be satisfied. If you do not satisfy it, you have all kinds of neuroses and repression psychoses. Sex is here to stay. Let us forget the prudery that makes us hide from it, throw away all those inhibitions, find a girl who is like-minded and let yourself go." One of the typical cartoons in *Playboy* depicts a boy and a girl locked in amorous embrace during which he cries out, "Why talk of love at a time like this?" The cartoon portrays Hefner's counsel of cultivated coolness towards the other.

FOUR ARGUMENTS AGAINST FORMAL MARRIAGE

Four basic arguments are typically presented by those advocating the right and propriety of having sexual relations without marital forms of "holy deadlock." The first argument maintains that being in love is its own justification. The important thing is "to feel." Feeling is more important than the pro forma protocol of the marriage license, the senseless "piece of paper."

The second argument insists that sexual relations openly arrived at by mutual consent are fine as long as "nobody gets hurt." After all, no one advocates seduction or coercion. If two people voluntarily wish to have such a relationship and nobody gets hurt, there is nothing wrong with it.

The third argument asserts that sexuality is important as a means of determining marital compatibility. How will you ever know whether you are compatible without experiencing sexuality?

The fourth argument claims that sexuality is morally neutral. It is a gratifying biological phenomenon and not qualitatively different from hand-holding.

An honest response to such arguments calls upon an understanding of our own ideals of marriage and love. Concrete, ad hoc responses to such arguments fail to deal with the whole network of values which envelop our expectations of authentic interpersonal relationships. To begin with, I, for one, cannot accept the underlying presuppositions of these four arguments. They are premised on the separation of the body from the total self, and the isolation of the self from the community. If sexuality is essentially a physical function, the purpose of which is to remove the overaccumulation of tensions, then the body is viewed as a machine. The machine is the model of our sexual self and of the other. Clearly, before you invest in a machine, you try it out. You see whether or not it works. If it doesn't work, you may discard it or trade it in or try to fix it up. Such mechanistic reductivism of sex describes the depersonalization of man and woman. Given the man-as-machine analogy, it is understandable that so much literature dealing with love and marriage is replete with technical advice and quantitative measurements. We enter a technological world of high frequency and low fidelity.

The body as a machine is subject to serious abuses. Psychiatrists report a rising concern with impotence and frigidity. Patients no longer come to psychiatrists with the old complaints of sexual inhibitions. They now come with a complaint of "affectlessness," an incapacity to feel, to be moved, to laugh or cry or love. The complaint of these emancipated men and women is of a numbness, a frozenness, an anesthetized self. The heroes of polymorphous sexuality cry and remain unsated. The lyrics of rock and roll resonate the misery of "I don't feel anything." At the core of Alexander Portnoy's complaint in the boudoir is the anguish of his affectlessness. "God, how have I become such an enemy and flayer of myself? And alone, so alone nothing but myself, locked up in me?" Why does Alexander feel alone when there are so many others in his bed? Why is there no feeling for the obsessive pursuer of feeling? Perhaps it is because there is no person, no self in bed with him. When the other is seen as an appendage of your body, an instrument of your physiological gratification, you are alone with your selfless body. Autoeroticism is not love. When the other is reduced to an object, sexuality only expresses the mirror of narcissism. I do not feel anything because I will not or cannot feel for any other.

Jean-Paul Sartre illustrates the *mauvaise foi,* the bad faith of such pseudo-relationships. A young man and woman go out on a date. They sit in a cafe drinking coffee. He seizes hold of her hand and squeezes it. She is now beset by an embarrassing dilemma. Should she squeeze back, she signals acceptance of his advances. Should she withdraw her hand, he stands rejected. She is prepared for neither consequence. What is she to do? She simply ignores the situation, continues the conversation as if nothing had happened. The hand hangs limp, unattached to the rest of the body. Similarly the entire body can be so dissociated from the whole self as to render its presence meaningless. The body then says nothing. It is the carcass of a machine.

To touch and not be touched, to feel one's self but not to feel for another is, in Buber's language, to make an "it" out of a relationship. The bumper signs which advertise "Make love, not war" are more revealing than they intend. You can make war as you can make an omelette or make your bed. But you can't make love. You cannot make another being unless you reduce the other to an instrument, to an object for your gratification. You can make war because war is an act of ultimate disrelationship. But love is quintessentially the art of relationship, which entails mutuality, reciprocity and responsibility.

The bifurcation of love yields no "feeling." One can have "feeling" in the sense that one feels sensations. One feels hot and cold, tumescence and detumescence. Or one may feel in the manner of Tolstoy's nobleman who sat himself on the shoulders of his servant. The servant carried the nobleman's obesity on his shoulders, groaning under his burden. The nobleman "felt" compassion for him and removing a large kerchief, mopped the sweat off the brow of the servant. His was a feeling of passive sentimentality, a feeling of no consequence. The feeling one discovers in love of another entails *Mitleid,* compassion, literally the capacity to suffer another's pain. To love and be loved is to be willing to be open to the hurt of another and to open one's own hurt to another. There is risk in such self-disclosures. Who can hurt us more than one to whom we have revealed our vulnerability? The stranger cannot hurt me. Towards the stranger one can "play it cool." Out of fear, we prefer estrangement, emotional distance in the midst of physical intimacy. Not lust but fear may rationalize sex without love. It is easier to "love" the stranger than the neighbor. Only towards the latter is the clause "as thy self" added. Without the self-disclosure that is part of the process of self-revelation, there is no other with whom to relate. But painless sensuous experiences will not overcome the emptiness of insularity.

Erotic action "without any strings attached," it is sometimes argued, offers opportunity for co-habitants to evaluate their marital compatibility. It is a pragmatic argument which employs sexual compatibility as the touchstone for matrimony. The position raises questions subtler than the accusation that promiscuity is being endorsed. For many the style of fidelity is unimpaired. But where sexuality is used as a test to determine love, it assumes that sex as a criterion for compatibility is qualitatively the same as sex as a consequence of compatibility. But while viewed physiologically the two acts describe the same phenomenon, they are critically different. From the view of the weighing scale, a day of dieting registers no differently than the Yom Kippur day fast. What differentiates the two is the intention assigned to the act and the purpose attached to it.

Moreover, sexual compatibility trivializes the meaning of marital compatibility. Premarital sexual competence is not even a valid indicator of marital sexual compatibility. A good deal of psychological literature reports the sexual disappointment of couples who prior to the marriage enjoyed more than satisfactory sexual liaison. Without understanding, patience, compassion and love, sexuality can become mechanical. It is difficult to repair such sexual disorder, because sexuality is not merely a mechanical event. Sexual disappointment often disguises such nonsexual areas as the unresolved conflicts over basic values, authority and self-esteem, just as infidelity may signify many different things besides sexual dissatisfaction with one's mate or the sexual attractiveness of another.

LIVING TOGETHER

Some critics of premarital sex have facetiously suggested that if a couple truly sought to determine their compatibility, they would take along a three-year-old on all their dates. The serious point is that there is more than sexuality that measures compatibility. One of the responses to this critique of sexual reductivism comes from the advocates of living together, an arrangement which simulates the total relationship of marriage without the commitments and complications of the latter. Responsibilities are less coercive and dissolutions less complex in the living-together alliance.

But living together has its own price tag. Increasingly, cohabitants report that the anguish over breaking up living-together arrangements and their unspoken declarations are no less painful than the severance of the marriage bond. It is too facile to declare that in sharing bed and board "nobody gets hurt." Moreover, making it easier to split may make it harder to bind. The very tentativeness of living together does little to encourage the couple to "work at it," or to resolve the normal strains and disharmonies of intimate relationship. The attitudes which inform a relationship which is admittedly experimental are significantly different from one which is committed to covenanted connection. How one enters a relationship, and with what expectations and responsibilities, is not irrelevant to the chances of its failure or success. The decision to declare oneself husband and wife before the witnesses of a particular community motivates and predisposes the character of that relationship. The private roots of the married couple are sunk in deeper soil than "thou" and "I."

MARRIAGE AND COMMUNITY

For Judaism marriage is not a *ménage à deux*, a private arrangement. The marriage vow which declares "Be thou consecrated unto me" is not complete without that added clause, "in accordance with the law of Moses and Israel." Along with the two persons covenanted to each other is a third presence. That witness is the Jewish community and its ideals of divinity. The nexus between the couple and the cosmos is the community.

If willful celibacy is in some traditions a religious statement that transcends the needs of this world, marriage in Judaism is a political declaration in which two people, in the presence of a minyan, affirm the community and the world. So the ritual act wherein the groom breaks the glass dramatizes the fragmentation of life and the imperatives to respond to that condition. The broken vessel symbolizes war and poverty, sickness and hatred. The breaking of the glass means that the bride and groom, as a Jewess and a Jew blessed with love, acknowledge the couple's task to enter the world, making whole that which is broken and binding that which is bruised. Consecrated love has cosmic meaning. It is to salvage the sparks of divinity lodged in the husks of the world.

The ultimate task of life is to overcome separation without absorption of the other. Such a union respectful of the other requires wisdom. "Therefore shall a man leave the house of his father and his mother, and shall cleave unto his wife, and they shall become as of one flesh." This new oneness refers to the union discovered through *da'at*, or knowledge.

Da'at, in biblical Hebrew, means both "to know" and "to love." To love is to know, and to know is to love. Such a unified wisdom of love informs the Jewish attitude towards sexuality in its dialogue with the dualists of ancient and modern times.

THE HYPHEN BETWEEN THE
CROSS AND THE STAR:
MIXED MARRIAGE

Pope John Paul II's pastoral visit to America brought a revival of Christian-Jewish anecdotes in its wake. One such story tells of Cohen's conversion to Catholicism, for reasons unknown. The Knights of Columbus host a banquet in Cohen's honor. Called upon to speak, Cohen looks at his audience—devoted lay Catholics, priests, bishops, and monsignors—and begins his address, "Fellow goyim."

Jewish humor of this genre is meant to console. It implies that the conversion has not "taken". A Jew always remains a Jew.

The true challenge to Jewish identity comes less from outright conversion than from quiet "deconversion." It is not the cross but the hyphen that dissolves Jewish identity. The Judeo-Christian hyphen is turned into a sign of identity. Blue and white lights, green and red fixtures, hot-cross buns or latkes, all signal the same directions. The threat derives from the common notion that deep down, Judaism and Christianity are twin faiths without significant differences.

IN THE RABBI'S STUDY

The two of them—attractive, intelligent, young, and very much in love—enter my study. Sam, a Jew, and Peggy, a Christian. Their object is matrimony, and their goal is to find a rabbi liberal enough to officiate at the mixed union or alongside a liberal priest. Neither seeks conversion. They seek an "equal opportunity" cleric.

They each have a vague sentimental attachment to the faith in which they were raised and genuine filial fidelity to their parents. They have thought out the dilemma of raising children; they will offer the best of two religious civilizations. "If it's a boy, we'll have him both circumcized and baptized," they agree. They do not see conflict in this arrangement. Instead, they are convinced that the wisdom of both Old and New Testaments will enrich their lives and confirm the prophet Malachi: "Has not one Father created us? Has not one God made us?" (2:10). They take courage from how alike the sister traditions are. Towards their own and each other's beliefs and practices they offer benign neutrality.

The discussion wanders. At one point, perhaps out of frustration, I ask what they think of my officiating as both rabbi and priest. They are taken aback.

"You're not serious?" they ask.

"Well, let's play it out. I know the church sacrament, the nuptial blessings, and I certainly know the seven blessings of Jewish tradition," I reply.

Peggy finds such ecumenicism a bit much. She can't quite conjure up the union of surplice and tallit, swinging rosaries and knotted tassels. Still, if we have one Father, why not one rabbi-priest?

They are not slow to see how I have taken their approach to its logical, but absurd, conclusion. So Peggy goes on to explain that she is not a practicing Christian. Why then, I ask her, would she have her child baptized?

She answers with a personal anecdote about a cousin whose infant had died. "If that happened to me, I couldn't face the thought that my child was unbaptized." Unbaptized, her child would be suspended between heaven and hell. I ask about the status of her husband-to-be. Would an unbaptized Sam be subject to limbo or damnation, or would he be saved? A long and deep silence follows.

In that silence, I ponder the neglect of Jewish theology and philosophy in Sam's life. Sam's Jewishness amounts to casual observance of a pastiche of rituals, a vague sentimentality towards Jewishness, and an attachment to his Jewish parents. No Jewish map of the world, no distinctive view of human nature, God, or the quest for meaning.

For Sam, and for Peggy as well, all religions are the same. Preferences for a colored Easter egg or the roasted egg of a Seder, a swaying evergreen or a shaking lulav, are more matters of taste than of principle. It seems such a shame to dissolve a love because of a few residual ethnic memories.

In truth, however, the differences between Christianity and Judaism are profound. They entail basic world-views and values that affect them more than they think.

The world-view of most of the people with Christian backgrounds that I meet—like Peggy's—is woven out of the fabric of Christian doctrine and symbol. They understand the nature of original sin, damnation and salvation in the manner of traditional Christian theology. As we shall see, this is a far cry from Judaism— a gap too large for a hyphen to bridge.[1]

WHOSE PRAYERS ARE HEARD?

To begin with, Christianity is rooted in the dogma of original sin. "Original" does not refer to the invention of new sins, but inherited sin traced back to the Bible story of Adam and Eve. They rebelled against God, who forbade eating of the Tree of Knowledge. The "original sin" is transmitted to every living human action. It is no longer the result of an individual's choice; it is a congenital curse from which there is no human cure. Only by faith in the incarnation of the man-God and his unmerited kindness in dying for God's children is the stain wiped out. The crucified Christ alone can loosen Eve's children from the grip of Satan.

During the 1961 trial of Adolph Eichmann, when a Canadian Christian minister flew to Jerusalem to offer Eichmann the chance to confess his belief in Christ, reporters asked him whether Eichmann's confession would save his soul. The minister affirmed that it would. Asked whether the souls of Eichmann's victims would be saved without such confession, he answered, "No. No one comes to the Father but by me," says Jesus (John 14:6); as Reverend Bailey Smith restates it, "God does not hear the prayer of a Jew." Outside the church, no one is saved.

For many of the church fathers, Judaism was a vestigial anachronism, a "has-been" whose purpose was to prepare the path for the good news of the advent of Christ. In the gospels of Matthew, Mark and Luke, we read that on the day that Jesus died, some forty years before the destruction of the Second Temple, the veil of the Temple was torn from the top to the bottom. The Temple, the priests, the sacrificial system and the authority of the rabbis collapsed, while the instruments for communion with God fell exclusively into the hands of the true believers in Christ crucified and resurrected.

In Judaism, salvation is not for Jews alone. Those who do not believe our way or pray our way are not thrown out of the divine court. In rabbinic literature, heaven and earth are called to witness that "whether you be gentile or Jew, man or woman, slave or free man, the Divine Presence rests on you according to your deeds" (*Yalkut Shimoni, Tanna de-Vei Eliyahu*). In the Book of Jonah, the people of Nineveh are spared because of their deeds, not their conversion to Judaism; because of their turning from evil ways, not their acceptance of the Sabbath and festivals. Jews do not seek to convert the world to Judaism, but rather to convert the world to righteousness, justice, and peace.

THE EUCHARIST IS NOT MATZAH

"Whoever eats my flesh and drinks my blood has eternal life, and I will raise him in the last day" (John 6:53). This promise is ritualized in the eucharist, mass, or communion sacrament. The wine and wafer are transformed into the blood and flesh of Christ on the cross.[2]

By contrast, the wine of the Jewish *Kiddush* remains wine, and the challah of the *Motzi* remains bread. The Yiddish writer Y. L. Peretz told a story that reflects these radically different outlooks. On the day before Pesach, husband Hershl and wife Sarah find themselves without money to purchase matzah and wine for the Seder. Forlorn, Hershl goes to the market and stops to watch a traveling magician performing tricks in the square. The trickster produces matzot and a bottle of wine, and offers them to an amazed Hershl.

Hershl runs to the rabbi for counsel. Are the matzah and wine permitted for Pesach use, seeing that they were produced by magic?

The rabbi asks Hershl, "Does the matzah break? Does the wine pour?"

Hershl breaks a piece of matzah and pours a drink of wine. They perform naturally.

"Then they may certainly be used for the Seder," the rabbi rules.

Matzah is matzah and wine is wine. No ritual item in Judaism is transformed into another substance. Nothing in the wine or matzah is intrinsically sacred. They are symbols to sanctify a festival and recall an event. The idea of the transformation of natural products into supernatural substances is alien to Judaism. After they have been used in the ritual, the remaining wine and matzah may be discarded. They possess no sacramental powers.

THE "OLD TESTAMENT" IS NOT THE JEWISH BIBLE

The Christian Bible includes the "Old Testament" with its "New Testament" but rearranges the order of the books. The Jewish Bible (Tanach) ends with the Book of Chronicles, a résumé of biblical history. The last verse in II Chronicles refers to King Cyrus of Persia, who is charged by God to rebuild God's Temple in Jerusalem. Cyrus, who in Isaiah 45:1 is referred to as a messiah—"the anointed one" *(mashiach)*—proclaims to the Jewish exiles: "Whoever is among you of God's people, may the Lord be with you. Go up!"

In the Christian reordering of the Hebrew Bible, the last books are those of the Prophets, which end with Malachi. Here the last verse reads, "Lest I come and smite the earth with a curse" (3:24). In this manner, the Christian order of the "Old Testament" has replaced the Jewish hope of return to Zion with the threat of Israel rejected. Thus Jesus is made to succeed and supplant the Hebrew prophets, and Israel's tragic destiny is foreshadowed. The old covenant is broken, and Israel depends for its redemption upon its acceptance of the new covenant and the resurrected Savior.

DEICIDE

Jews have a special taint in Christian thought. Guilt for the killing of Jesus is added to the contagion of original sin. The episode of the Roman procurator Pontius Pilate, who washes his hands of the bloodshed, and the stubborn mob of Jews who are crying, "Crucify him, crucify him," is dramatized in Easter Passion plays and in such commercial dramas as *Godspell* and *Jesus Christ Superstar*. The chilling words in Matthew 27:25, put into the mouths of the Jewish mob, "His blood be on us and on our children," augur the history of contempt for the "perfidious Jew" so virulent in the hands of the mobs as to defy even the restraints of higher church officials.

BAPTISM IS NOT CIRCUMCISION

Baptism and circumcision are rites with differing theological roots and psychological import. They are far from complementary dramas.

Baptism is based upon an anthropological pessimism. Human beings are born in the womb of sin. Since there is nothing a sinner can *do* to expiate that innate blemish, the sole recourse is to rely upon a supernatural Other, who has assumed the burden of suffering atonement for all others. As Luther expressed it, the believer becomes *velut paralyticum,* as one paralyzed, abandoning the conceit of his or her own deeds, utterly dependent on the self-sacrifice of the innocent lamb of God.

Baptism is crucial for Christian salvation. The Roman Catholic rite includes exorcism of the Prince of Darkness. The priest blows on the infant's face, ordering the spirit of Satan to depart. He moistens his thumb, touches the ears and nostrils of the infants, and asks the child's sponsors to renounce the power of Satan. Those who are baptized and who believe are saved; those who refuse are stigmatized by the inherited sin that remains indelibly inscribed in the unredeemed soul. We can understand Peggy's concern over her infant's baptism and her silence over its absence in Sam's life.

Circumcision is the initiation into the covenant of God and Abraham. The eight-day-old boy carries no baggage of sin into the world. Prior to baptism, the Christian infant is a pagan; by contrast, the Jewish boy is Jewish even before or without the rite of circumcision. The Jewish infant is born innocent, created and sustained in God's image. No eternal damnation hovers over him. As a Jew, he will be raised in a tradition that commands him to save lives rather than souls.

According to Christianity, humans sin because they are sinners. According to Judaism, a person sins when he or she sins. Of course, we do sin—not because we enter the world condemned as sinners, but because we are fallible human beings, and "there is no righteous human being who has done good and does not transgress" (Ecclesiastes 7:20). The sin is his or hers, the choice is his or hers, and the reparation to be done is his or hers.

No one can sin for another, cry or die for another, or absolve another. "Wash yourself clean," Isaiah addresses the penitent (1:16), "put away the evil doings from before My eyes; cease to do evil, learn to do well; seek judgment, relieve the oppressed, the fatherless, plead for the widow." The rabbis add, "Blessed are you, Israel. Before whom are you purified, and who purifies you? Your Father who is in heaven" (*Yoma* 8:9).

Whereas in Christianity, the relationship between self and God is vertical, the Jewish connection with God is horizontal. Horizontal human transactions call for reparation, forgiveness and apology for the injuries done to others. They cannot be skipped over by a vertical leap between the individual and God in heaven, ignoring the proper relationships with God's children on earth. The prophet Ezekiel makes it clear what the truly penitent is to do. "If you the wicked restore the pledge, give back what you have robbed, walk in the statutes of life . . . you shall surely live. . . . None of the sins you have committed shall be remembered against you" (33:15 ff.).

Baptism focuses on the paralysis of the human will, helpless without God combating Satan. The covenant of circumcision stresses that the human being can exercise control over his life. As God counseled the sulking Cain, "Sin crouches at the door, but you may rule over it" (Genesis 3:7).

Sam and Peggy must learn that circumcision and baptism are not a knife-or-water option, but ritualized dramas of values. They affect our relationships to God, world, neighbor and self. Baptism depends upon belief in a specific divine person who walked the face of the earth.

FLAWED FOUNDERS

Philosophers have noted a unique aspect of Judaism. The late Walter Kaufmann observed that Jinna and Buddha, founders of the sixth-century B.C.E. religions of Jainism and Buddhism, were worshipped in later years; Confucius and Lao-Tze came to be deified; the Greek heroes were worshiped as gods; Jesus was adored as God.

Only in Israel were the flaws of the religious founders openly revealed. Moses is buried in no-man's land, powerless to enter the

Promised Land, without statue, icon, or shrine. David is found by the prophet Nathan to have sent an innocent man to war to be killed, so that the king might enjoy Bathsheba, the victim's wife.

The heroes of Israel are splendid, but not so special that they are to be obeyed without question. No sacrifice of intelligence is demanded. Consequently the people are all bidden to learn, know and ask questions. The rabbis declared that Ezra the scribe would have been worthy to be the bearer of the Torah if Moses had not preceded him (Tosefta *Sanhedrin* 4:7). Could that have been said if Moses were a man-God? The Israelite priest and high priest were to be honored, but not revered blindly. "The learned bastard takes precedence over the ignorant high priest" (B.T. *Horayot* 13a).

The Jewish Messiah is wholly human, mortal, and fallible. The Messiah's coming offers no excuse for being passive. As Rabbi Yochanan ben Zakkai taught, "If there be a sapling in your hand, when they say to you 'Behold the Messiah!' go and plant and afterwards meet him" (*Avot de-Rabbi Nathan* 31).

Jews live according to a different calendar. For them, this is not *anno domini,* the year of the Lord; the world is far from redeemed. The saplings in our hands are not to be put aside. We see poverty, bickering, jealousy, sickness and hunger. The Messiah has not yet come.

FAMILY

Peggy spoke warmly of the Jewish family. Family is one aspect of Jewish life that rabbis hear praised over and over by non-Jews. The primacy of family fits the horizontal world-view of Judaism. It is rooted in a tradition that makes no schism between love among humans and love between humans and God. In no Jewish religious text can one find the approach to the family that Jesus expresses in the Gospels of Luke and Matthew. "If any man come to me and hate not his father and mother and wife and children and brothers and sisters, yea and his own life also, he cannot be my disciple" (Luke 14:26).

In Judaism, Jews come to God through their families and friends, not at the expense of these relationships nor through the sacrifice of self. Divinity yields its nature through the love and care of human others and self.

By contrast, Jesus declared, "For I have not come to bring

peace on earth but a sword. For I have come to set a man against his father, a daughter against her mother, and a daughter-in-law against her mother-in-law." For Jesus, the believer is confronted with a hard, sharp break; either heaven or earth, either Christ or family, either Jesus or self. "He who loves father or mother more than me is not worthy of me" (Matthew 10:34 ff.).

In Christianity one cannot come to the Father except through the Son. In Judaism one cannot come to the Father except through the sons and daughters of the human family.

These are not easy teachings for Peggy and Sam to hear. But the differences in the birth traditions are not trivial. Theological differences are likely to cast large cultural and moral shadows.

Peggy and Sam may come to understand that true tolerance does not entail wholesale adoption of all faiths, and that openness does not mean reducing all traditions to sameness. They may come to see that conversion does not discredit a faith but flows from an awareness of the profound dissonance between religious cultures.

Their resolve to hold clashing traditions in one household not only distorts the uniqueness of each faith civilization, but compromises their own integrity. With the best of intentions, Peggy and Sam hope to offer their offspring the best of religion. But, to paraphrase Santayana, to attempt this would be trying to speak in general without using any language in particular. Judaism and Christianity are particular languages, with their own precious syntaxes, which when thrown together, produce a babble of tongues.

I am aware that there are Christian theologians who take a far more liberal view of original sin and damnation and salvation. I point this out to Peggy. But the more liberal views of modern Christian thinkers have not filtered down to Peggy. The interpretations of Paul Tillich or Reinhold Niebuhr or Hans Kung are as foreign to her understanding of Christianity as the Judaic interpretation I present to her. Peggy has not come to me for a course in Christian theology. I deal with Peggy as she presents herself, as she has been instructed by the church and religious school she attended.

Sam and Peggy have crucial decisions to make. If they build their lives on the narrow edge of the Judeo-Christian hyphen, they offer their children the fate of Disraeli. Converted to Christianity by his father, he became Britain's prime minister in the time of Queen Victoria, and yet he held pridefully the glory of his Jewish ancestry. Queen Victoria is reported to have asked him, "What are you, Disraeli? Which Testament is yours?" He replied with sadness, "I am, dear Queen, the blank page between the Old and the New Testament."

It is to be hoped that Sam and Peggy will learn to see and respect the difference between the Jewish and Christian outlooks and not lead their children to inherit the blank page. For all that Christianity and Judaism are alike, the hypen between the Cross and the Star of David is no sign of identity.

NOTES

1. True, some modern and present-day Christian theologians interpret the doctrines of sin and salvation in a far more liberal manner. But their influence has not been wide, and so their views will not be included here.

2. How literally this transformation is understood remains a Christian debate that need not concern us here.

RITELESS PASSAGES AND
PASSAGELESS RITES

Even when the rabbi believes he has the answers, he must know the *Fragestellung,* the form the question takes. The answering text must respond to the context of the questioner's life situation. Questions often conceal more than they reveal. The rabbi must learn to read between the lines. Who is the person who asks this question?

But "in order to answer a question, one must have something in common with the questioner" (Paul Tillich). Here the graduating rabbinic student begins his career at a decided disadvantage. The world of the seminary in which he has been immersed is not the world of the synagogue, and neither one is the world of the individual Jew. And it is the individual Jew—not some abstract metaphysical construct—whose questions or silences must be compassionately understood and addressed.

For the most part, the three worlds—seminary, synagogue, individual—have nonintersecting agendas, isolated from each other. So the task before us is to make connections, to integrate the public and private agendas of Jewish living. This requires the cultivation of mediating structures and the development of mediating roles within the synagogue community. It calls for building bridges between communal wisdom and the values of individualism, between tradition and modernity.

The historian Jacob Katz describes the theory of traditionalism as the belief that public and private life can be regulated by law, and that meaning and values are derived from "the total reliance on the distant past" (quoted in Charles Liebman's "The Sociology of Religion and the Study of American Jews," *Conservative Judaism,* May–June 1981). Despite the modernity of its scholarship, the rabbinic seminary is largely, in Katz's terms, a traditional institution.

By the same token, the world of the synagogue, despite its modern dress, operates on the basis of a traditional outlook, reflected in the manner that its ritual and liturgical life is conducted.

But the world of the individual Jew, whether within or without the synagogue, is increasingly non-traditional. He or she owns a private agenda of personal hopes and fears that have little in common with the traditional public agenda. The individual's concerns range over the disharmonies of marriage, the disenchantment in raising children, the deaths of parents, fears about personal illness and death, the weightlessness of his or her career, the unarticulated hopes for interiority. The Jew's modernity is expressed in a fundamental voluntarism of thought and deed: Free to choose, the individual finds deeper pride in choosing than in chosenness. This Jew is suspicious of "groupism," of the imperatives of Jewish law, and of his or her implication in the fate of the community. "Modern consciousness," Peter Berger reminds us (in his *The Heretical Imperative*), "entails a movement from fate to choice." Voluntarism, individualism and pluralism create the atmosphere the individual Jew breathes.

The rabbi breathes the same air. Upon seminary ordination, the rabbi is thrust into a world very different from the one he is leaving. From the seminary, he carries the assurance that he is the authoritative teacher, the decisor, the judge of *issur ve-heter,* of that which is forbidden and that which is permitted. He has law on his side, and the law has its mandates. In a revealing paragraph of his *Guide for the Perplexed,* Maimonides characterizes the law and, by implication, the traditionalist model of the rabbi.

Whatever the law teaches, whether it be of an intellectual, a moral, or a practical character, it is founded on that which is the rule and not the exception; it *ignores the injury* that might be caused to a *single person* through a certain maxim or a certain divine precept. For the law is a divine institution and (in order to understand its

operation) we must consider how *in nature* the various forces produce benefits which are *general,* but in some solitary cases they also
cause injury. . . . We must consequently not be surprised when we
find that the object of the law does not fully appear in every
individual; there must naturally be people who are not perfected by
the instruction of the law, just as there are beings who do not receive
from the specific forms *in nature* all that they require. . . . From this
consideration it also follows that the laws cannot *like medicine* vary
according to the different conditions of persons and times; whilst
the cure of a person depends on his *particular* constitution at the
particular time, the divine guidance contained in the law must be
certain and general, although it may be effective in some cases and
ineffective in others. If the law depended on varying conditions of
man, it would be imperfect in its totality, each precept being left
indefinite. For this reason it would not be right to make the fundamental principles of the law *dependent on a certain time or a certain
place;* on the contrary, the statutes and judgments must be *definite,
unconditional,* and *general* (in accordance with the divine words,
"as for the congregation, one ordinance shall be for you and for the
stranger"; they are intended . . . for *all persons* and *all times*).
                    —*Guide for the Perplexed* 3:34 (emphasis added)

In this formulation, the fate of the individual is secondary to the
judgment of the law. In a traditionalist society, where obligations
and practice of the rules and customs are natural, the analogy
between law and nature seems more convincing. But that is quite
remote from the world of the Jew of modernity, who will not
submit his lot to the generality of the law or consent to suffer
injury because of the law. The ethos of modernity does not
cultivate easy acceptance of the dictates of the group or of the law.
The Jew of modernity may be polite enough to say nothing, to act
out personal unhappiness by abstention, but in confessional moments admits resentment at being told when, where, how and what
to eat; when, where, how, and whom to marry; when, where and
whom to mourn. The rabbi cannot simply mandate the behavior of
the individual Jew by citing from traditional texts; quotational
Judaism falls on deaf ears. If he seeks to persuade, it is not on
legal arguments that he must rely, but on the wisdom of the law or
its therapeutic benefits, its advantages for the well-being of the Jew
and his family.

THE RABBI CAUGHT BETWEEN

A *mara de-atra* with the power to "bind and to loosen" implies a community of consent, a community of common beliefs, settled convictions, shared practices. Without such a common network of belief and conduct, the authoritative voice loses its resonance. The rabbi feels compelled to turn ventriloquist, to acquire the talent to so throw his voice that a dialogue of *she'elot* and *teshuvot*, of questions and responses, appears to be taking place. The rabbi finds himself answering questions that were never asked. For real questions emerge from a real community, a *kehillah* of common faith and practice—whereas the rabbi faces an audience of separate individuals. With the community transformed into an audience, the synagogue becomes theater, the *bimah* a stage, the cantor a vocalist, and the rabbi a monologist.

So it is that the rabbi is caught between the traditional and the modern. His training is in and for the world of tradition; the demands he confronts, if he is lucky enough to be confronted with demands, are of and about the world of modernity.

Take, for example, the arena in which rabbi and individual Jew relate most personally; namely, the rites of passage, from birth to death.

The energies and intelligence of the rabbi trained by tradition are concentrated on the performance of the rite, not on the process of the passage. De facto, the rabbinic focus is upon the proper performance of the ritual act, not upon the emotional and spiritual growth of the individual involved in the passage. The rabbi sees himself and is seen by others as dealing with the technicalities of performing a proper *milah* circumcision, not as a specialist in working with parents to understand the religious and moral meaning of the *berit* covenant; with the proper writing of the *ketubah* and the rites of wedding, not with the spiritual preparation for the marriage; with the *tevilah* and *milah* (ritual immersion and circumcision) of the proselyte, not with the emotional and attitudinal changes involved in becoming a Jew by choice; with the prescriptions and proscriptions of the *levayah* (funeral), not with the internal dynamics of grieving and mourning. The layman has learned to approach the rabbi as he approaches the bench. The rabbi, like the judge, hands down decisions—how, when, where the rite is to be done. The layman receives *not the how of the passage but the how of the rite; not the rite as it expresses the meaning and significance of the passage, but the mechanics of the rite itself.*

As for the passage—that may be left outside the Jewish religious domain, to secular agencies, to psychological or spiritual groups unrelated to the Jewish juridical process. The rabbi deals, in short, with passageless rites.

DIVORCE

Consider how the Jew who seeks a religious divorce experiences the rabbinic court, the Beth Din. The entire focus of rabbinic energy and time is concentrated on the correctness of the form, the writing of the twelve lines, the presence of qualified witnesses, the legally appropriate delivery of the *get,* the document of divorce. As for the passage from the status of *kiddushin* (marriage) to that of *gerushin* (divorce), the Beth Din appears to have nothing to say or to do with helping the couple cope with the trauma. What Jewish wisdom or ethic is imparted by the Beth Din to the pained parents who are clearly in need of spiritual counsel and support? What has the court to say to the frightened children whose loyalties are pulled in different directions? Is it not clear that *passageless rites are as religiously scandalous as riteless passages?*

Religiously scandalous—for if the emotional, moral, and spiritual dimensions of the passage remain extrinsic to the halachic process, the process of applying Jewish law, then the halachah is trivialized, is made into an irrelevant protocol that will be derided as empty legalism. If, for example, the passage is not regarded as organically part and parcel of the halachic process, the *get* is impersonal and pro forma, indistinguishable from the civil divorce. (Indeed, the civil courts these days sometimes demonstrate more concern for the human issues of the divorce than the religious courts do.) Perhaps, in premodern times, the expectations and needs for individual attention and personal wisdom may not have been felt as deeply as they are today, or perhaps they were ignored, or perhaps they were satisfied by the close-knit community. But today?

The split between rite and passage is symptomatic of the split between tradition and modernity, between the public agenda of tradition and the private agenda of the modern individual. If the schism is to be overcome, an end must be put to the view that tradition and modernity are hard disjunctives requiring either/or choices.

Hard disjunctive choices between tradition and modernity, between halachah and aggadah, between law and ethics are not found where the relationship between each of these pairs is understood as dialectical, not oppositional. The law is for the sake of the people, and the people is for the sake of the law. But their complementary relationship calls for an expansion of the domain and interest of the halachah. It is not the retraction but the enlargement of halachah that promises to restore the unity of rite and passage. Enlargement suggests a way to combine attention to the individual's emotional and spiritual needs with the more traditional legal concerns that bind the individual to the structure of community.

It is not enough to tell stories of the ethical sensibilities of a Chatam Sofer, Chafetz Chayyim, or Israel Salanter. The gifts of unique leaders inspire us, but they do not solve the problem of how to make our institutions respond to the moral, spiritual and emotional needs of our time. Their tales show us how to integrate such dimensions into the contemporary practice of Jewish law. Appropriate mechanisms and vehicles must be established as indispensable elements within the halachic process that will enable it to respond to the questions Jews ask—and to the questions Jews are reluctant to ask out of fear there are no answers, at least from within the halachic system. The forms and apparatus of tradition must be stretched, not shriveled.

THE "WHY" OF HALACHAH

This calls for a serious evaluation of the teleology of halachah. Moses Maimonides' contrast of the character and function of law and the judge as opposed to medicine and the physician must be reconsidered. Jewish men and women are bleeding. The rabbi must be as much physician as lawyer. Ways must be found to pay attention to the individual in pain and to prescribe medicines according to the particular ailments. If Judaism is a way of life, not simply a catalogue of rites, the practice and teleology of halachah must be greatly enlarged.

The rabbi is mistaken if he sees it as his task to present himself to his modern congregant as the unconditional defender of tradition. The apologistic role forces a false choice upon the congregant. Doubts turn into heresies. Moreover, for all that his seminary training has focused on the tradition, the rabbi himself is not immune to the ethos of modernity.

The rabbi properly points out the perversions in our society that transform individualism into privatism, expressivity into anarchy, interiority into irresponsibility. But the rabbi cannot dismiss as the conceits of modernity the cries for personal help, spirituality, and moral relevance. It was, after all, no antinomian figure but J. B. Soloveitchik himself, who bemoaned the shallowness and mechanical forms of "the majestic community"; no anti-traditionalist but Abraham Joshua Heschel who chastised the sages for having neglected the individual in the Jew. It is not enough to demand the individual's deference to community and tradition; what of the rights of the individual, the obligation of the tradition to the individual Jew?

To dismiss the Jew of modernity as a feckless soul fallen prey to the culture of narcissism turns a deaf ear to the genuine cry for attention and the mounting disaffection with many of the public institutions of Jewish life.

"If I had the power, I would provisionally close all synagogues for a hundred years. Do not tremble at the thought of it, Jewish heart. What would happen? Jews and Jewishness without the synagogue, desiring to remain such, would be forced to concentrate on a Jewish life and a Jewish home." We do not have to approve of Samson Raphael Hirsch's proposal in order to appreciate his frustration. He understood that sanctuary Judaism is no surrogate for Jewish living.

But the contemporary home is no oasis of Jewish life. In the words of the sociologist Arnold Gehlen, the Jewish home today is "underinstitutionalized." The Jewish individual is left to his or her own devices to create Jewish ambience and content—yet the individual Jew cannot do it alone. The Jewish individual who comes from the naked Jewish home into the synagogue finds it an alienating institution. Coming without a whiff of Jewish nostalgia, the individual enters an impersonal megastructure that only heightens his or her estrangement. Too many of today's grandsons and granddaughters neither know nor feel nor believe nor practice what the synagogue leaders insinuate is the belief and the praxis of all congregants. Even public honors turn into private disgrace; called to the Torah for an honor, they are embarrassed in front of family and friends. (We may recall here the earlier rabbinic innovation, which established the role of a professional *ba'al keri'ah,* reader of the Torah, so as to lessen the humiliation of the layman who could not himself read from the Torah.) In any case, it is more than synagogue skills that they require.

Bibliography is not the answer. Classes in adult education do not meet the needs of the individual Jew, for they do not respond to the problems of estrangement, of discomfort, of doubt, of lack of a sense of real belonging. As Rosenzweig understood, "Books are not now the prime need of the day. What we need more than ever are human beings—Jewish human beings." The founder of the Frankfurt *Lehrhaus* was expressing no anti-intellectual bias. But he understood that Jews need Jews to be Jewish. Belonging is essential to behaving and even to believing.

OUTSIDE THE SANCTUARY

Jewishness cannot begin nor end in the sanctuary. It must be experienced outside the threshold of the synagogue, *pro fanum.* Jewishness is brought into the synagogue from without. By contrast, sanctuary Judaism only manages to supplant the individual; it sponsors community celebrations of what were once family traditions, it purchases prayer shawls and skullcaps and prayer books, all once proud private possessions, now inscribed as temple property. The individual becomes a passive auditor, an attender of services.

For the individual Jew caught in the interstices of the underinstitutionalized home and the overinstitutionalized synagogue, a halfway house must be built. The individual needs mediating structures.

The synagogue havurah is the liveliest illustration of such a mediating institution. It provides the individual with an association small enough to see and hear him, large enough to move him beyond privatism. The synagogue havurah is a single example of what religious leadership can do to create a nonthreatening environment, a peer group with whom the individual can express doubts and fears, and taste the joys of decision and choice. It is only one model of the way the lonely individual Jew may take her first steps towards the larger institutions of her people. Through the havurah she has the opportunity to experience peoplehood, Torah, and *gemilut chasadim*—acts of redemptive loving-kindness. The synagogue is thereby humanized, personalized, rendered accessible.

Nor is the havurah the only mediating institution we can imagine and invent. *If Jews need Jews in order to be Jewish, then the rabbi needs Jewish allies.* He needs lay colleagues who can help him relate Judaism to Jews face-to-face. Realistically, no rabbi has the time or energy to engage the individual Jew person-to-person and to sustain such a relationship. The rabbi therefore needs to enter into a collegiality with lay leaders dedicated to serve the synagogue community as para-Judaic counselors. He needs to train fellow *ba'alei bayit,* landlords, not as custodians of the temple building or its material contents, but as his own allies in fostering the spiritual life of the individual Jew.

Before every congregational rabbi lies a significant untapped reservoir of lay people who want to do more than serve on fiscal committees or join the critics' circle. There are altruistic men and women in every congregation willing to learn in order to teach, to solicit Jews for spiritual contributions to their own lives and to the lives of their families and their community. Yet is there, outside the philanthropic organizations, a laity that operates on such a person-to-person model? Is there a cadre of competent and compassionate Jews trained to serve individual Jews?

Such a cultivated cadre of men and women would serve as mediators who would create a blood-and-flesh nexus between the synagogue and the individual, and between the rabbinate and the laity. They could enter the homes and the lives of diffident individuals who are too intimidated to enter the corridors of the megastructure by themselves. The para-rabbinic or, if you will, para-Judaic counselors would help bring the Sabbath and festivals into the home, not through classroom exercises but personally, not as abstract and threatening norms but as comforting and natural ways. They will have been trained to help make the rite of passage more than a routinized pro forma exercise, to make it instead a vital stage in the Jewish growth of individual and family.

The rabbi cannot do it alone; he is not ubiquitous—nor ought he to be, for he is not the community, and it is community that is wanting and wanted. But the rabbi can tap the creativity and altruism of the laity as partners in the sacred task of making Jews. Alone, the rabbi becomes as indispensable as a master plumber— and as meaningful. He is called upon, mostly in emergencies, to perform his mysterious rituals; when his work is done, he is expected to leave so that his employers can go about their normal business.

Experience with pararabbinic counselors has convinced Jewish leaders that through these lay people the rabbinate can achieve a new level of relevance. The rabbi's authority and influence increase as the lay leaders begin to understand through their own involvement how complex and critical are his tasks and aspirations. The counselors do not replace the rabbi, they extend his scope and influence. The lowering of the *mechitzah,* the partition, between seminary, synagogue and individual is imperative in our times. To do so, mediating structures and the training of mediating religious leaders must be placed high on the agenda. The relevance and credibility of the Torah, "which makes wise the simple and restores the soul," is a correlate of the new collegiality between professional lay Jewry that reaches into the lives of individual Jews where they are.

INREACH: WAYS TOWARDS
FAMILY EMPOWERMENT

We Jews belong. We belong to organizations and institutions, synagogues and centers, federations and defense organizations. We contribute to building drives and to Jewish appeals and we give generously.

We are public Jews led by public officials and public personnel carrying out the mandate of public agenda. We maintain social welfare, educational, recreational and cultural Jewish activities, support Israel, fight anti-Semitism locally and abroad. We serve on committees, commissions, task forces, boards of directors and boards of overseers. We attend meetings, conventions, conferences, assemblies. We have been trained in the skills of public life. We know Robert's Rules of Order, how to formulate a motion, add an amendment, call the motion. We are organization Jews.

Who are we, alone after the conference is over, after the last gavel has been pounded? Who are we after *Ne'ilah,* after the last shofar is blown? Who are we, not as delegates or solicitors or representatives or dues-paying members or members of the minyan, but as individual Jews?

Who am I alone in the hospital bed after the visitors have gone, after the *shivah* mourning period is over and the minyan has left? What personal Jewishness do I have to draw upon to respond to the loss of job, the loss of parent or spouse or child, or our own mortality? Who am I as Jew, behind the locked doors, drawn drapes, with my family? What songs do I sing, what is my poetry? What stories do I tell? What convictions do I own?

For public institutions, the problems, targets, and agenda are public and outer-directed. Out there young people are caught up in Eastern and Christian cults; out there mixed marriages, out there assimilating Jews and unassimilable Jewish immigrants proliferate. And if the problems and target population are out there in the public domain, then the solution lies in the public domain. The "outreach" metaphor is right. The direction is wrong.

It pays greater attention to external symptoms than to internal causes, hearing the echo as if it were the origin of the outcry, repairing the damage from without—better institutions, better management, more and better schools and camps and temples and personnel. Consider intermarriage, the issue that engages so much interest in the Jewish community. Consider the not atypical instance of Susan, who has studied with rabbis, attended public classes, religious services, retreats. Susan is a Jew by choice, moved by the shiver of Jewish history and ritual symbolism, attracted to the nondogmatic character of Jewish theology and the centrality of the Jewish home. She has immersed herself in the waters of the mikvah, passed the test of the Beth Din. Now, at last, she is invited to her Jewish in-laws-to-be on a Friday night. The home is finely furnished, the table exquisitely set. It is her first experience with Jews outside the public arena. Susan reports her disappointment. The Sabbath evening was far different from what her textbooks and teachers had given her to believe. It was an evening bereft of benediction, no blessings over the candles or wine or bread. She had been told of *zemirot,* the Sabbath songs around the table, the chanting of grace after meals. But here are songless, graceless Jews, with table talk as pedestrian as the weekday dust. No. The integration of Susan into the Jewish family is not the problem. Neither ethnic nor theological identification. The problem is with the Jewish integration of the family into Judaism. What is Jewishly distincitve? What is culture, faith, ritual choreography, particular wisdom, ethos, culture, faith, ritual choreography? How is the Jewish home different from the middle-class home in general? What do we have to say Jewishly to Susan, who takes Jewishness to heart? Thoreau, told about Morse's invention of the telegraph, which would allow a man from Maine to instantly send a message to a man in Texas, asked, "But what have they to say to each other?'' What have we to say to Susan-Shoshana?

The problem is not out there. It is here. The problem is not with Jews by choice; but with Jews by genes. The problem is not what does Susan, the proselyte-to-be see in us, but what do the native born see in themselves. The problem is not Susan, the stranger in our midst, but the Jewish estrangement of her husband-to-be and her in-laws.

It is a self-deceptive projection to cast the problems outward. Intermarriage is a *symptom* that is treated as a *cause* of Jewish weakness.

Hear the cry of Philip Roth, not his alone, ''What a Jewish child inherited was no body of law; no body of learning, no language and finally no Lord. . . . But what he did receive was a psychology that can be translated in three words: 'Jews are better.' ''

But in what sense better; better in what respect according to which meanness of excellence? Better in the sense of Duddy Kravetz or Sammy Glick?

Reach out—with whom?

Reach out—with what?

Reach out—from where?

There can be no outreach without inreach. Public Jews and public institutions have ignored the individual and his family, neglected the private sector in Jewish living. We have succumbed to Spinoza's treatment of Judaism as nothing more than a ''social organization,'' a polity to which we owe allegiance.

We have rejected Whitehead's statement that ''religion is what one does with one's solitariness,'' by emphasizing only institutional togetherness, only membership, only belonging. But public belonging without private believing and private behaving is like praising public forests without attention to private trees.

Heschel was right. ''Unless a person knows how to pray alone, he will remain incapable of praying with the congregation.'' No public institution, no public prayer or public theology can cry my tears, mourn my loss, discover my conviction, wrestle for my faith. Inreach is prior to outreach. ''If we meet no gods it is because we harbor none'' (Emerson).

We have ignored the Jewish inwardness of the individual Jew and his individual family. We have dismissed his wanderings into spiritual experience in EST, Scientology, Transcendental Meditation, Arica, as some idiosyncratic expression. But there is a cry for attention here. "Don't tell me what I can do for Judaism—tell me what Judaism can do for me. Don't tell me what I can do for the synagogue, tell me what the synagogue can do for me. Don't tell me what Jewish tradition can do for me—in my existential aloneness, in my disillusionment, in the weightlessness of my life, and the barrenness of my family."

Public Jews are spiritually unsupported. Even in their private castles they are overwhelmed by a mass culture that has penetrated the walls. Television is the paradigm of that culture. It is the major educational medium and message shared intergenerationally by the entire family. Taken seriously, it represents a serious challenge to Jewish values.

Big Brother has invaded the sanctuary of the home. Not that Big Brother is watching the family. The family is watching Big Brother. Ninety-eight percent of American homes own television sets, a higher percentage than have indoor plumbing. The average American household watches television seven hours a day, teenagers eight hours a day. Children spend fifteen hundred hours each year watching TV—more than attending school or any action except sleeping. If you are forty years old, you have seen one million TV commercials, and before you reach your sixty-fifth birthday, you will see another million commercials. Such are the gifts of longevity.

Complain to Marshall McLuhan that there is nothing serious on TV, he would reply, "Nonsense, there are commercials." Commercials are serious. What we subliminally absorb is more than cars and deodorants. Through commericals we ingest values, an understanding of self and the world, a folk theology. In thirty- or sixty-second intervals the parables and sermonic homilies inform us of what is real, what is valuable, and how to cope with life's challenges. Neil Postman suggests that television commercials are a form of religious literature.

A couple sits relaxed in a restaurant. A waitress approaches the table, notices the dark lines around the man's collar. She stares boldly with ill-concealed contempt at the ring. She is offended. The husband glares at his wife. The look is full of blame and recrimination. The camera now focuses on the accused wife, and her face reveals self-loathing and an admission of culpability. She knows how to effect expiation. She is shown using a new detergent. Proudly she shows the cleansed shirt to the camera. "Yea, though your sins be as scarlet, they shall be as white as snow." They are returned to the restaurant, to the scene of the original sin. They eat their meal oblivious to the waitress. Expiation, exculpation, redemption within sixty seconds.

The debate over the cause or effect of television is poorly framed. Television doesn't affect culture or reflect culture. Television is culture. "Culture," Einstein said, "is what remains after you've forgotten everything you learned in school." Television is the lingua franca of the modern family. We know its parables and homilies and the lessons it teaches about facing crises. The parable of the lost traveler's money on his vacation, the man with halitosis, the woman with the heartbreak of psoriasis, the crisis of the spotted glassware before the arrival of the mother-in-law, the embarrassment of the unsophisticated dolt who orders just Bud or just beer without knowing the correct name. This is not just commercials. This is folk theology. It preaches that not to own certain things, not to know what or how to order things is to fall from grace. The ethos of the commercial culture teaches our children that owning certain commodities gives you grace and elegance, gains you favor, esteem, or love, but not owning them will bring about a crisis in your life. When Catherine Deneuve purrs, "Of course it's expensive, but I deserve it," more than an advertising message is brought home. The commercial preaches a powerful moral lesson in hedonism. My value is expressed in the perfume or clothes I wear or the money I spend on myself. There is no need to transform yourself or to struggle with the environment. Salvation is as fast as a purchase. It is found in things bought, possessed, or used.

Television commericals preach a theology of hedonism. Pursue pleasure and avoid pain. The smallest irritation—traffic jams, a long line at a theater, noise, a delay—is intolerable. From infancy on we are raised to avoid the slightest pain. Our pain threshold is increasingly lowered. The television set has stocked the sacred chest of the family—the medicine cabinet—the pharmacopoeia of potions and pills promising salvation. Twenty billion dollars a year spent on sleeping pills, stomach settlers, headache tablets, analgesics, Dexamils, Halcion, Restoril, Valium, amphetamines, barbiturates, stimulants, and sedatives. "Cause us, O Lord, to lie down in peace and raise us up again unto life." Marx was wrong: Religion is not the opiate of the people, opiate is the religion of the people. Ours is an addictive culture feeding on a hedonistic theology.

Television indoctrinates our children with heroes and role models. In a study conducted by the Electronic Learning Laboratory at Columbia University's Teachers College, high school students asked to name some role models chose TV characters more often than any other fictional or real figure. Clint Eastwood and Sylvester Stallone. Rambo and Dirty Harry present a heroism that has the character and competence to handle the real world. The new commercials of Phillip Morris do not argue that cigarettes are dangerous to your health, but, knowing who we are, they point to the successful men and women who smoke. The Marlboro man may spit up blood from his lungs, but he rides a white horse, and it sells and it teaches. We live in an opticizing culture. "We are instructed by words but educated by our eyes" (Burckhardt).

In the absence of well-defined parental attitudes "heavy violence viewers are highly likely to approve aggression and to be willing to use violence as a means of solving problems." The home viewer is bombarded by twelve hundred different images each day of heroes impatient with dialogue and debate, muscle-bound men who cut through the palaver, the frustrations of court procedure with a sharp machete. Television is no diversion. Television is more than the babysitter, television has become the true parent.

Television binds the family. TV is the "Equalizer." Television has wiped out the generation gap within our families. There are no secrets to be hidden. What is there in our private imagination that is off limits or off camera? There are no private parts or impulses in a society in which all you have to know is to watch.

In pretelevision days, you had to wait to know about those things until you could read *Studs Lonigan* or Boccaccio's *Decameron,* which my papa kept hidden behind the front row of decent books. But my grandchildren needn't be literate to see it all. Prime time is for parents. According to Frank Mankiewicz's book on TV, *Remote Control,* approximately three million children, ages two to ten, watch TV every night between the hours of 11:00 p.m. and 11:30

p.m., and an equal number between 11:30 and 1:00 a.m. It is midnight. Do you know where your children are at home?

No secrets. Where there are no secrets, there is no shame. Blushing is obsolete, a sign of unsophistication. Television has adultified our children. They are not embarrassed. Without a capacity for shame, nothing is sacred, nothing is really private.

So we deceive ourselves into thinking our homes are private. It is in the sanctuary of our private homes that the family watches, over and again, salacious, violent scenes that sell the products we consume. But they also sell the by-products of character education our children ingest.

Television is a nervous and impatient medium, fearful of pauses or conversations. Thinking is not a performing art. Car chases and crashes are. And so we witness the rise of a new form of uncivil discourse. Programs like the *Morton Downey, Jr. Show* may surpass Ted Koppel's *Nightline,* or the analytic, slow-paced *MacNeil Lehrer Report.* The verbal attack on the jugular, the confrontation that rips apart guests and turns audiences into jeering, hooting intimidating mobs cannot be laughed away. These shows are not listed as comedies but as information, conversation, dialogue. Insult has been elevated to a state of the art.

How ordinary these concerns. What has mass culture to do with Judaism and the Jewish future at the dawn of a new century? Why not speak about the challenges without? The challenges of Christianity or Islam or the cults or atheism or communist ideology?

Because the Kulturkampf, the daily battle of culture, is not so high-blown. It is not fought over theological doctrines. I hear it in my conversations with the couples who come to see me about their contemplated mixed marriages. They are either ignorant of or indifferent to the theological differences between Christianity and Judaism. They stand in the naked public square, religiously neither/nor. As the Yiddish quip has it, they are akin to the celebrated cross-breed of a hen and a rabbit, *"nisht a hen un nisht a hin."*

The conflicts are not with great religions or the missionizing of our children. But over the internal conversion of the home into the vulgarity of narcissism, hedonism, materialism, the exploitation of sex and violence that sponsors and sells along with its merchandise, a style of life and values. The surrender of the family to the sovereignty of the television media is taking place in the private domain. Jewish parenting, the indispensable apparatus for transmitting character, the refinement of the spirit, is being surrendered to new parents, the commercial manipulative media. The family parlor room—called parlor from *parler,* "to speak," the room used for conversation—is obsolete, replaced by Oprah Winfrey and Geraldo Rivera.

Christian writers understand: Christianity is rooted in church, in its celebration of the eucharist. Judaism is rooted in family.

The home is the substructure of Judaism, and with its erosion, the superstructures of all Jewish agencies tremble: federation center, synagogue, temple, defense organization. Charity begins at home, not in public relations rhetoric. The love of Zion begins at home, not in propaganda releases. Jewish theology begins at home. Children have fears and doubts. Children ask and wonder about God and death and miracles. December is the season of Jewish claustrophobia, Santa Claustrophobia. Children ask about Christmas trees and mean more than "Why can't we have Christmas trees?" they mean "Why can't we be Christians?" Parents are fearful, theologically bankrupt. And the children are not answered by parents who increasingly act as referral agents—"Ask your teacher" or "Ask the rabbi"—wrongly believing that others "can do it better." Send them outside. The home has become an empty nest even before the kids have flown the coop. That is wrong. Parents are gods to their children in their formative years. Parents create memories that support our lives. Parents teach by the songs they sing, the stories they tell, the poetry they recite, by the sayings of the fathers and the mothers.

Children pick up parental convictions and beliefs, and where there are none, a vacuum is created that is readily filled by gurus and sects and cults. Again, the problem is not with the proselytizers out there, but within. As Chesterton put it, "Where man ceases believing in something, it isn't that he believes in nothing, but that he believes in anything." Human nature abhors a vacuum. The vacuum is in the home.

Surveys and studies of religious schools of all denominations have shown repeatedly that "a school cannot be expected to carry out a religious socialization process for which there is little sympathy at home" (Greeley and Rossi, *The Education of Catholic Americans,* 1966).

The school can teach dates, history, and geography, but not the language that penetrates the soul. Around the Passover table, I experienced the democratic character of ritual. I, a child, and my bearded grandfather and uncle, and my uncles and aunts—people of different ages and opinions—all ate the bitter herbs, dipped the parsley in salt water, and counted aloud the ten plagues. I experienced peoplehood, the warmth of belonging to a family bound to a transcendent history.

I remember the year my parents allowed me to fast for a half-day on Yom Kippur. It was a boost to my self-esteem. It was for me the first small measure of heroic self-denial, the first small suffering for something beyond my hedonistic conceits.

I learned more about ethical sensibility from mama-papa's *"es past nisht"* than from courses on moral philosophy. Asked why she believes in God, the little girl said, "I guess it just runs in the family."

The Jewish family is in trouble. Scattered, shattered, and shriveled, it has been left to fend for itself, to shoulder responsibilities it cannot bear on its own. Sociologists like Arnold Gehlen and Peter Berger have recognized the "underinstitutionalization" of the family. The family is unsupported culturally, spiritually, morally, ritually. The chasm between public institutions and the private sector of the family must be overcome.

It cannot be done by institutional surrogation. The family cannot be bypassed. The family cannot function vicariously.

My grandfather came to the synagogue because he was a Jew. His grandchildren join to become Jewish. But the synagogue is not mishpachah, the sanctuary is not the home, and it cannot pretend otherwise: public sanctuaries are not private homes.

For decades the synagogue has attempted to fill the gap by assuming the role of family. In the process the house was emptied. The sukkah adjoins the walls of the synagogue; the lulav and etrog have become properties of the institution. The Passover Seder has been removed from the living room to the social hall, the Haggadah has been taken out of the hands of the family into the hands of the rabbinic and cantorial officiants. The inside cover of the siddur, machzor, Bible does not record handwritten inscriptions of births, deaths, anniversaries. It is stamped with the imprimatur, "Property of Valley Beth Shalom."

The family has been projected outward, externalized, congregationalized. Inadvertently, the institution has robbed the home of its sancta.

This must change. It is easier to substitute for the parent than to motivate and teach the parent to parent. It is easier to lecture than to turn the student into a lecturer himself. It is easier to give charity than to help a fellowman learn to support himself. But to offer the family parenting competence and confidence is the highest and most significant task confronting the community. It is easier to outreach than to inreach.

The Jewish family needs to be strengthened and confirmed. The Jewish home needs to be reclaimed. The parental roles need to be restored. This means that the public institutions must redirect its intents, energies and projects to enter the home and restore its moral, cultural and spiritual centrality. The public rhetoric, rituals and issues must be personalized, harmonized, familiarized so that they become part of the table talk. The songs and stories and ritual choreography heard and seen in the public square must be brought back to the family. The family must be freed from its muteness and its expressivity encouraged.

This is a call to public institutions: the community requires *mechanchei mishpachah,* family educators, a cadre of men and women motivated by one superordinate goal, one major task: *the empowerment of the family.* The teleology of the *mechanchei mishpachah* turns to a new methodology. Their world is not of textbooks and blackboards and tests, knowledge for the sake of knowledge. Their world is the home, their desk is the table, their students are members of the family, their tests are the Sabbaths and festivals, the rites of family passage, the table talk. The goal is for Jewish expressivity, Jewish competence, performance, Jewish doing, speaking, singing, decision-making. It is a far cry from the passive audience of adult education. They are to be trained to do, to learn in order to teach, to become ancestors, to encourage questions.

Jews need Jews to be Jewish. Mishpachot need mishpachot to become mishpachot. The community's task is to match mishpachot so that they join at each other's tables to share stories, to learn from each other the art of raising Jewish children, to enjoy their Jewishness—and to know that within the larger circles of their affiliation there are skilled and caring friends of the family to enrich their lives.

There is a need for "perestroika"—restructuring of public institutions. The models of the havurah and the para-Judaic counselor were meant to decentralize and personalize the members of the institutional megastructure. Their skills and goals may be refined and readjusted to enter the sanctuary of the home, wherein lie the most powerful energies for our sanity and sanctity.

The public institution must bend its efforts to fulfill the promise of the home as "a safe haven from a heartless world," where children learn what is right and what is wrong; to be kind and generous, where another channel is played to experience how conflicts are resolved without fangs and claws.

It is not in the institutions above or beyond the seas but within us, and in our families. A Hasidic master towards the end of his days looked back at his life's choices. "When I was young, I thought to repair the world. When I grew older, I thought it wiser to begin with my own village. Older yet, I thought to begin the repair with my own family and myself. I regret nothing of those decisions. I only wish that I had first begun with my family and myself." It is time to reach in.

THE STRANGER IN OUR MIRROR: JEWS BY CHOICE

Why is so much of the Jewish agenda centered around the convert? Why is so much Jewish energy spent on outreach programs, on Jews by choice, on proposals and arguments dealing with patrilineal descent, on the legitimacy of proselytizing agencies and procedures, on the intermarried and mixed-married? Why is the major issue shaking the foundations of Jewish solidarity focused on the amendment to the Law of Return—a matter that has now appeared forty-three times before the Knesset—and which again focuses on the convert?

Why the convert? Why the *ger* and why now? The connection is symptomatic of an internal cultural and religious crisis, a Kulturkampf among our people. The controversy over the Law of Return is not simply the manifestation of a political power play between religious factions in Israel or in Israel and the diaspora. The depth of feeling expressed by world Jewry on the "Who is a Jew" issue evidences an intuitive folk awareness that something deeper than definitions and demography is involved. Consider that this time even the appeal to the Holocaust, that ultimate argument for Jewish unity, failed to keep the lid on the seething cauldron of Jewish disputation. This time the glue failed to keep in check the anger and threats to Jewish unity. It was perhaps the first indication of the exhaustion of the Holocaust as the unifying memory.

We are concentrated on the *ger*, the stranger in our midst, because the *ger* has become a litmus test for the character and destiny of Judaism. How we see the *ger*, how we relate to the stranger in our midst, reflects the way we relate Judaism to the world around us. The *ger* who stands on the threshold of our home is a metaphor for our relationship to Western civilization. The attention focused on the proselyte is a paradigm of the emerging cultural struggle. Hermann Cohen wrote, "In the stranger man discovered the idea of Judaism." I would add that in the stranger Jews discover the moral ideal of Judaism.

Towards the *ger* there is an ambivalence within our tradition. In the words of Aaron Lichtenstein, the rosh yeshivah of Har Etzion, there is "encouragement on the one hand and repulsion on the other; some esteemed the ger while others approached him with cautious apprehension" ("On Conversion," *Tradition,* Winter 1988).

I identify two dominant strains in Judaism towards the *ger,* two fundamental attitudes towards the proselyte that express two basic philosophies of Judaism. At one end of the spectrum is the Ezra strain, named after Ezra the Scribe, who, returning from Babylonia, saw calamity in the intermingling of the "holy seed" with foreign wives whose assimilated children spoke "half in the speech of Ashdod and could not speak the Jew's language."

For the Ezra strain, a conversionary solution for this tragic entanglement is not possible. It presumes that there is a primordial foreignness in the *ger* that cannot be Jewishly assimilated. The unique purity of the people can be restored only by excluding the alienating partner. "Make confession unto the Lord God of your fathers . . . separate yourselves from the people of the land and from the strange foreign women" (Ezra 10:11).

At the other end of the spectrum is the Ruth strain, which stands genealogical conceits on their head and transforms alleged genetic flaws into providential virtue. The ancestry of Davidic royalty and messianic status is doubly flawed, audaciously traced back to incestuous unions with biblically forbidden peoples. On the mother's side, David stems from the Moabite Ruth, but according to Deuteronomy, a Moabite "shall not enter the assembly of the Lord," and the eponymous ancestor of Moab was the child of an incestuous union between father Lot and his daughter. On the father's side, David's lineage is derived from Peretz, the product of an incestuous union of father-in-law and daughter-in-law, Judah and Tamar (Ruth 4:12). The Ruth strain contradicts with a vengeance the genealogical purity of the Ezra strain. The convert is as the newborn. "Whoever brings another person under the wings of the Shechinah is considered as having created him, shaped him, and brought him into the world" (Tosefta *Horayot* 2:7). "A *ger* is like a newborn babe" (T. *Yevamot* 22a).

THE BODY REVEALED

The Book of Ezra and the Book of Ruth are both canonized biblical texts. Each approach has its own *gilgulim*, its transformations. The Ezra strain is evident in the thinking of Judah Halevi, the Maharal of Prague and the School of Chabad. Its most contemporary resurrection is found in Professor Michael Wyschograd's book *The Body of Faith* (1983). A graduate of Yeshiva University and a teacher of philosophy at Baruch College of the City University of New York, and one of the principal Jewish spokespersons in the international Jewish-Christian dialogue, Wyschograd boldly articulates the Ezra strain. Judaism is a carnal election. God chose the route of election through a biological principle. The *berit* (covenant) of God with Israel does not take place as an ideological, spiritual, disembodied covenant. Israel's election is transmitted through the body. God chose to elect "a biological people that remains elect even when it sins." The Jew is corporally chosen, chosen in the flesh, regardless of his spiritual or moral merit. The frontispiece of Wyschograd's book carries a statement from the *Sifra*, "Even though they [the Jews] are unclean, the Divine Presence is among them."

Those not elected, those not born Jewish, will of course be hurt, for they are not of the seed of Abraham whom God loves above all others. And election has nothing to do with the virtues of the person or people. Wyschograd argues a theology of the Jewish body, a metaphysical sociobiology down to the putatively Jewish facial physiognomy and culinary predilections. "There are those for whom their Jewishness means gefilte fish, bagels with lox and cream cheese, or the smell of chicken simmering in broth. Those who think of those things with derision do not understand Jewish existence as embodied existence. Just as the gait and face of a person is that person, at least in part, so the physiognomy of the Jewish people is, at least in part, the people" (p. 26). "Anatomy is destiny," Freud observed. I have heard such arguments, not from philosophers, but from Jews for whom the unassimilability of the proselyte is "alimentary". *De gustibus non disputandum est.* The people of the book favor an Ashkenazic menu.

Following the Ezra strain, Judaism is not essentially a matter of faith or ethics or ideology but a matter of mysteriously inherited traits. The *Tanya,* the Hasidic classic authored by the founder of Chabad, Schneur Zalman, is the sacred text studied daily by the Lubavitchers. The *Tanya*'s metaphysical biologism runs throughout the text, distinguishing Jewish souls from the souls of the nations of the world, which emanate from unclean husks that contain no good whatever.

All the good that the non-Jewish nations do is done only from selfish motives. "From the lower grades of the *kelipot,* altogether unclean and evil, flow the souls of all the nations of the world and the existence of their bodies, and also the souls of all living creatures that are unclean and unfit for human consumption" (chap. 6). Within the Ezra strain, pure, impure, clean, contaminating, are the critical categories that divide the souls of God's creation.

Still there is a felt embarrassment in the exclusionary Ezra strain. If Jews inherit character, how can someone not born a Jew acquire the congenital virtues by a sheer act of will? And yet there is an unambiguous legal possibility of conversion. Here the Ezra strain feels compelled to put some limits on the elevation of the proselyte. For Judah Halevi it is clear that "those who become Jews do not assume equal rank with born Israelites, who are specially privileged to attain prophecy" (*Kuzari* 1:115). No other nation besides Israel knows the true meaning of the Tetragrammaton, no other people has the connection with God. For the *Zohar,* while the proselyte receives a new soul from heaven, it is not of the same caliber as the souls of Jews by birth (see Jacob Katz, *Exclusiveness and Tolerance,* chap. 12).

THE ATTRACTIONS OF THE EZRA STRAIN

If I dwell on the Ezra strain and barely mention the rabbinic traditions endorsing the Ruth strain, it is because liberal Jews are rarely exposed to the Ezra tradition. The books we read, the tradition we select, the rabbis we hear have filtered out the Ezra view of Judaism. But if we are to understand the implications of our outreach program for Judaism, we must understand the Ezra strain, because it is more alive than we may think, and its presuppositions and implications are very much a part of the contemporary Kulturkampf.

The arguments I hear mostly contend that the "Jews by choice" are hopelessly deaf to the ethnic strains of Jewishness. This is, I suspect, a more polite way of saying that Jewishness is an ascriptive not an acquired character, something you are born with, or as one of my patient congregants put it, "Jewishness, dear Rabbi, comes with the mother's milk." Indeed, it seems to me that the less practicing and believing the Jew, the more insistent the contention that Jewishness is something born into. The weaker the Jew, the more powerful the attraction to make Jewishness a genetic affair.

Ruth followers must understand the heart of Ezra. Ezra cannot be simply dismissed as bigoted or xenophobic. Ezra has no trust in the viability of a community of choice. Choice is too fragile to assure the Jewishness of his grandchildren. He seeks something independent of choice, a covenant in the flesh, a circumcision in blood. *Be-damayich chayi*, "In thy blood shalt thou live," is recited at the *berit*. The Ezra strain seeks a genetic transmission of loyalty as certain as a transfusion of blood.

There is something reassuring in the genetic fixity applied to Judaism. The sociologist Nathan Glazer argues that "the converted may be better Jews than those born within the fold and indeed often are, but it seems undeniable that their children have alternatives before them that the children of families in which both parents were born Jewish do not—they have legitimate alternative identities" (Nathan Glazer, *New Perspectives in American Jewish Sociology*, American Jewish Committee, 1987). Choice is chancy. Jews by choice chose. But he who chooses for Judaism one day may opt to chose out of Judaism another day, or else his child may. In halachic terms, the infant of a Jewish womb, whatever he/she may later choose, is irrevocably Jewish—*Yisrael af al pi shechatah yisrael hu;* no theological or ritual text is called for. But a non-Jewish infant converted before his/her majority can protest the conversion. The biological Jewish infant is safe. He cannot protest and cannot revert.

CHOICE AND HERESY

There is in the tradition a greater confidence in being chosen than in chosing, in chosing because you are commanded rather than chosing out of your autonomous decisions. The election of Israel (*Avodah Zarah* 2b) took place without consultation with Israel. God overwhelmed Israel. He suspended a mountain over Israel like an upside-down vault, declaring, "If you accept the Torah, it will be well with you, and if not, there you will find your grave." It is God's choice, not Israel's choosing, that assures the irrevocable election and singularity of the Jew.

But it is precisely here that the *ger* in our times challenges the presuppositions of the traditional society. The very title "Jews by Choice" challenges the genetic understanding of Judaism and the preference of biological fate over chosen faith. It raises root questions that touch the nature of our identity and the character of our education. Is Judaism essentially a biological affair, a congenital matter determined by the ovum, or is Judaism an ideological, spiritual matter of faith to be chosen? While formally these alternatives are not contradictory—for Israel is a community both of birth and of choice—de facto the Ezra and Ruth strains pull at either end oppositionally. There are pragmatic advantages for the Jewish community in retaining elements of both, i.e., accepting a Jew by birth without any theological or ritual test and accepting a non-Jew as a Jew by religious and cultural decisions. And yet there are powerful theoretical and pragmatic arguments for rejecting the extremes of the Ezra strain that border on metaphysical racism.

Outreach to the proselyte affects our self-understanding. In the conversion of the *ger,* the native-born is forced to confront himself. The *ger* of adoption places greater weight on choice, will, faith, ideology. The contemporary calls for greater Jewish "spirituality," the growing emphasis on theological clarification within the religious movements, the disenchantment with mere belonging, all reflect the shifting of the pendulum from destiny to decision, from being chosen by an external fate to freely choosing by inner conviction.

"Heresy" comes from a Greek word, *hairein,* which means "to choose." In the closed society of the premodern world, choice was heretical. In the open society, choice has become the nobler spiritual imperative. "Modern consciousness," Peter Berger summarizes, "entails a movement from fate to choice." In modernity, the pendulum shifts from Ezra to Ruth. The *ger* challenges the presuppositions that value biological fate over faith, that make of Judaism a theology of the inherited body-soul and ignore the willful attachment to faith, the longing for spirituality.

All this affects the consciousness of the native-born. The Jewish attitude towards the *ger* presents in concentrated form a clue to the Jewish relationship to Western civilization which lies at the heart of the contemporary Kulturkampf. The *ger* is the microcosm of the world outside us.

We are shaped by those we shape. The artist is revealed in his art. The *ger* comes to us from the outside and leads us to look inside. In the process of *giyur* (conversion) the native Jew is enlarged. The *ger* enters a new covenant with God and us, transforming us, reinforcing the genius of Jewish universalism. The *ger* who brings *bikkurim* (first fruits) to the Temple is entitled to declare that God has sworn to his fathers to give them the land, for when God spoke to Abraham He said, "I have made you a father unto the multitude of nations" (Genesis 17:8). In this sense, Abraham is transformed. For, as the Talmud Yerushalmi has it, while in the past Abraham was only the father of Aram, through the acceptance of the *ger* he became "father of all those in the world who ever become Jewish" (*Bikkurim* 1:4). Through the *ger,* the view of Judaism is enlarged. A universal community of faith is added to the particular community of birth. When the *knesset yisrael* turns away from the *ger, knesset yisrael* turns away from the world; turning towards the *ger, knesset yisrael* enters the wider world. The Kulturkampf struggling over our posture towards the *ger* entails a struggle over our attitude towards Western civilization.

THE CAVE

A celebrated talmudic episode adumbrates the depth of our burgeoning Kulturkampf. The Talmud records a conversation among a group of rabbis around the year 130 C.E., when Palestine was under Roman rule (*Shabbat* 33b). Rabbi Judah ben Ilai observed, "How fine are the works of these people [the Romans]. They have made roads, built bridges and markets, and erected bath-houses." Rabbi Yose remained silent, but Rabbi Simeon ben Yochai noted caustically, "All these edifices and structures they make for themselves. The marketplaces are to put harlots into them, the bridges are to levy tolls for themselves, the bath-houses are to pamper their bodies."

The Roman government issued a death decree to punish Simeon ben Yochai's seditious statements. He and his son Eleazer escaped to a cave and remained there, praying and studying, for twelve years. When it was rumored that the decree had been annulled, the two left the cave and went into the world. They were aghast at the activities they saw. Men were plowing and sowing a field, and the two condemned them: "People forsake life eternal for the business of temporal life." Whatever they looked at was immediately burned up. Thereupon, a heavenly voice cried out: "Have you come to destroy My world? Get back to the cave!"

Chastened, they returned to the cave, there to pray and study another twelve years. And then they again heard the heavenly echo cry out, "Go forth from your cave."

It was on the eve of the Sabbath when father and son emerged and saw an old man holding two bundles of myrtle. They asked him, "What are the myrtles for?" He answered, "They are for the honor of the Sabbath." "And why two myrtles?" "One is in honor of the commandment to 'observe the Sabbath.' And the other in honor of the commandment to 'remember the Sabbath.' " The minds of Simeon ben Yochai and his son Eleazer were set at ease. The myrtles were not in the cave. They were in the world among the thorns and thistles.

The retreat of Simeon ben Yochai from the world, his contempt for the culture and civilization of his day, is echoed these days in many circles—not all fundamentalist. It is a critical aspect of the contemporary Kulturkampf. Particularly after the profound disillusionment of the Holocaust era, the cave looms large as an attractive option. For the cave mind-set, there is no good in Western civilization, and in associating with it there is the risk of a contamination that poisons Jewish identity and continuity. Democracy, pluralism, humanism, science, tolerance, conscience, the Enlightenment are the seductions of foreign wives that eat away at the unique holiness of Israel. The *Tanya* warns against those who occupy themselves "with the sciences of the world, for the uncleanness of the science of the nations is greater than that of profane speech'' (chap. 8).

There is peace in the cave. In the cave there are no foreign elements to intrude. Out there in the world at large there is an innate, irreconcilable conflict between "them" and "us" in the very womb of Rebeccah. Rabbi Elie Munk in his commentary *The Call of the Torah* explains that the hostility between Esau and Jacob is "prenatal," a "providential factor in history which escapes the control of the will." The intrauterine hostility between Esau and Jacob, projected in talmudic and medieval times onto Rome and the Christian world, is not to be explained in natural terms, on economic, political, or psychological grounds. Jewish and non-Jewish hostility is an a priori fact, something born in conception. "Two nations are in your womb, and two kingdoms will separate from your entrails. One kingdom will be stronger than the other, and the elder will serve the younger."

The long and wicked history of anti-Semitism aggravates the Ezra strain and gives it credibility beyond its historical context. The impotence of the victim seeks compensation in the malediction that characterizes the oppressor as evil to the core. "If someone is cruel and does not show mercy," Maimonides writes in *Hilchot Matnot Aniyim,* "there are sufficient grounds to suspect his lineage, since cruelty is found only among the other nations." The angers and resentments of the persecuted must be understood. But indiscriminate curses extending beyond historical context and appropriate targets hurl boomerangs dangerous to our spiritual being.

The conclusion of the Simeon ben Yochai aggadah repudiates his *contemptus mundi,* the xenophobia that cremates the products of civilization. The heavenly voice teaches that there is no safety in the cave, only the smothering self-incarceration of the Jewish spirit. For the Ezra mind-set there is no foreignness in the cave, no *gerim,* no synthesis, no contaminating association with civilization. But to turn away from the world and its civilization is to turn against God's gift of opportunity to us. The Jewish task is not to escape civilization, but to refine it. Civilization is not divine, and it must not be indiscriminately embraced. But neither is it the work of Satan. The land must be sowed and plowed. The two myrtles in honor of the Sabbath of creation are reminders of a society that is yet to be. The rabbis would not dismiss Roman civilization in the time of Simeon ben Yochai. What then should be our attitude towards democratic Western civilization, which has enriched Judaism and elevated the lot of our people?

The Ezra advocates of Jewish isolation are fond of citing the verse from Deuteronomy 33:28, "Israel dwelleth in safety alone." But they ignore the talmudic passage (*Makkot* 24a) that rejects the alleged value of Jewish insularity. In the rabbinic interpretation, Amos the prophet arose to challenge Moses' benediction. "How shall Jacob stand alone?" The Talmud continues, "The Lord repented concerning Moses' acclamation. This also shall not be, saith the Lord God" (Amos 7:5–6).

RUTH, NAOMI, AND BOAZ IN OUR TIMES

Much of the conflict between the followers of Ezra and of Ruth lies beneath the surface of the Kulturkampf. But for Jews for whom the Ezra strain is outmoded and irrelevant, the Ruth strain presents its own challenges. Who is the Ruth of our time? The Ruth of our era who approaches us is not the Ruth of pagan times nor of Christian dominance. The Ruth of modernity is less likely than before to come to us with church dogmas from alien theologies. She comes from a highly secularized culture, a neutral society. She seeks in Judaism the warmth of a family attached to the rootedness of tradition, the joys of festival celebration and commemoration, the sense of superordinate purpose that can overcome the shriveled culture of secular neutrality. She seeks songs to be sung, stories to be told, choreography to be danced, memories to be relived, wisdoms to be enacted, faiths to be revered. She seeks a family of spiritual literacy and refinement.

The Ruth of modernity comes to us with great expectations. She has felt the shiver of history. She has immersed herself in mikvah and study. She comes to the promised Sabbath table of her beloved and to the Sabbath table of her betrothed's Jewish family. The table is beautifully set, but the evening is graceless and without benediction. The conversations are pedestrian, banal, materialistic, hedonistic, indistinguishable from any non-Jewish middle-class family. The native-born family is Jewishly mute. they are pseudo-universalists like those who would "speak in general without using any language in particular" (Santayana). But Ruth seeks the particular language of Judaism. In her adopted Jewish family she finds no ethnicity of song or narration, no Jewish poetry or ritual choreography or theology. Ruth is prepared to pledge to her beloved: "Thy people shall be my people, thy God, my God." But where are the God and people in the native-born husband and in-laws? Ruth's Jewish family are in most things neutral souls, living spiritually in the naked square.

The question is not whether Ruth, the stranger, can be integrated into the Jewish family, but whether the estrangement of the Jewish family from Judaism can be overcome. It is the foreignness, the alienation of the Jewish family, not the purported foreignness of the proselyte, that is haunting. The Ruth of modernity is not the Ruth of the tradition, and neither are the Boaz and Naomi of our times those of the Scriptures. The *ger* challenges us to think deeply about our noblest intent to reach out. Reach out—with whom? Reach out—with what? And after touching the *ger,* bring her home—where?

There can be no outreach without inreach. Outreach without inreach is not only premature, it results in frustration, embarrassment and disillusionment. Outreach must be doubly targeted. It must be simultaneously directed towards the alienation within as much as towards the stranger without.

You cannot reach the *ger* except through the native-born. And especially in Judaism, whose substructure is the family, it is in the private home, not in the public institution, that the Jewishness of belonging, believing and behaving is most effectively transmitted and lived. Outreach to the stranger must be coupled with the Jewish empowerment of the host family.

The *ger* cannot be converted to Judaism as a theological abstraction. The *ger,* like the native-born, cannot thrive in the megastructure of Jewish society. The *ger* needs a sustaining, personal environment. Jews need Jews to be Jewish. The *ger* needs Jews to be Jewish. The *ger* needs a Jewish home. To support that home must be the primary task of our Jewish public institutions. Each synagogue, temple, Jewish center must plan the formation of *mechanchei mishpachah,* lay and professional family educators resolved to enter the private domain, the *reshut ha-yachid,* for the purpose of enhancing the Jewish home. Outreach begins with inreach. The education of the *ger* cannot be isolated from the education of the native-born. Both need to cultivate Jewish talents, competencies and sensibilities. Therein is the twin goal, the dual task of a lay and professional teaching collegiality. One law and one pedagogy for the homeborn and for the stranger that dwells among us.

The *ger* is our mirror. We have only to look at it to discover that the stranger is us. It is a shock of recognition that holds the promise of renewal. On the evening of return, on *Kol Nidrei*, we pray, "And the congregation of Israel shall be forgiven as well as the stranger that dwells in their midst."

TYING ONE'S SHOELACES: A PARABLE FOR HOME AND SCHOOL

Reb Leib Saras said, "I do not go to Rabbi Dov Baer of Mezritz to learn interpretations of the Torah. I go to him to observe his way of tying his shoelaces." Why? Because with the demonstration of his fingers a person teaches meaning.

Dig your hands in your pockets or put them behind your back. Then instruct someone verbally how to tie their shoelaces without the benefit of moving your hands. "First tighten the laces in the eyes of your shoe. Then, holding the shorter lace under your left thumb, press it down against the tongue of the shoe, and with your other hand hold the longer right lace, loop it and cross it over . . ." It is an exhausting exercise bound to leave you tongue-tied and exasperated. It is far less frustrating to take your hands out of your pockets, bend down, and show the student hands-on the practice of thumbs and fingers to accomplish the tying of the knot.

The difference between the two ways of teaching was termed "knowledge by description" and "knowledge by acquaintance" by the philosopher Bertrand Russell. The two kinds of knowledge apply equally to teaching how to ride a bike, swim or play baseball.

And what might this tell us about transmitting Judaism? Much of Jewish education falls into the category of "knowledge by description." From the pulpit, the adult education platform, the teacher's desk, Judaism is talked about. This "aboutism" (Fritz Perl's term) speaks about Jewish practice and beliefs. It yields a meta-Judaic knowledge, talk about Judaism. Those who listen learn about the Seder, about prayers, about the lulav and ethrog, about the Sabbath, and kashrut. It is a theoretic and not unimportant way of knowing. At its best it communicates the history and rationale behind Jewish acts. It informs the listener as to the meaning of the prayer and the purpose of the observance. Such teaching is a response to the pedagogic behaviorism which puts on the tefillin, shakes the lulav, sounds the prayers, but knows neither why nor what for.

But doing is not knowing, and knowing is not doing. The gap between "theoria" and "praxis" is a constant challenge to the educator. To overcome the chasm, behaviorist educators adopt the *na'aseh ve-nishma* pedagogy that contends we learn by first doing and thereafter offering a rationale. They have found that examination of the genesis or teleology of ritual, for example, ends up as a spectator sport. The instructed sit observing those who observe.

The presupposition of pedagogic behaviorism maintains that people believe what they do more than they do what they believe; that people feel what they do more than they do what they feel. Cognition and affect are consequences of activities rather than their cause. Performance overcomes the fissure between theory and practice. Behaviorist pedagogy endorses the leap of action. Its confidence is in orthopraxy, straight practice. There are strengths in knowledge-by-acquaintance methods, and as we shall later indicate, limitations.

Many parents prefer knowledge by description because practice is not their major motivation for giving their children a Jewish education. As they express it, they want their children to know. And the knowledge they have in mind is theoretic. They want them to know the history of our people and the story of its practices. They abhor ignorance. Ignorance is not knowing what the phylacteries are or how to don them. It has nothing to do with whether or not the tefillin are put on. They are more interested in the phylacteries of the head than in the phylacteries of the hand.

However commendable, behavioral pedagogy often produces routinized and mechanized action devoid of the poetry, philosophy and ethics of the ritual act. Not a few students of such behaviorist instruction complain that they were taught "how" without knowing "what for." They boast fluency in reading but confess that little comprehension or spiritual feeling attends the recitation. They are proud of their skills in performance but embarrassed by their failure to understand, believe, or feel. They have been told that understanding and spirituality will come "later." Philosophy and poetry are postponed till tomorrow. But tomorrow never seems to come.

Midrash without *ma'aseh* and *ma'aseh* without *midrash* are half-wisdoms. Theory without practice is empty. Practice without theory is blind. And here the shoelace parable breaks down. A shoelace is a functional string, but a pair of tefillin is a religious symbol. Tying a shoelace is a mundane function calling for literal instruction. Whether it is a single or a double knot is of little consequences. But tefillin tied seven times around the weaker arm, in a particular order and with specific prayers, require a different attention. To drop a pair of phylacteries is not to drop a pair of shoelaces. Holiness requires intention, thought, reverence.

To put on the tefillin simply routinely is to rob them of their intellectual, moral and spiritual meaning. We have seen proselytyzing pietists putting the phylacteries upon the limp arms of half-willing people who pass by and repeat the mumbled prayers. The teacher is convinced that performing the act itself is the mitzvah. "Later," he may reason, rationale may come. Inadvertently, an act of immense potential meaning is trivialized.

The Jewish educator must not separate doing from thinking or acting from feeling. To divide these realms would inadvertently create a gnawing schism of Jews who practice mindlessly, and Jews for whom Judaism is a speculative game. It would destroy the holism that unites head, heart, and hand in the unifying gestures.

Cognitive, affective and active dimensions of Jewish practice must be taught simultaneously. "Knowing how" and "knowing what for" are interdependent forms of knowledge. When the rabbis were puzzled by the two biblical versions of the same Decalogue, one reading "Remember the Sabbath," the other reading "Observe the Sabbath," they resolved the apparent contradiction of the unity by declaring, *Shamor ve-zachor be-dibbur echad*—"observe" and "remember" were spoken at once with one divine word. It is a difficult but important Jewish pedagogic task to transmit at the same time "what" and "what for," "how" and "why," knowledge by description and knowledge by acquaintance.

IV
Rituals and Festivals

KIDDUSH

It seems odd
to use wine to sanctify the Sabbath.
Wine can intoxicate, confuse the mind.

But *Kiddush* is for lucidity
for twin remembrances
of creation and redemption
of nature that begins with God's word
and of history, the exodus from Egypt
that combines faiths and will.

The choice of wine seems odd.
Some deified it, grew drunk on it, cut their flesh
with knives in frenzied piety before pagan gods.
Others spilled wine upon the ground
prohibiting its use, the squeezed vine of Satan.
But we raise the cup of wine
dedicate it, sanctify the Sabbath through it.

We drink philosophy, a mighty analogue.
As wine is neutral, ambivalent, ambiguous,
as wine is potential, holding in it
the capacity to lose awareness, to desecrate
and the talent to consecrate life,
so all energies that flow from the Creator-Liberator,
can raise up or pull down, rejoice or depress.

Power—this hammer that can knock nails into boards
that holds together homes and hospitals
can ruin the walls of our sanctuaries.
Intelligence—this brain that can discover
and invent cures and continents
can plot and design for death and destruction.

Wealth—this power that can support the fallen
can reduce men and women to slaves,
build shelters for the homeless
or smart bombs to shatter lives.

This wine can rejoice the heart with grand purpose
or render us powerless,
a seductive escape from responsibility.

We raise the wine recalling the seventh day
of creation and the first day of liberation
We raise the wine to remember the potentiality,
the possibility in us to consecrate our talents
and sanctify our worlds.

KIDDUSH: JEWISH PHILOSOPHY SQUEEZED IN A CUP OF WINE

Philosophy and theology are found in prose and poetry. In Judaism they are expressed as well in the body-language of rituals. If, as Israel Zangwill noted, Jews eat history on Passover, then on the Sabbath and the festivals Jews drink theology. Consider the ritual ceremony of the *Kiddush,* the blessing over the wine for the sanctification of the Sabbath and festivals. Why, of all the substances available, did the tradition decide upon wine for santification?

A strong case could be made against such a choice. Our first biblical encounter with wine ends in disaster. Noah, after the flood, planted a vineyard, "drank of the wine and was drunken," lay uncovered before his children, and was shamed. The incident resulted in the curse of Canaan. Wine in the prophetic tradition is often associated with pagan orgies and bloody struggles. "Wine," the Book of Proverbs noted, "is a mocker, strong drink a roisterer; he who is muddled by them will not grow wise" (Proverbs 20:1).

Despite its unsavory reputation, wine is exalted in the Jewish liturgy. And therein lies a valuable piece of Jewish insight. Wine, like any energy in creation, is an ambivalent power. The intellect, for example, is a neutral energy that can invent heart-lung machines to rescue life or chemicals to poison innocent persons. Affluence can build sanctuaries for people in search of godliness or gambling parlors to rob people of their money. Beauty can enhance the enjoyment of the world or serve as a cosmetic masking malevolence. And wine can either cause the hearts of men and women to rejoice or blind their eyes with stupefaction. Ascetic tradition poured the wine upon the ground, proscribed it as the potion of devils. Dionysian traditions reveled in its inebriating power.

The Jewish tradition rejected both attitudes. Wine, like all other powers, is subject either to consecration or to desecration. In the *Kiddush,* wine is purposed to sacred twin memories: the remembrance of creation and the remembrance of deliverance from bondage. The *Kiddush* elevates drinking into a toast in honor of the world that is created and the world that is formed in history. With God, human beings are the co-consecrators and co-sanctifiers of the universe.

Note that the blessing over the fruit of the vine is not over grapes. Though the fruit of the vine is of God, the human element requisite for the blessing of consecration is absent. Consecration is in the transaction between nature and humanity. To exclude either is to miss the divine-human partnership celebrated in the covenant. Similarly the *Motzi* blessing is not recited over the sheaves of the field, but over the bread which derives from nature coupled with human labor and intent. We recite the blessing not over the grape, presented whole on the vine, but over the wine squeezed and fermented through human agency. And if there is no wine, the *Kiddush* is recited over the challot with the *Motzi* blessing instead of the blessings over the wine. The *Motzi* too is recited not over the sheaves of wheat and barley, presented whole, but over the bread grown and kneaded and shaped by human hands. Through human and divine cooperation, in the givenness of sun, seed, and soil transformed by the purpose of sustaining the body and rejoicing the soul, santification takes place.

The theological humanism in the *Kiddush* is exemplified in the talmudically recorded debate between the House of Shammai and the House of Hillel. The former believed that the *Kiddush* should begin with the santification of the day and then be followed by the blessing over the wine. Clearly God sanctified the Sabbath before man and woman were created. The Sabbath then arrives with the sinking of the sun and the appearance of the stars.

The House of Hillel saw consecration differently and preceded the sanctification of the day with the blessing over the wine. God sanctifies the Sabbath. Human beings sanctify the wine that proclaims and recalls the Sabbath. Human beings remember the Sabbath, human beings observe the Sabbath, human beings initiate the Sabbath with the presentation of the wine, the transformation of potentiality. The House of Hillel added another reason for the priority of the blessing for wine. "The blessing for the wine is constant, while the blessing for the day is not constant—and of that which is constant and that which is not constant, that which is constant comes first" (T. *Pesachim* 114). Here, the *Kiddush* is tribute to the constancy of human effort in helping God improve the universe. God, not men and women, blessed the Sabbath. "And God blessed the seventh day and hallowed it" (Genesis 2:3). If so, why is human blessing needed? So that the Sabbath will be remembered and observed.

And what makes the seventh day Sabbath? It is told that a group of Hasidim once wondered whether the intrinsic holiness of the Sabbath came from the chronology of the seventh day or from another source. Their rabbi suggested an experiment. Let them observe the Sabbath on an ordinary Wednesday and let them test whether it is the seventh day or something else that possesses Sabbath holiness. Tuesday evening the disciples gathered together, lit the candles, chanted the *Kiddush,* broke bread together, ate the delicacies of the Sabbath meal, recited the grace after meals and sang *zemirot,* prayer-songs in honor of the Sabbath. On Wednesday they acted as they did on the Sabbath—prayed and studied and read the Torah and sang and danced. Then they came to report to the rabbi the results of their experiment. Lo and behold, Wednesday had felt just like the Sabbath. They concluded that it was not the chronology of the day, the physical setting of the sun and the appearance of the stars, that made the Sabbath, but the spiritual intensity and intention of the disciples that endowed the day with sanctity.

Is the wine of the *Kiddush* different from other wine? Wine is wine. Nothing is transubstantiated, turned into something else. When the wine in the *Kiddush* cup is left over, it is poured out, as with any other liquid. Like the many other religious accessories that are used for a religious observance and may be discarded after having served their purpose, e.g., sukkah, lulav, shofar, the fringes of a tallit, wine possesses no intrinsic sanctity. Y. L. Peretz tells the story of a poor family that had no money for the Passover meal. Disconsolate, the father of the household wandered about the village and came upon a fair at which a magician performed his sorcery. Out of his hat the magician pulled unleavened matzot and a bottle of wine and presented them to the astonished man. He ran home satisfied that he had bread and wine for the Seder. But as he related the story of the magician and the fair to his wife, he wondered whether wine and bread from sorcery was kosher. He sought the advice of the town's rabbi, who asked him, "Does the wine pour? does the matzah crumble?" On hearing the father's affirmative responses, the rabbi responded, "If the wine pours and the matzah crumbles, it is permissible to drink and eat." Wine is wine and bread is bread.

Jews, prior to the ravages of assimilation, possessed a proud record of sobriety despite the permission to drink alcohol. Philo of Alexandria, the first Jewish philosopher, wrote of *sobria ebrietos* (sober drunkenness) and attributed that paradoxical virtue to the Jews. Here is a people with endless opportunities to drink wine, mandated to intoxication on Purim and yet celebrated for its sobriety. This unique trait even moved Immanuel Kant in the eighteenth century to write a monograph to explain the Jew's exception to drunkenness. There are multiple explanations for Jewish sober intoxication: Sociological, psychological, and theological. To be drunk is to lose oneself, to be blind to the world. For the Jews, this world is to be taken seriously. And to be taken seriously means that the world must not be avoided. The religious goal may be to unite with God, but in Judaism one does not unite with God by subtraction. One cannot come to God absent from the world, not even through the mysteries of God-intoxication. Ernst Simon and Martin Buber among others taught that the Jewish insistence upon the dignity of the self discourages what other traditions seek: merger with God. To lose oneself in God is to lose the "I" essential in genuine dialogue. For an authentic I-Thou relationship, distance is required. Though Jewish mysticism speaks of the importance of *bittul ha-yesh,* the nullification of the self, the aim is to eradicate the self-control conceit of narcissism, not the dignity of the self. To drink a toast to God is to raise a cup for life, *le-chayyim,* for this life in this world with which we are bound.

Le-chayyim is plural, literally "to lives," to the life in community. Life requires attention to others. To live in this world is to live with responsibility towards self and other. In a state of inebriation, one can wrecklessly drive a vehicle into another human being, because blind drunk there is no other, only the confused self.

Kiddush is celebrated as part of a meal with and for others. It originally appeared in the synagogue not as an isolated ritual gesture, but as part of the meal prepared for travelers who found a temporary home in the synagogue. It is pertinent that only on the first and second evenings of Passover is the *Kiddush* not recited at the synagogue service. On those nights, no traveler is to remain alone in the synagogue lodgings. The "stranger in thy midst" is to be taken home to rejoice with the family the redemption that freed us all. Detached from the meal, the synagogue *Kiddush* at best is pedagogic. The *Kiddush* recited on Sabbaths and festivals in the synagogue serves as a public lesson preparing congregants for the *Kiddush* to be recited at home.

While Judaism loves life and the pleasure of life, it retains its sobriety by remembering the ambitions and responsibilities of Jewish life—to sanctify the incompleted world. God is *asher kiddeshanu*—He who has sanctified us so that we may in turn sanctify the world. We are co-sanctifiers. Who would extinguish the power to bless by deliberately obliterating human awareness? Drunkenness is an injury to the self, a neglect of the world, and an insult to the Creator. We who prepare the wine that makes the hearts of men and women to sing remain sober, so that we may rejoice the inhabitants who dwell in God's world.

HAVDALAH: THE WISDOM OF SEPARATION

Havdalah takes place "between the suns" (*bein ha-shemashot*), between the setting of the sun and the appearance of the stars, at a time when faces and forms are indistinct. It takes place at twilight. "Twilight," Rabbi Yose declares, "is as the twinkling of an eye, one entering and one departing, and it is impossible to determine it" (T. *Shabbat* 34b). But precisely at the time of indeterminancy, distinctions are to be made. "Blessed art Thou . . . who distinguishes *between* holy and profane, *between* light and darkness, *between* Israel and the nations, *between* the seventh day and the six days of working."

"Between" is a preposition that connects and separates relationships. In Hebrew the word for between is *bein*. It lies at the root of the Hebrew word *binah,* the wisdom of discernment. *Havdalah* celebrates discriminating intelligence, the act of differentiation first introduced in the liturgy at the conclusion of the Sabbath. *Havdalah* is deliberately incorporated in the first petitionary prayer of the weekday. It is associated with the praise of God for bestowing knowledge upon human beings and concludes by asking God for knowledge, understanding and discernment. As the Talmud puts it, "If there is no discerning knowledge, how can there be prayer?" If one cannot distinguish good from bad, right from wrong, how does one know for what to pray? "If there is no knowledge, how can there be *havdalah?*" "Great is knowledge, since it was placed at the beginning of the weekday blessings" (T. *Berakhot* 33a).

The discernment dramatized by the *havdalah* draws upon the

creative intelligence of divinity that divides the elements of the "blooming, buzzing confusion" of chaos to form a cosmos. Out of the unformed void God creates an orderly, harmonious universe through the act of *havdalah,* separation. God creates by separating and disentangling the admixture of multiple powers. In the beginning was separation. God divides the waters under the firmament from the waters over the firmament. The sun, which is to rule over the day, God separates from the moon, which is to rule over the night. He creates seeds after their kind, tree-bearing fruit after its kind, the winged fowl after its kind, cattle, creeping things and beasts of the earth after their kind. Each kind has its assigned domain, its proper limitations. All transgression is stepping beyond set boundaries. Transgression is the disrespect of limits. Prior to creation there were no limits, no borders, no discrimination. Before God's act of separation, there was only undifferentiated energy, formless, purposeless, "darkness upon the face of the deep." Through the wisdom of separation a universe is formed out of anarchy.

Havdalah ritualizes God's creation of the universe through wisdom, which we renew symbolically. Through *havdalah,* the presentation of the categories of differentiation, the world is recognized as intelligible.

The universe is One. Its unity is revealed not by blurring distinctions, but by understanding the interdependence of the separate elements. Removing the spectacles from our eyes, everything may appear as one. But the uniformity of a blurred vision is not the unity born of discriminating wisdom.

The benedictions of *havdalah* separation signify that the world is not monistically one, drawn from one substance or character. The universe is not all holy or all profane, all light or all darkness, all Sabbath or all weekday, all Jewish or all gentile.

The benedictions of *havdalah* focus attention on the ambiguities of the world we inhabit. The world created is diverse. Both sides of the duality are real, neither is to be ignored.

The temptation is to dichotomize, to treat contrasts as if they were warring opposites, adversaries bent on extinguishing each other. The lure of dualism urges us to split the world into hard disjunctives, exclusive either/or choices. Either darkness or light, the holy or the profane, the Sabbath or the weekday, Israel or the nations. Therein, the wisdom of *havdalah* is seriously misunderstood. When complementary attributes of reality are turned into contradictory energies that cannot coexist, the dialectic of *havdalah*, the connections of "betweenness," the interdependence of the dual categories of *havdalah* are severed.

"Between the seventh day and the six days of creation." *Havdalah* differentiation, however, knows that the Sabbath is not the enemy of the weekday. Both coexist. They are not mutually exclusive options. They enhance each other. The weekday transforms the given world. The Sabbath contemplates its work. It is the balance between labor and appreciation that is the intention of the inclusive week. The goal is neither a Sabbathless world nor a world without weekdays. The ideal is not seven days of Sabbath or seven days of work. The term *shabbat* does not even appear in the *havdalah* blessings—only the "seventh day," as if to emphasize that the whole week includes the day of rest as its natural part. In God's created world, the sought end is the harmonious interrelation of both modes of time.

"Between light and darkness." Darkness is not the opponent of light. The sun and moon are separated. Two regal spirits may not share the same crown, but they are both vital luminaries, both to be blessed. The rabbinic sages so composed the liturgy that in the evening prayers we are to remember the light of the day, and in the prayers of the morning we are to recall the darkness. The *Zohar,* in the name of Rabbi Judah, declares that the reason why it is written "and there was evening and there was morning" for each day is to show us that there is no day without night (Isaiah 46a).

"Between the holy and the profane." The profane is not the antagonist of the holy. The profane is *chol,* secular, potential energy that can be consecrated or desecrated. The world of the secular possesses ambivalent energies. It is not the consecrated that needs to be consecrated. It is the ordinary, the neutral potentialities that inhere in the created world which are to be sanctified. "Profane" refers to the neutral area outside the sanctuary (*pro fanum*), not to a contaminated arena.

"Between Israel and the nations." The distinctions between Israel and the nations of the world do not make them deadly enemies. Israel and the nations are not the same, and the attempt to reduce them to one indiscriminate sameness is not only intellectually dishonest or a mark of ignorance, but a disservice to each. Israel and the nations are each blessed by God. Israel is not holy and the nations contaminated. Israel and the nations have chosen to enter different, at times overlapping, covenants. There are wisdoms and truths in each, so as to elicit from the talmudic rabbis a blessing for the sages of the non-Jews with whom God shares His wisdom.

The eradication of either side of the polar duality is a diminution of God's goodness, wisdom, and power. Fixation on one side of the duality is idolatrous. Idolatry, the error of worshipping a part as if it were the whole, improverishes divinity.

Havdalah-wisdom separates in order to unite. Without separation there can be no authentic integration. As in the Jewish myth which tells of the androgynous character of the original Adam, half-male and half-female in one body, the undifferentiated oneness before the divisions of creation contains all that is, but for all that fullness is no universe. The hermaphroditic Adam, for all his/her self-sufficiency, remains lonely until God divides Adam into two separate parts. Separated, each yearns for the other half to find fulfillment. Separated, they can turn to see each other face-to-face. For the macrocosm that is the universe and the microcosm that is the human being, separation and differentiation is necessary for unification. Distance is essential for union.

The differentiations articulated in the *havdalah* are essential for the sake of integration. To achieve the wholeness which imitates the oneness of God, the diverse energies in the universe must be sorted out, identified, and finally held wisely together. The left side and the right side must be balanced to achieve the ambidexterity suited to take hold of the complexity of the world. Neither side is expendable.

The *Zohar* states that when God created the world and revealed what was hidden in its depth, light and darkness were entwined with each other; the holy and the profane, the good and the evil impulses cleaved to each other. The task of God's human partner, as co-creator and co-consecrator, is not to eliminate one side from the other, but to recognize the powers and uses of each and order them as complementary pairs: justice with compassion, law with spirit, power with mercy.

Havdalah-wisdom is not a metaphysical abstraction. It offers counsel for the human microcosm reflected in God's mirror. In us, as in the macrocosm, is an admixture of talents and temperaments. In us darkness and light, holy and profane, altruism and selfishness cohere. It is folly to expect that we should live on one side of the *havdalah* spectrum, forever cheerful, forever generous, forever studious. In each of us is a pluralism of moods and insights. We are not made of one disposition, one attitude, one impulse. In us are temperaments hard, strict and judgmental; and others soft, empathetic, permissive. In us are moments of pessimism and cheer, parsimony and generosity, anger and forgiveness. In us are ambivalent impulses, libidinal energies, that may be sublimated or suborned. The dual inclinations within need each other. Without the *yetzer ha-tov,* the good inclination, conscience would not be developed. Without the *yetzer ha-ra,* the evil inclination, there would be no family, no commerce, no civilization. As the rabbinic sages observed, without the libido, no egg would be found throughout the earth. With wisdom we come to discover the spark buried in the husks of the unattractive: the grain of responsibility for self and family within the shell of parsimony, the passion for fairness within rage, the need for approval within our ostentation. Ambivalence, ambiguities, contradictions pull at us. They require patient wisdom to acknowledge the conflicting claims, to respect the virtues of each and to embrace them in one hold. Separated out and properly counterbalanced, traits that appear mean-spirited when isolated reveal their unique strengths and virtues.

The admixture of good and evil in the world calls for cognitive and moral disentanglement. Those who do not make distinctions, those for whom it is all one, risk a reductivism that ends up in perversion. "Woe unto them who call evil good and good evil, who change darkness into light and light into darkness, who change bitter into sweet and sweet into bitter" (Isaiah 5:20).

The categories of *havdalah,* e.g., the holy and the secular, provide us with the conceptual tools with which to seize hold of the world. Reality is *chol,* neutral, amoral, natural. Reality is obdurate enough but not entirely intractable. Reality is tough but malleable enough to be adjusted, altered, modified. Reality has limits, but how far they may be stretched is an ongoing search in living. There is an elasticity in facts which purposes seek out. The Jewish categories of existence entail an expanded view of reality that includes ideality. "Ought" is as real as "is," "should" is as real as "must," "will" is as real as "necessity." The reality and limits of each must be acknowledged and respected. Therein lies an essential element of the insights and projects of *havdalah*.

To enter at night into the weekday world after a Sabbath of no petitions and no labor requires courage and hope. Legends in the Talmud and Midrash speak of Adam at the termination of the Sabbath when the sun sank and darkness began to set in. Terrified, Adam thought, "Surely indeed the darkness shall bruise me." God inspired Adam with knowledge and made him find two stone flints. One was marked with the name *afelah,* which is darkness. Upon the other was inscribed the name *mavet,* which is death. With inspired knowledge Adam struck the flints against each other. The friction produced a spark with which he lit a torch. It comforted him throughout the night, and in the morning Adam saw the rising of the sun. He then observed, "This is the way of the world." Out of darkness and death, a spark is created. There is darkness and there is light, the fear of death and the hope of survival. Therefore we recite a blessing over the fire at the termination of the Sabbath because it was created for the first time. And we begin the *havdalah* separation prayer with a benedictory prologue of courage. "Behold, God is my salvation. I will trust and will not be afraid, for God, the Lord, is my strength and song, and He is become my salvation."

HAVDALAH: A SONG OF DISTINCTION

Black into white
light into shadow
Blessing into curse
Doubt into belief.

Nothing divided
neatly severed
cut off
one half from another
Trimmed polarities.

Nothing given pure, simple, unalloyed.
Nothing given in halves
Except—idolatries.

In strange worship
halves and quarters
pretend wholeness.
A coin held close to the eye
blocks the world,
all is draped in darkness.

Simple solutions
blur distinctions,

Confusing blindness
with wholeness.

Light shadow
sweet bitter
the admixture inseparable.

Accept it whole
fragrance galbanum
together
elements of sanctified incense.

Accept it whole
Yet not without distinction.
Yours is not theirs
day is not night.

Accept it whole
not with cruel division
amputating organic wholeness.
And not with absorption
that swallows the shadow side.

Accept it whole
not rending whole cloth
into convenient rags.
Sundering the universe
into segregated parts:
Good evil
Week Sabbath
Them us.

Divisions desecrate
Hard disjunctives
rip apart
the underlying unity,
the possibility of reconciliation.

Hallow the link between
darkness light
mundane festive
others us

Hallow the circles
demarking separate styles
but also the outer lineaments
penetrate each other
without assimilation.

Creation, separation
Kiddush, Havdalah
Different wines
different candles.

HA-MOTZI: SOCIAL ETHICS IN A LOAF OF BREAD

"With savages the weak in body or mind are soon eliminated; and those that survive commonly exhibit a vigorous state of health. We civilized men, on the other hand, do our utmost to check the process of elimination; we build asylums for the imbecile, the maimed and the sick; we institute laws for the indigent, and our medical men exert their utmost skill to save the life of every one to the last moment. . . . No one who has attended to the breeding of domestic animals will ever doubt that this must be highly injurious to the race of man." So Charles Darwin opined in his *Descent of Man*. Thomas Malthus in his *Essay on Population* disapproved of relief for the poor on the grounds that war, disease and poverty are natural antidotes to the rapid explosion of the population. Adam Smith projected an ideal laissez faire state which would not interfere with society, leading many to oppose government assistance to the poor.

There is a considerable history of contempt for the poor. Its echoes sound even louder these days. "There must be something wrong with people who can't or won't take care of themselves, who live off charity, depend upon the public dole." I never heard anything like this in my home. Poverty, if it was a disgrace, reflected poorly upon God, not upon the hungry. It raised questions not about the character of poor men and women, but about the powerful and good God who—as we are reminded by the grace after meals—nourishes the whole world with food, and sees to it that we never lack for food. "Blessed are You, Lord, who feeds everyone.'' The *Birkat ha-Mazon* (grace) concludes with the bold assertion: ''Once I was young and now I am old, yet in all my days I never saw a just person abandoned and his children begging for bread. The Lord will give His people strength. The Lord will bless His people with peace.''

Poverty is no virtue. As Mendele Mocher Sefarim put, ''It is no disgrace, but neither can you be proud of it.'' Incorporated in the grace after the meal is the poignant prayer that we ''not be in need of gifts from flesh and blood nor of their loans.'' However benevolent the donor, it is no joy to receive alms. ''Make us dependent only upon You, whose hand is open, ample, full, so that we may not be embarrassed or ashamed.

In my home, not poverty but wealth was something of an embarrassment, and the tradition, for all its this-worldliness, kept us at arm's length from opulence.

—A Torah written in gold is *pasul,* invalid; and legend reports that when Alexander of Macedonia ordered such a Torah written, it was discovered by the rabbis and summarily buried. God's name in gold?

—A shofar covered with gold may not be used, and its sound is invalid. The sound of the broken notes from a sobbing heart out of a shofar of gold would make it lose its voice.

—The high priest on Yom Kippur must shed his vestments of gold and silver before entering the Holy of Holies. Who could appear to ask forgiveness in gold and silver apparel?

—On Shavuot, the *bikkurim* (first fruits) could be brought into the outer court in gold baskets, but into the inner court only in baskets of straw.

—On Shabbat, money is to be neither touched nor seen. Before the Sabbath, the mitzvah is to search one's clothes, to break off relations with ''the pocket.''

BREAD

At home I was taught that if a piece of bread fell from the table, it should quickly be picked up and kissed. Bread was God's gift. I heard wondrous stories about the sacredness of a *shtikel broit* ''a little piece of bread''. Once, around the third meal of the Sabbath, the disciples of the Rebbe persisted in asking him to tell them where God is. He remained silent, but at last recited the *Motzi* and pointed to the loaf of bread on the table. God in a piece of bread? There is theology in a piece of bread. And it is important, particularly for children of entitlement living in the Garden of Gucci, to understand Ben-Zoma's observation: "What labors did Adam have to carry out before he obtained bread to eat. He plowed, he sowed, he reaped, he bound the sheaves, he threshed and winnowed and selected the ears, he ground, then sifted the flour, kneaded and baked, and then, finally, he ate. And I get up and find all things done for me" (*Berachot* 58a).

Ha-motzi lechem min ha-aretz—that which brings bread out of the earth is godly. Consider the process, the givenness of earth and water and seed, as well as the human energy and ingenuity to turn sheaf into edible cake. "Which is greater, the works of man or of God?" the pagan Tinneius Rufus asked. Rabbi Akiva replied that the works of man are greater than those of God, and illustrated his contention by presenting Tinneius Rufus with sheaves of wheat and loaves of cake. The cakes are greater, not that the works of God are less worthy, but that the full measure of divinity is expressed through the interaction between God's nature and the crown of His creation. The *Motzi* is not recited over sheaves of wheat and the *Kiddush* is not recited over clusters of grapes. The *Motzi* is recited over the bread, which is made through human effort and the *Kiddush* is recited over the fruit of the vine, which human ingenuity cultivates. Both benedictions exemplify the power and goodness of God expressed through the works of human beings.

Our sages knew that "a blessing does not prevail except through the work of human hands." And it is in our hands to give bread to the hungry and to do so without ulterior motives, even for the sake of piety. Consider the Hasid who boasted to his rebbe that he had made a fellow Jew pray. A poor man had come asking for a meal, but the Hasid sought to save his soul. "First we must pray," the Hasid insisted. They both prayed *minchah*, then *ma'ariv*, and before the Hasid gave him the bread, he had him wash his hands and recite *al netilat yadayim*. Hearing his story, the rebbe grew sad. "You meant well, but you have not acted well. There are times when you must act as if there were no God in this world." "No God in the world?" the Hasid wondered about this blasphemy. "Yes, no God. When a person comes to you in need, you must act as if there is no one, no God, no man, in the world except you yourself and that needy person." "And what of his soul, his neshamah?" "Take care of your soul and his body," the rebbe answered.

Poverty is no blessing, but abstemiousness is no virtue. If you are blessed with wealth, you are bound to live accordingly. Once some disciples overheard the rabbi chastising the village *gevir*, the wealthiest man in town, not because he was profligate with his money, but because he was stingy with himself. He would eat only black bread and drink water. The rabbi reminded him that he was a man of means and ordered him to eat fine meats and drink good wine. "Why such strange counsel?" they asked the rabbi. "Because if such a wealthy man is content to eat bread and drink water, he will be more likely to tell a poor man who comes to him, 'If I, a man of affluence, can make do with food and drink, it is enough for you to eat rocks and sand.' " This wisdom the rabbi likely learned from the genius found in the book of Deuteronomy, where those who go up to Jerusalem with the second tithe are told to bestow the money "for whatsoever the soul desireth, for oxen or for wine or for strong drink, or for whatever thy soul asketh of thee." But in the third and sixth years of the Sabbatical year, instead of consuming the second tithe, let the tithe be given for the "Levite, because he has no portion nor inheritance with thee, and the stranger, and the fatherless, and the widow" (Deuteronomy 14:22 f.). He who experiences the joy of food and drink may more likely feel the anguish of those who hunger. "Ye shall eat and be sated and bless the Lord thy God" (Deuteronomy 8:10). The chronology is suggestive. On an empty stomach, blessings grumble in resentment.

And whom are we to feed? For whom is the Passover *Ha Lachma* cry, "Let those who are in need come and eat; let those who are in need come and celebrate the Passover"? Why the redundancy? Rabbi Jacob Emden, the Yavetz, a distinguished talmudist of the eighteenth century, offered this explanation in his commentary on the Haggadah. The first call to "all who hunger" refers to non-Jews who are *ra'ev la-lechem ve-lo le-dvar ha-Shem*, those who are hungry for bread and not for the word of God. The second call is for Jews who require the ritual celebration of the Passover, for whom matzah, not bread is needed. Our obligation,

Rabbi Emden declared, is towards both Jews and non-Jews. Here he cites the Talmud *Gittin* 61: "Our rabbis have taught: we support the poor of the heathen along with the poor of Israel, and visit the sick of the heathen along with the sick of Israel, console the bereaved of the heathen together with the bereaved of Israel, and bury the dead of the heathen together with the dead of Israel." We do this for the sake of peace, for the sake of God.

We begin the meal with bread, among other reasons, to remind us that we are men of flesh and blood, not angels. So it is told of Rabbi Israel Salanter that he would recite *Shalom Aleichem*, the hymn which greets the angels who visit us on Shabbat, *after* the *Motzi*, and not, as others practice, before the breaking of the bread. For angels do not eat or drink, but we and our family and the guests around the table are not angels. We have bodies and hungers. Eat first and greet the angels later. There is much instruction in a piece of bread.

OVERVIEW: CELEBRATION AND COMMEMORATION

The Jewish calendar structures our awareness of time and self. There is a syncopation of collective wisdom with which our individual and family lives are synchronized. The Jewish calendar is the record of experienced values inscribed in time. Celebrations and commemorations repeated annually, each year adding another layer of meaning. We grow older along with the calendar of our people.

The three pilgrimage festivals—Passover, Shavuot and Sukkot— each distinct and each interconnected. Three biblical festivals, each retaining the ancient flavor of an agricultural event—harvesting, ingathering—is transformed into a historical event and spiritual opportunity.

Passover. The beginning of Jewish self-awareness. Through the breaking of the chains of physical, moral, and intellectual bondage, the reality of *Elohut* (godliness) is discovered. Coerced living is destructive of religious sensibility. A slave cannot tie the thongs of the phylacteries around his arm because he is still fettered to the will of others. Only the emancipated is free to tie himself voluntarily to a transcendent purpose.

Shavuot. Freedom tied to task. Without a Decalogue of deeds and prohibitions, freedom degenerates into unleavened anarchy, liberty sours into caprice. Commandments must be freely accepted and their purpose understood. Commandments thrust down upon us from above are dreary burdens. Held joylessly, without knowledge, the letters of the tablets dissolve in the air of rhetoric. The

Decalogue falls from our hands, shattered into bits and pieces of stone.

Sukkot. To live with dreams and limitations. The sukkah is as fragile as our lives; the palms spread over the tabernacle barely shield us from the beating of the sun. But the stars must be seen through the interstices of the protecting cover. To live in a temporary abode, with the courage of laughter and song, calls for a stability that does not come from physical security but from an inner architecture. The foundation of the sukkah is within.

Shabbat incorporates all the festivals. It celebrates the Jewish triad: creation, redemption, and revelation. *Creation:* We are born into the world; not thrust into it by some enigmatic force. The world is not our enemy. *Redemption:* We are born into freedom. No doctrine of fatalism rationalizes away the power of our decisions to affect changes within and without. *Revelation:* We discover each day new things about ourselves and our environment. Self-revelation is a never-ending phenomenon. It is coterminous with life itself.

The High Holy Days. We do not wait for fantasies of postmortem confrontations with our Maker. The Day of Judgment and Decision is here and now and in the presence of the community of faith. We are not judged posthumously. The verdict is passed during our lifetime; the book is open for us to see the hand which writes our own judgment.

The root symbol of Rosh Hashanah and Yom Kippur is the scale. At birth, the scale is balanced. Our decisions tip the scales one way or the other.

Chanukah, Purim, and Yom Ha-Atzma'ut. Jewish life does not end with the Book of Deuteronomy or the Second Book of Chronicles. The Bible is the centerpiece and Israel the matrix of our Jewish destiny. But Chanukah is not reported in the canonized Jewish Bible. Purim took place in Persia. And Yom Ha-Atzma'ut (Israel Independence Day) is testimony to the ongoing character of the Jewish miracle: the incredible will of a people to live with meaning.

Fasts and Yom Hashoah. No tradition loves life more than our own. Enemies are real, no figment of a sick imagination. But friends too are real. Tishah Be-Av and Yom Hashoah, remembrances of the destruction of the Temple and of one-third of our people, cannot and must not be forgotten. We are gifted with a sense of humor but possess as well a sense of tragedy. To live isolated with either sense alone is untrue to life. To live with an unrelieved and undiscriminating sense of humor turns laughter into madness. To live with a single sense of tragedy turns sadness into self-destruction.

The calendar of Jewish life marks a zodiac of multiple values, a reflection of many moods and temperaments. Celebrated with wisdom they offer us a precious sense of balance and make whole people out of fragmented selves.

Was, is, will be—*hayah, hoveh, yihyeh:* the name of God is formed out of the three tenses of the verb "to be." Blessed is *Elohut,* which enables us to celebrate seasons and times.

SPACE AND TIME: THE SERIOUS SIDE OF HIGH HOLY DAY SEATING

The philosopher Abraham Joshua Heschel emphasized time rather than space as the major category of significance in Judaism. The first divine hallowing in creation was the seventh day, the Sabbath, not any place or thing. When the child asked Menachem Mendel of Kotzk "Where is God?" he answered, "Whenever you let Him in." Not "where" but "when," and not place but time is the locus of godliness.

But masses of people seem to distrust this spiritual notion of holiness. More time is spent on securing good seats in the sanctuary before Rosh Hashanah than in the preparation of the heart. More energy and passion are spent at board meetings over the allocation of tickets than over any theological issue. The board is sensitive to the "territorial imperative" which grips grown men and women. Reassign the location of a seat and temple membership itself is at stake.

There is a mystique about where we sit that no single rational explanation can properly fathom. It's not a matter of seeing or hearing the pulpit celebrants better. It's not a matter of sitting beneath the air-conditioning vent or under a poorly lit lighting fixture. There's something magical about where we sit, and especially about changing the seats from last year to this coming one. As the Hebraic proverb has it, *meshaneh makom, meshaneh mazal*—change the place, change the fortune.

241

The disputes over the allocation of seats reached the point that they brought the issue to the rabbi. Half-jokingly, they asked him to resolve the raging debates regarding the place distribution of seating. It was a *she'elah* (inquiry) he had not prepared for but which he knew had deeper roots than psychology or sociology. The issue, in the last analysis, was theological. And the rabbi was the best person to deal with it, for he was above such pettiness. Besides which, his own seat was cushioned, as close to the Ark of Holiness as could be, one facing the eastern wall. What is involved here is a theology of space, a struggle between pagan and Judaic attitudes.

In archaic, pagan religions, there is a phenomenon of "sacred space." There is a central place where communication can take place between the cosmic planes of heaven and earth. The rabbi recalled the insight of the late religious anthropologist Mircea Eliade about the space that "makes possible ontological passage from one mode of being to another." There are places on earth that are closer to divinity than others. Recall the Ziggurats, the towers of Babel, cosmic structures seven stories high, representing the seven planets, which were ascended by the priests in order to reach the summit of the universe. There is a place where the gods sit. But these are pagan notions of archaic religion. For Judaism, God has no such celestial geography, and we recall the awesome fall of those who sought to build the Tower of Babel. Solomon is embarrassed about building the House of God. He senses the crudeness of closeting God in the building space. "Will God indeed dwell on earth? Behold, the heavens cannot contain Thee—how much less the house that I have built?" (II Kings 8:27). He is heir to the earlier biblical articulation wherein the Divine Presence rests in the lives of the people, "And let them make Me a sanctuary that I may dwell in them" (Exodus 25:8).

Where indeed does God reside, or in the language of Hebraic liturgy, "where is the place of His glory?" The answer is immediate and unequivocal. His glory fills the world. To look for God in a particular place is to commit the spiritual fallacy of simple location. As the rabbis declared, "God is the place of the world, not the world God's place." On Sukkot, the lulav is not pointed to any location at the mention of God's name. It is not only rude to point; towards God it is downright blasphemous.

We Jews don't ascend to the heights to find God. When the psalmist asks rhetorically, "Who ascends into the mountain of the Lord?" he answers, "He who hath clean hands and a pure heart, who has not lifted up his soul unto vanity, nor sworn deceitfully" (Psalms 24:3–4). The place of God is within, between, among us. "Place" is a visual metaphor, not to be taken literally when applied to God. Godliness is in relationship, not in Row A. God is in morality, not in geography. Is that not what Isaiah declared in the name of God? "Where is the house that ye build unto Me? Where is the place of My rest?" God does not respond to the best tickets in the house, but "to the poor and broken-hearted who is concerned about My word" (Isaiah 66:1–2).

The issue of seats may well be more important than we have suspected. The preoccupation with seats may reveal a perverse theology, a greater attachment to external, material places than to internal, spiritual experiences. To be nearer to sanctity can never be a matter of place. "The idol is near and yet far. God is far and yet near. For a man enters a synagogue and stands behind a pillar, and prays in a whisper—and God hears his prayer. So it is with all of His creatures. Can there be a nearer God than this? He is as near to His creatures as the ear is to the mouth" (Yerushalmi *Berachot* 9:1).

It is a revolutionary idea in the history of religion to find God not in statues, shrines, palaces of marble and stone but in the human spirit. The rabbis interpreted the verse in Exodus 17:6 audaciously. What does it mean that God announces to Moses: "Behold, I will stand before thee there upon the rock of Horeb; and thou shall smite the rock, and there shall come water out of it, this the people may drink" God said to Moses "In every place where you find a trace of the feet of man, there am I before you." God is where men and women are in need. God places Himself in the footprints of men and women, not upon the isolated mountain.

There are fears about limiting God to place, and not simply because it seems to reduce the dignity and power of God. The deification of place leads to dangerous idolatry. The rabbinic imagination in the midrash suggests that the murder of Abel came about because he and his brother Cain both argued that the sanctuary of God should be built on their own exclusive property. Together they owned the earth, but each wanted God's lodging to be in his own jurisdiction. In our times, the controversy over the place of the temple has led to the bombing of holy places and threats of jihad. It is a reminder that not places but lives are holy.

So what had begun as a half-serious question developed into an earnest answer. What began as a question of seats ended in a question about self. Does the place confer real status upon me? Is location the validation of my significance? Is the best seat in the sanctuary up in front? Is the synagogue theater? Is the *bimah* the stage? Is the writing in the Book of Life the inscription on the ticket? Is the answer to spirituality space?

"Master of the Universe—where will I find you, and where will I not find you? . . . In heaven, Thou art on earth, Thou art wherever I turn, wherever I stir Thou, Thou, Thou."

CREATION AND CREATIVITY: MEANING AND MEANINGS

How is it that on Rosh Hashanah, the day commemorating the creation of the world, no passage from the first two chapters of Genesis is found in the machzor? How is it that among the multiple biblical verses which comprise the *Malchuyot-Zichronot-Shoferot* trilogy, part of the order of the Rosh Hashanah service, none are selected from the Book of Genesis? What more appropriate and obvious readings for the Torah service on Rosh Hashanah than those describing God's creation of the universe and man? In its stead the tradition chooses to recite the biblical narrations dealing with the banishment of Hagar and Ishmael and the conflicts surrounding the near sacrifice of Isaac.

Such omissions suggest a deliberate decision to deflect attention from the creation event and place emphasis elsewhere, upon the human moral struggles of the patriarch and matriarch of our people. It is as if the rabbinic or prerabbinic focus meant to repudiate the ideology that archaic religions, according to Mircea Eliade, the celebrated scholar of comparative religion, have at the heart of their New Year celebrations—the ritual miming of the cosmogonic act. At each archaic New Year, the victory of the gods in creating cosmos out of chaos was celebrated through a choreography which relived the primordial event. In reactualizing the eternal repetition of this myth of creation, the religious man of archaic religion found the meaning and guarantee of the meaning of his life. Only the sacred time exemplified in this original event was truly real. History offered no meaning and no hope for salvation. Man was not a historical being, and the preservation of his memories had no value. After the mythic act of divine creation, it was all over. The liturgical time of the calendar, cyclical time, had been created only to be periodically repeated. The circle was closed, the serpent held its tail in its mouth, profane time was swallowed by sacred time. Is it conceivable that during the twelve-day Babylonian New Year, the epic of creation would be omitted?

A JEWISH PERCEPTION OF CREATION

The Jewish tradition relates differently to creation, and the conspicuous deletion of the creation legend throughout the High Holy Days dramatizes that unique relationship. The rabbis never weary in their insistence that everything created is incomplete, unfinished, imperfect. Creation is the beginning, not the end, of the world. What is celebrated on Rosh Hashanah is not the sacred time of creation but the plenitude of potentiality which enables humanity to continue shaping moral order out of amoral energy. The mustard seed must be sweetened, the lupine made soft, the wheat ground, and human nature worked at—for everything created requires repair. Not the metaphysics of creation but the ethics of creativity is celebrated. Our attention is therefore drawn not to the seven days of creation, but to the struggles of father Abraham with sibling claims and contradictory voices from heaven testing his faith and moral sensitivity. His salvation is not found through ritual identification with the gods of creation; not through imitation of nature. Meaning is discourse in the process of moral transformations.

If the sacred time of archaic religions may be symbolized by the circle, Jewish sacred time may be symbolized as an arrow. The circle expresses the idea of perfection as complete. There are no surprises, the target has been reached. The arrow is in motion. It covers new ground. It is on its way.

Meaning is not handed down by creation or by belief in creation. Meaning is wrested out of the obduracy of personal and collective history, out of concrete, profane time, which is real. We build our meaning-cosmos out of selected memories, e.g., Abraham at Sodom and Moriah rejecting genocide and infanticide as incompatible with his understanding of *Elohut*.

The quest for meaning is not over, for meaning is no more complete and finished than is creation. Meanings are not one nor are they given once and for all. Events are prismatic and meanings are varied. They go through endless *gilgulim* (cycles) of refinement and qualification. And there is no guarantee that this is "the" meaning for all times and for all men. It is, of course, tempting to proclaim that the divine plan is given and secure, that meaning is absolute, immutable, and guaranteed. But history, profane and concrete, has taught us the terrible price that such certitudes demand. To promise meaning on the grounds that creation has God's purpose in it, and later to admit that we cannot know His purpose, is to raise a dust of expectations and then complain that we cannot see. If meaning is related to divine purpose, then not to know what God wills smothers the promise of meaning under a blanket of ignorance.

Even if creation may be argued to imply purpose, it offers little evidence for meaning. Pagans too believed in creation, and so presumedly did Satan. Not sheer purpose but the moral quality of that purpose, not the will of God but the moral character of that will can satisfy the hunger for meaning. For Jews it is the morality of revelation, the morality of purpose, the morality of creativity that must be known before revelation, purpose, and creation may be sanctified in celebration. Not the mysterious Subject and His inscrutable will in creation and revelation, but the moral sacredness in creativity, choice, and discovery is essential for the celebration of meaningful *Elohut*. We are not forced to accept the loaded options offered us: God's guarantee or moral anarchy, one absolute meaning or absurdity. Other alternatives assume a more modest appreciation of the human predicament that is destined to filter every claim, whatever its alleged source, through human heart and mind. The relativism of meaning derives from our human condition. The predicament is not avoided through reading one's own idea of meaning into a text only to get it back with the blessing of absolute authority.

Meanings there are which are not invented nor flung down upon us from above. There are meanings discovered by our people through their experienced transactions with their environment. Not "the" beginning but many beginnings shape our world; not one meaning, one revelation, one interpretation but many are called for. And all remain open and subject to scrutiny, rational debate, and judgment on the table of consequences.

Menachem Mendel of Kotsk counseled a Hasid who had experienced "terrible thoughts" questioning Judge and Justice and meaning in the world. To every anguished doubt of the Hasid, Menachem Mendel retorted, "And so—what do you care?" And seeing that the Hasid truly cared, he advised him not to worry about his doubts, "for if you care so deeply, you are an honest Jew, and an honest Jew is entitled to such doubts." In beginnings, worlds are created. In creativity, meanings are formed.

AS SERVANTS OR AS
CHILDREN?

Is our relationship to God like that of children or that of servants?
On Rosh Hashanah, we recite a series of biblical verses declaring
God's sovereignty (*Malchuyot*), remembrance (*Zichronot*), and
redemption (*Shoferot*). At the conclusion of each of these three
collections of verses, the congregation ends with a conditional
prayer: "This day all the creatures of the universe stand in judgment before Thee as children or as servants. If as children, have
pity on us as a father pities his children; and if as servants our eyes
beseech Thee to be gracious unto us and pronounce our sentence
clear as light, Thou who art revered and holy."

There thus appears to be a choice in the way we stand before
God; and a corresponding difference in the way God responds to
us. The parent-child relationship is softer than that of the master
and servant. The latter refers to justice, law, sentence; the former
speaks of pity. How do I relate to God as a child and how as a
servant?

A talmudic passage (T. *Bava Batra* 10a) introduces a significant
distinction between the two roles which bear on this prayer. The
passage is introduced with a common argument: "If God loves the
poor, why does He not support them?" God knows their condition
and God can act; and if He does not intervene, might it not be
because people get what God believes they deserve? Pursuing this
argument, the Roman governor of Judea, Tinneius Rufus, offers
Akiva a pointed parable: A king was angry with his servant, placed
him in prison, and ordered that he be given neither food nor drink.

If someone were to give the servant food and drink, wouldn't the king, upon learning of this interference with his edict, be angry with him? For it is written, "For unto Me the children of Israel are servants" (Leviticus 25:55). Rabbi Akiva counters with another parable. A king was angry with his child and ordered that no food or drink be given him. Then another man gave his child food and drink. Would the king not reward him with a present? For it is written, "Children are ye to the Lord your God" (Deuteronomy 14:12). When you carry out the desires of God, you are called "children," and if not you are called "servants." From the parables one can conclude that a servant does that which he is obliged to do according to the commands of his master. The relationship is not one of love but of duty. But a devoted child knows the heart of his parent and in turn is treated with compassion.

What of God's support of the poor? We mortals have options, we can regard the poor as the responsibility of the Lord. We can act as servants, and rationalize our nonintervention as the nonaction of piety. Or we can act as God's children, following the prophet Isaiah, "Is it not to deal thy bread to the hungry and bring the poor that are cast out to thy house."

The parables are clear enough. If we bear no responsibility for the well-being of God's children who are impoverished, if we treat them as God's servants, we too are as His servants and may expect to be treated accordingly. But if we relate to God's creatures as children, with compassion, we may pray for compassionate reciprocity from God. The prayer reflects the talmudic statement, "He who is merciful to others, mercy is shown to him by heaven, while he who is not merciful to others, mercy is not shown to him by heaven" (T. *Shabbat* 151b). Our status is formed by our behavior and self-image.

Passivity wears a modest face. After all, who are we, fragile and finite beings, to interfere with God's inscrutable will and alter the condition of man? *Gott vet helfen,* "God will help," mocks a reverence for the providential power beyond our understanding. Akiva sees through such false acquiescence as a betrayal of the divine image that enables us to share God's burdens. The posture of resignation turns away from the ultimate dignity and purpose of human existence. But to turn away from the world is to turn away from our closeness to God. "To walk after the Lord your God."

To clothe the naked, to visit the sick, to comfort the bereaved, is to imitate God (T. *Sotah* 14a).

The task is not to read the wretched condition of our fellows as a divine sentence against the impoverished. On the contrary, to love God is to love His children. To be regarded as one of God's children is to recognize the suffering of others as that of our siblings.

In the aforementioned parable, Akiva contends that the poor are left for us to support so that we may be saved through them from punishment. Through them, as well, we are rewarded, with purpose. His parable ends with a rhetorical question. "When do you bring the poor who are cast out to your house?" He responds *now*. Procrastination is death. The rabbis recalled the fatal delay of Nachum Ish Gamzu's charity. When a poor man asked him for something to eat, he replied: "Wait until I have unloaded this burden from the donkey." He waited, fainted, and died of starvation. *Now* is the time to respond. "This day the world was created." This day the world must be sustained by us, not as servants but as children of God.

CONCEALMENTS AND REVELATIONS

Seeing their nakedness, Adam and Eve fled from before the presence of the Lord.

When Jonah heard the voice telling him to go forth and to prophesy to the people of Nineveh, he hid himself in the gray womb of the whale.

The Rizhiner Rebbe, when he came home one day, noted the fact that his little boy was crying. He asked his son why, and the boy answered, "Because I have been playing hide-and-seek." "But that's no reason to cry," said the Rebbe. "It is, Papa. I was hiding, but nobody was seeking."

So it is, said the Rizhiner, with the soul of man, that it hides, and nobody seeks.

A midrash: when the angels heard that God was going to create the image of His own being, and breathe the breath of His life into it, they conspired with each other to hide the image of divinity. One angel proposed to put it on the top of a mountain. A second proposed to hide it at the bottom of the sea. But the wiliest angel of all said, "Let us hide it by putting it in man and woman, because that is the last place anyone will look for it."

Our tradition talks a great deal about the fact that human beings are hiders and gravediggers and concealers. We're always looking for getaways, whether through work or through leisure, in health or in sickness. There are appointments to be kept, and there are patients, and there are clients, and there are customers, and there are investments; there's jogging and there's dieting and there's bleaching and there's dyeing. There are mountains and seashores and cathedrals and museums, all to get away to. And there are committees. All these are ways for us to hide from the very first question that is posed in the Bible: *Ayeka?* Where are you?

We hide so cleverly that when we hear that question, we think it is the bank teller who is asking. So we produce our wallet, and our Social Security number or our credit card. (When I show my American Express card, they will know who I am.) We confuse identity with identification.

The ultimate question—the question of identity, the question of where we are, of who we are—that question gets drowned in small talk, or in doubts, or in quarrels, or in drink, or in infidelity. Most of all, people hide the question behind a complaint: "I am bored." People tell me that they are bored and I ask them how they can be bored, observing that they have everything to live for. Nevertheless, they tell me, they are bored. What is it they want, I ask. And they tell me they do not know what they want; all they know is that they are bored.

Once in a while, in a crisis situation, when one has to face the gray walls of a hospital or a mortuary or a divorce court, the boredom ends, the strategies of evasion crumble, and the question comes out in the form of a scream: Where is the life I have lost while living?

Mi ani: Mah ani? Le-mi ani 'amel? Mah yeshu'ati? Mah gevurati? Mah kochi? Who am I? What am I? What do I stand for? What shall I say before myself? What does life demand of me—or is there absolutely nothing demanded of me?

These are uncomfortable questions and people avoid them. These are spiritual, metaphysical, philosophical, theological questions, questions of purpose. Such questions make us uncomfortable because we are practical people and we live in a marvelously technological society. Technocrats do not ask, "What for?" They ask, "How much?" or "How?" or "When?" They say, "I will get you there faster, I'll get you there more efficiently, but once you get there, I have nothing to say to you. That's not my job."

Ours is a society that is concerned with means, with instruments, with gadgets, not with ends. Ends petrify us. It makes us terribly uncomfortable to be asked, "What for?"

We prefer to live out Kafka's parable of the messenger, he who traverses long distances until finally, exhausted, he arrives at the palace of the king—and has forgotten the message.

Now comes Rosh Hashanah. Rosh Hashanah can be treated as we treat any other holiday, or it can be respected for its radical uniqueness. There is no other time like the time from this day through Yom Kippur. On every other festival we can hide behind the skirts of the community. We can hide behind historical events, we can have our own lives swept up by history: On Pesach we were redeemed, and on Sukkot we wandered in the desert, and on Shavuot we received the Revelation, and on Tisha Be-Av we suffered the destruction of the Temple, and on Chanukah the Temple was rededicated, and on Purim we won a great victory over the enemy, and on Yom Hashoah we suffered the loss of six million and on Yom Ha-Atzma'ut we witnessed the establishment of the State of Israel.

But Rosh Hashanah has nothing to do with community and nothing to do with history. The focus is not on "we" on Rosh Hashanah and Yom Kippur. The focus is on the first-person singular. The commandment for each of us during these days is *Mi-besarcha lo titalem*—"You shall not hide from your own flesh."

Strip aside the small questions, and have the courage to ask the big, hard, scary questions that suit this day. Let us set aside, for a time, Judaism as a system of means or of ceremonies, and even the Judaism that is going to redeem the world or redeem the Jewish people or keep the family intact, and concentrate on the holy self-centered Judaism that has to do with finding *my* meaning, *my* self, *my* esteem. Is there anything that I can do with myself in confronting the ultimate that will enable me to live out my life *be-chol levavi u-ve-chol nafshi u-ve-chol me'odi*—with all my heart and with all my soul and with all my might. Without hiding place, without retreat. The rabbinic statement "For my sake the world was created" expresses a holy selfishness.

What does Judaism tell me about the way that I am supposed to live my life?

When we look at the texts or listen to the preachers, the answer seems plain enough. Study, learn, attend a school, become a master of the text. Which other people holds that the House of Study is holier than the House of Prayer? A church is called a church, a mosque is called a mosque, but we call a synagogue a shul—which comes from the world *schola* and means "school." We believe in the power of learning. That is why 85 percent of our youngsters who are eligible are in college, four hundred thousand in all, that is why 10 percent of the college faculty members in this country, and 20 percent in the elite institutions, are Jews.

But that is not what the rabbis had in mind by study. Why study? The great rabbis also asked, *tachlit?* (what for?). And they answered, "The function of wisdom is to do repentance and to do good deeds, so that a man should not study Torah and Mishnah and Gemara and then kick his father and his mother and his teacher." Beware, you who are given to cerebral conceits, beware of the boasting of the *yiddishe kop,* because the *yiddishe kop*—a Jewish brain—may kill the *yiddishe hartz*—the Jewish heart. The rabbis concluded, "He who studies Torah, Torah, Torah, only Torah, and has no other considerations is considered as if he does not believe in God."

They taught, "If somebody studies not for the purpose of doing something, it would be better if he had not been born." Adam's sin is that he eats of the tree of knowledge. If we are punished for eating of the tree of knowledge, it must mean that knowledge is not the end.

How can that be so? I recently met with a rabbinic colleague who is a Jewish historian of some note. He had contracted a disease that involved the wearing out of the fatty substance at the end of the nerves. He was told to see a neurologist. The neurologist had to perform a very painful procedure, electrical conduction on the nerves. And because it was painful, the doctor said to my friend, perhaps to take his mind off the procedure, "That's a Mengele machine." "What did you say?" my friend asked. "That's a Mengele machine." It developed that my friend the Jewish historian was being treated on a machine perfected by that sadistic monster, Dr. Josef Mengele, during the course of his experiments to determine whether there was sensation in the vagina, a curiosity he satisfied by placing electrodes in the vaginas of Jewish women, most of whom died in excruciating pain.

So much for the idolatry of the brain. Mengele had a Ph.D. Hitler's doctors and Hitler's lawyers and Hitler's scientists had wall-to-wall degrees, some were very bright people, and so were the engineers of I. G. Farben and Krupp, those who invented Zyklon-B gas.

Adam's transgression was that he chose to eat from the Tree of Knowledge and not from the Tree of Life. When we put the Torah back into the Ark of Holiness, we don't sing, *etz da'at hi lamachazikim bah*—"it is a tree of knowledge to them that cling fast to her." We declare, *etz chayyim hi*—"it is a tree of life." While we revere the Torah and recite blessings over it, Jewish law rules that if you need money to redeem hostages, you sell the Torah. If you know of a poor orphan girl who needs money for her dowry, you sell the Torah. The function of the Torah is not to be owned or to be quoted, but to be *used,* to be used as a tree of life for life.

To *be* the truth is more important than to *know* the truth. When the yeshiva bocher came to his rebbe and boasted that he had gone through the Talmud five times, the rebbe asked him, "And how many times has the Talmud gone through you, my son?"

No, the cultivated intellect does not answer the ultimate question of purpose we seek.

PRAYER

Maybe the answer lies in prayer.

How about prayer, the tallit and the tefillin, the liturgical life, the yearning to be part of a spiritual community? Is the purpose of prayer to pray? The purpose of prayer is to pray into your hands. Prayer is not spiritual theurgy. Prayer begins with the trembling of the lips, but it should end with the movement of the legs. Twenty-eight centuries ago, the prophet Isaiah, in the time of the First Temple, the time of sacrifices and priests, proclaimed: "In the name of God, when you spread out your palms, I, God, will close My eyes to you; even though you utter many prayers, I will not listen. Wash yourselves clean; remove your evil acts from my sight; cease to do evil; seek justice; aid the oppressed; uphold the right of the orphan; defend the cause of the widow."

The radical character of Judaism's teaching is that holiness has to do with morality. That revolution has still not been absorbed by the world, not even by the Jewish people.

Israel Salanter was the founder of the Musar movement, a movement of ethical revival. A man of vast ethical concern, and fastidiously observant. Yet he was suspicious of public swaying, the "shokling" of davening, of intense prayer. "Even when you are in intense movement, and you are doing things for the glorious God, and you are praying with such avidity, make sure that you do not trample the foot of your neighbor. Make sure that when you put on your tallit, you don't slap the face of your neighbor with its fringes."

No, it's not prayer that is the end. And it's not study. So what is it that's left?

KASHRUT

How about kashrut, how about yom tov, and ritual observance in general? A midrash on Genesis from the sixth century of the common era: "What difference does it make to God whether you kill the animal by the throat or by the nape of the neck? Is God helped by the one way or frustrated by the other? Rather, the function of the mitzvot is to sensitize the character of the human being." Ritual is a means, and to make a means into an end is the essence of idolatry.

Israel Salanter, citing the law that prohibits eating an egg in which you find a speck of blood, said, "The law applies to more than eggs. If you take money in which there is blood, the blood of exploitation, is that kosher?" "It is prohibited to swallow an insect alive. And if you eat up another human being with your eyes, in envy, in jealousy, in corruption, is that not tref?" He was suspicious of people so overly scrupulous in their observance. Before the *Motzi,* the tradition is to take a jug of water and pour it over the hands up to the wrists. But Israel Salanter would take a few drops of water and put them on the tips of his fingers. When he was asked the meaning of his way, he answered, "Did you see that maidservant over there? She carries the water from the well, two large buckets at a time in a yoke on her back. I don't want to earn mitzvot on her shoulders."

CHARACTER

So what is the end, what is the "what for"?

The answer is the cultivation of a *yiddishe neshama,* a soul and a character of *rachmanut,* of *erlichkeit;* of sensitivity, of dignity, of care, of compassion. Otherwise sancta turn into broken branches, dead wood. What good kindling the Sabbath lights if we extinguish them with the breath of quarrelsomeness? When we shout at each other, we make dark our home. Children speak to us of their pain and their sadness at such darkness. What meaning has the sweetness of the *Kiddush* wine? It sours at a table that is full of accusation and fault-finding. What good is the soft challah when life has become so hard and judgmental? What good is the grace after meals when we are so graceless during our meals?

From Proverbs: "Better a dry morsel, and quiet therewith, than a house that is full of meat and sacrifices—with strife." What good is fasting, whose purpose is to make our heart soft, when the home is full of labeling and stigmatizing?

From Isaiah: "You fast in strife and you fast in contention and you smite each other with the fist of wickedness." If there is no kindness to family and friends, the house may be kosher, but it is tref.

Does this mean that it is not important to observe the ritual or to go to shul. But that too is a way of hiding, evading the question. The question is not whether you believe in morality *or* in ritual, the question is not whether you believe in ethics *or* in kashrut. The question is whether you understand the end, the purpose, the meaning, the thrust behind behavior and thought. If you do, you will daven, but differently; you will keep kosher, but differently; you will come to the synagogue, but differently; you will recite the blessings differently: "Blessed art Thou, O Lord our God, who has commanded us by Thy commandments and *sanctified* us." I am a sanctifying power, a hallowing power. There is holiness in me. I can be moved to tears, I can be stirred into action when I see bitterness, helplessness—that is my meaning, and that is the answer to the question of my Jewish being.

Ultimate questions cannot be answered with money orders. They are answered through behavior called *gemilut chasadim*, acts of love performed without money—not only for the poor, not only for the living. *Gemilut chasadim* means comforting the bereaved, making records for the blind, settling the stranger in our midst. *Gemilut chasadim* heals, but it heals not only the recipient but the donor. The giver, who pledges not his money but his soul, is important. In *gemilut chesed*, the donor transforms not only the external situation but his inner character.

There is no blessing for *gemilut chasadim*. There are blessings for apples and pears, for cucumbers and lightning bolts, but no blessing for acts of *gemilut chesed*. Perhaps because the acts are blessings that nothing should interrupt, not even the benediction.

For you or me to act for others is a beginning. But it is only with a beginning that God creates the universe. *Bereshit bara Elohim.*

IMAGINING ZAYDEH'S SUKKAH

It was incongruous even in imagination. Though I never witnessed the actual construction with my own eyes, I did see it and everyone testified that Zaydeh had built it.

But how? On the tar-pitched roof of a two-story building on South Ninth Street in Brooklyn was a sukkah with three sides leaning against a brick wall. Incredible to think of that old man with gray-white beard and black derby hauling boards and palm branches up to the roof from the street. Where did he find the material, and who could imagine Reb Avraham pounding nails into the wood, he whose commitment to study led him to look down on working with one's hands? He could never understand my playing with the interior workings of an old clock. It was *bittul zeman,* a waste of time taken away from the study of Torah. Who could imagine the wasted time Zaydeh had to have spent constructing the sukkah?

Zaydeh sitting in a hut, outside the home, eating at a table surrounded by the aroma of leaves and fruits, a sight as strange as imagining Zaydeh at a camping jamboree. There he was outdoors, sitting hunched up with his suit collar raised, eating and drinking while it rained through the thatched roof. In the sukkah, Bubbe never ran short of soup. The law, of course, exempted him from dwelling in the sukkah if it rained. "If one suffers discomfort in a sukkah, he is exempt from the obligation of dwelling in it" (T. *Sukkah* 25b). If there is no joy, the mitzvah is suspended. But protected by his derby and his sense of mitzvah, Zaydeh felt no discomfort.

260

Jewish codes state that if guests are invited to the sukkah on the first night and rain begins to fall, one should wait until midnight to eat in the sukkah. Perhaps the rain will stop by that time. But if the invited guests are poor, one should not wait for the rain to stop. Being poor the guests have most likely not eaten anything all day. For them to wait is discomfort enough. Let them eat with you in the dining room and forgo the mitzvah of dwelling in the sukkah. So my Zaydeh taught.

The sukkah brought out an unsuspected side of Zaydeh even as the holiday revealed an unexpected side of Jewish piety. Sukkot is different, especially when contrasted with the days of Rosh Hashanah and Yom Kippur which precede it. Rosh Hashanah is cerebral, a matter of the head; Yom Kippur is affective, a matter of the heart. But Sukkot is physical, a mitzvah of the entire body with which one enters the sukkah, even in one's boots. As if to compensate for the fast and solemnity of the Day of Atonement, Sukkot is insistent upon rejoicing the body and the spirit, celebrating the taste and aroma of nature and reading the almost not canonized biblical text of Ecclesiastes. The wisdom of Ecclesiastes doesn't quite fit the conventional view of piety. "In the morning sow thy seed, and in the evening withhold not thy hand . . . truly the light is sweet, and it is a pleasant thing for the eyes to behold the sun . . . rejoice, young man, in thy youth, and let thy heart cheer thee in the days of thy youth."

Even the stories told about Sukkot possess an eccentric, irreverent Jewish charm. There is the one told about the rebbe whom the villagers entrusted with money to buy an ethrog. He prepared to travel to the nearest city to select a choice citron-like fruit, one fresh, firm, with a fine aroma, and wrinkled. Why wrinkled? Because the ethrog symbolizes the heart, and which heart that feels the anguish of the world can be smooth? A smooth-skinned ethrog is a symbol of a callous heart.

On the way to the city the rebbe came upon a wagoner crying beside his horse who had fallen dead. Without a horse, a wagon is as useless as a man without *mazal,* the wagoner explained. Without a horse, he and his family would starve. The rebbe asked no questions, handed over to the wagoner the bag of money allocated by the villagers for the purchase of an ethrog, and returned home.

He explained what had happened to the distraught villagers, who cried aloud, "What will we do when Sukkot comes?" The rebbe consoled them. "Do not be sad. The whole world will recite the benedictions over an ethrog, but we here will recite them over a dead horse." Irreverent but true to the spirit of Sukkot. For if the meaning of the festival of joy is gratitude, what greater rejoicing can there be than to lift up the lot of the fallen and thereby to rejoice God as well? If on Yom Kippur the way to expiate sins is through fasting and repenting before the King who dwells on high, on Sukkot one turns away from transgression by means of laughter and rejoicing. Along these lines Zaydeh taught us that there are two different ways to turn, to do *teshuvah*. One way is through fear, remembering that God transcends the world and is enthroned on High. That is the way of the solemn Day of Atonement.

The other way to turn is through love, remembering that God dwells in the midst of the sukkah. One way is the way of self-judgment, the other the way of self-forgiveness. Both are needed, and that is why there are so many feasts and fasts in our tradition. So Zaydeh taught.

COMMENTARIES ON THE SEDER

LIGHTING THE CANDLES

The first word in the creation of the universe out of the unformed void and dark earth was God's "Let there be light." Therein lies the hope and faith of Judaism and the obligation of our people—to make the light of justice and righteousness and knowledge penetrate the darkness of our time till the prophecy be fulfilled, "that wickedness vanish like smoke and the earth shall be filled with knowledge as the waters cover the sea" (Isaiah 11:9). We co-creators with God pray, "Let there be light."

KIDDUSH

We recite the blessing not over the fruit of the vine—the whole grape—but over the wine, squeezed and fermented through human agency. So too the *Motzi* is recited not over the sheaves of barley or wheat but over the bread, leavened or unleavened, ground and kneaded and prepared by human hands. The blessing is over the product cultivated through human and divine cooperation: the givenness of sun, seed, and soil transformed by human wisdom and purpose to sustain the body and rejoice the soul.

KARPAS

Passover is both nature and history. A springtime festival in the month when kids and lambs are born, and when the grain harvest begins with the cutting of the barley; and the root-history of our people's liberation from oppression breaks through. The convergence of spring and the breaking of the shackles of slavery signify a basic value in nature and in history: freedom. Vegetative life submerged beneath the icy winter breaks forth to reveal its liberation; human life fettered by chains of slavery bursts forth to claim its freedom. "Those who sow in tears will reap in joy." We raise the green parsley out of the salt of tears and praise the Power which raises fruit out of the earth.

YACHATZ

We are free, but we remember when we were slaves. We are whole, but we bring to mind those who are broken. The middle matzah is broken, but it is the larger part which is hidden (*tzafun*). Because the future will be greater than the past, and tomorrow's Passover nobler than yesterday's exodus. The prospects for the dreamt future are overwhelming to the point of making us mute. So it is in silence, without blessing, that we break the matzah and long for its recovery and our redemption.

HA LACHMA

Written in Aramaic this statement begins the narration of the Seder by inviting the hungry to our table. Aramaic, Jewish legend has it, is the one language which the angels do not understand. Why then the *Ha Lachma* in Aramaic? To teach us that where there is poverty no one should rely upon angels, no one should pray to the uncomprehending celestial horde for help. We know the language of the poor, for we were poor in the land of Egypt. We know that we are called to feed the poor and to call them to join in our celebration of freedom.

FOUR QUESTIONS

The Haggadah cannot be recited without questions. What good are answers if no one asks? The question is sacred. It is the mark of a free human being to ask. Slaves do not question. Slaves bite their tongues and obey their masters. We have no masters but One, and that Master, loving us, delights in our inquiry and is saddened by our apathy. Not the wicked, but the one not motivated to ask, is placed on the lowest rung of the four children. And it is our obligation, we who are called upon to answer, to open that one up, to share our past and our vision. May the one who cannot ask anything this night question next year and climb towards the higher level of the wise and caring.

IN THE BEGINNING: MI-TECHILLAH OVDEI AVODAH ZARAH

We were not born free men and women; we were not born believers in one God. We came from an ancestry of slaves and idol worshippers. Tonight we celebrate, not our genesis, what we were or what our ancestors were, but what we have become. We are a choosing people, and our choice has come out of tragic encounters with pagan superstition and political enslavement. We are choosing people, and we have discovered the meaning of our choice: to live as witnesses to one God who calls upon us to mend the world, to make whole the broken vessels of this incomplete world.

VE-HI SHE-AMDAH

Ours is not entirely a happy history. We have suffered much for daring to be different, for the audacity of saying "no" to pharaohs, princes, priests, potentates. But every "no" is a more powerful "yes." We say "yes" to the present and the future; "yes" to the real possibilities for shaping a happier society for ourselves and our children; "yes" to the men and women outside our own circle who are our real and potential allies in the struggle to attain the Passover of the future. None of our sufferings are wasted if, when recalled, they strengthen our resolve to engage in the struggle towards wholeness and freedom for our people and for humankind.

THE PLAGUES

The Passover victory is tempered by our consideration of the innocents who died, drafted to serve in the Pharaoh's chariot corps. We do not sing the whole *Hallel* on the last six days of Passover. Who, witnessing the death of God's children, dares sing "When I was brought low, God saved me," or taunt the dead by recalling their idols who had ears but could not hear, hands which could not save? We recall the ten plagues with ambivalence. We and our children were saved through the river turning red with blood and the storm and hail which destroyed the crop. But the angel of death, once released, does not distinguish between the guilty and the innocent. Our triumphal hymn is muted. The cup of wine does not spill over with unrestrained joy.

A medieval Jewish custom placed the ten drops of wine onto a broken plate. Some believe that doing so signifies the broken vessel of our world. Our attention is directed to the shattered vessel, to our obligation to redeem the sparks hidden among the husks, shards and ciphers in our midst.

MATZAH

This matzah for the Seder is baked from wheat or rye or oats or barley or spelt. Curiously, when moistened and allowed to ferment, these five types of grains become *chametz,* leavened food prohibited to be eaten during the Passover. Matzah derives from the same grains which are *chametz.* So too are the vices and virtues of our lives interwoven, our energies for good and evil intricately connected. Of itself the grain is neither good nor evil, neither matzah nor *chametz.* What makes it one or the other is the intention and use to which it is assigned. Each, in its proper place, has its purpose. It is we, not the neutral grain, who consecrate or desecrate the grain, who turn it into leavened bread or matzah.

MAROR

On Passover we eat theology and drink ethics. On our plates, in our cups, with the posture of our bodies, in the gestures of our hands, in the way we eat and drink and sing, in the way we converse with each other—are found the teachings of a people's faith and ethics.

The bitter herbs may not be swallowed. They must be chewed and tasted. It is not enough to talk abstractly "about" oppression, to analyze the causes which led to slavery, to read "about" the forced labor camps. To the best of our ability we are to experience the lives embittered by totalitarian punishment. To fast on Yom Kippur is part of the process of "afflicting the soul"; to taste the bitter herbs is part of the process of feeling the afflictions of body and spirit which a submerged society experiences.

Yet when the maror is eaten, it is mixed with the cinnamoned charoseth, perhaps to teach us that memory cannot be immersed only in darkness and despair. The sweet mixture is not the dominant taste as the maror is dipped in the charoseth. The charoseth is not meant to eradicate the bitter, only to remind us that there is goodness in the world, however small, and hope in the future, however slight. Without the charoseth, the only lasting memory would be that of the torture and the shame.

THE PRAYERS AROUND ELIJAH'S CUP

Our people suffered in Egypt and yet we are told, "You shall not abhor an Egyptian, because you were a stranger in his land" (Deuteronomy 23:8). Pharaoh decreed the drowning of the Hebrew children, but when the Egyptians drowned in the Red Sea, our rabbis told a tale of the angels being chastised by God for rejoicing at the death of His children. The Bible remembers Shifra and Puah, the two Egyptian midwives who saved Jewish infants from Pharaoh's decree of death at the risk of their own lives. The Bible records the gifts and loans which the Egyptians offered the Israelites before their exodus. The rabbinic commentator, Rashi, points out that Egypt opened its land to Israelites when there was famine in the land of Canaan. Jews do not exult in the fall of our enemies. We pray for the day when reconciliation among peoples will prevail over divisive hatred. We pray with Isaiah, "Blessed be Egypt My people and Assyria the work of My hands, and Israel Mine inheritance."

HALLEL

After the painful cry of Psalm 136 is recited, "Pour out Thy wrath upon the nations who know Thee not . . . for they have devoured Jacob and laid waste his dwelling place," our celebration is muted. But the Passover will not allow us to linger in despair. Melancholy introduces a slavery of its own, a defeat of the spirit, paralysis of the will. We turn quickly to the second section of the *Hallel* and to the vision of the Passover of the Future. We point to the Fifth Cup not yet lifted, not yet drunk. We recite the psalm which prays for the time "when all nations and all peoples will laud Thee; when the House of Israel and the House of Aaron will be joined by all who revere Thy name and when the soul of every living being will bless Thee." Like the three matzot, the Passover is woven of three tenses. The Passover is not over in recollection. The future is a magnet moving us towards the messianic era.

THE AFIKOMAN

There is something hidden, something to be discovered, something to be revealed. How fitting that the larger part of the broken matzah is searched for by the children. Is this not the meaning of our retelling the story of stories, to transmit to our young the shiver of our history and the will to recover the vision of our ancestors?

When the Baal Shem had a difficult task before him, he would go to a certain place in the woods, light a fire, and meditate in prayer—and what he had set out to perform was done. When, a generation later, the Maggid of Meseritz was faced with the same task, he would go to the same place in the woods and say, "We can no longer light the fire, but we can still speak the prayers"— and what he wanted done became reality. Again a generation later, Rabbi Moshe Leib of Sassov had to perform this task. And he too went into the woods and said, "We can no longer light the fire, nor do we know the secret meditations belonging to the prayer, but we do know the place in the woods to which it all belongs—and that must be sufficient"; and sufficient it was. But when another generation had passed and Rabbi Israel of Rishin was called upon to perform the task, he sat down on his golden chair in his castle and said, "We cannot light the fire, we cannot speak the prayers, we do not know the place, but we can tell the story of how it was done." And the story told had the same effect as the actions of the other three.

TZAFUN: EATING THE HIDDEN AFIKOMAN

No prayers, no benediction precedes the *yachatz,* the breaking of the middle matzah. The matzah is broken silently and its larger part is hidden silently. And when, at the end of the meal, it is retrieved by the children and eaten as the afikoman, it is consumed silently, without a benediction. We may have forgotten the prayer of our ancestors, the meaning they gave to this curiously mute ceremony—but reliving the event, we may speculate as to its significance. Was it fear of the Romans that kept this act wordless? Was the retrieval of the matzah symbolic of the messianic redemption which was yet to come, when the yoke of repressive foreign sovereignty would be broken? What knowing glances were passed among our ancestors around the Passover table? The ceremony is called *Tzafun,* which means "hidden." The mystery is yet to be revealed, the Passover of the Future is yet to be celebrated.

ELIJAH'S CUP IS EMPTY

At my Seder I have adapted an innovation attributed to Rabbi Naftali of Ropshitz (died 1827). Elijah's cup, symbolizing the coming of the Messiah, he left unfilled. But before the door was opened and Elijah greeted, he would pass the empty cup around the table. Everyone, man, woman, child, would pour a portion from his wine glass, into the empty vessel, during which the traditional melody of *Eliyahu ha-Navi* was repeatedly sung and hummed. When the cup returned to Reb Naftali he would lift it and recite the rabbinic statement, "Israel will not be redeemed except through its own efforts."

The Ropshitzer's ritual involves the participation of the Seder guests ceremonially and theologically. Redemption does not come through waiting. Belief in the Messiah is no surrogate for active involvement. The sages meant no slight of God or Messiah. They expressed their conviction that divine power is expressed through a living people's exercise of their moral will. The midrashic legend crediting the tribe of Benjamin for splitting the Red Sea by an active leap of faith accords with God's rebuke of Moses' prolonged cry for divine intercession in the Bible (Exodus 14:15). The first signs of redemption were manifest in Moses' appeal to the people to go forward.

In the Bible, Moses casts aside the rod, and instead of using the staff, he stretches out his hand over the Red Sea (Exodus 14:21). A rabbinic commentary offers this to teach the people that reliance upon the miracle rod is misleading. The rod, which once turned into a serpent and turned the Nile a reddish hue, is no magic wand. Its earlier use was for purposes of morale, meant to impress the

Egyptians, who respected only the powers of magic. But Israel is to learn that divine power is not in the rod. The same rod used to smite the tyranny of Egypt led to Moses' downfall when, in a fit of frustration and arrogance, he smote the rock to force it to yield water. The cup of Elijah stands empty before us. It will remain empty until we each give of our strength towards the fulfillment of the promise. The ritual of filling Elijah's empty cup is in keeping with Jewish mysticism's emphasis on the power of the world below to give strength to the world above. The Lurianic meditations before prayer and ritual acts are predicated on the belief that human beings are able to uplift the heavens. From the viewpoint of the *Zohar,* a Jew is to relate the Exodus story on Passover night not simply for himself. He must tell it joyously, fervently, with song and food and drink, to rejoice the Shechinah, the God who is in exile with us. "Rejoicing brings forth rejoicing."

Laughter below resonates in the heavens above. It is good to bring happiness to God. God rejoices in our joy and in our redemption as His own. With the family below, Jews call forth the Family above. God exults: "Come and hear the praises which My children bring unto Me." Then all the angels and supernal beings break forth into jubilation that the Holy One possesses people on earth who have not forgotten how and why to celebrate the joy of freedom.

All these legends of angels and Shechinah rescue us from the self-imposed chains of passivity; they remind us that actions produce other actions, waves upon waves of consequences flow from every stirring of the human spirit. We have powers within and between us which reach the heavens. One does not need a dungeon to remain insulated. The self-paralysis which is called by many names is subtler and heavier than chains. What fetters of the human will are disguised behind the gray "wisdom" of realism.

We "build worlds" through prayer, meditation, and deeds. However removed we may be from its metaphysics, however odd the imagery, we must surely sense our kinship with the *Zohar's* fervent faith in our people's capacity to affect the world. To lose faith in ourselves and in our task is to turn back to Egypt and away from the Passover of the Future that redeems us from emptiness.

"Ascribe ye strength unto God" (Psalm 68:35). The "ye" refers to each of us who knows himself to be part of a greater Jewish

community. He who separates himself from the community reduces his own power to choose and weakens the strength of
godliness in the world we inhabit. The Haggadah's "wicked" deny
the root principle of Judaism by uprooting themselves from the soil
of community. Unbelonging, they forsake the matrix out of which
belief is born and nurtured. Only in, with, and through community
can the self be raised out of sorrowful impotence. No individual
alone, no sectarian group alone can fill the cup of Elijah. Only
together, as a united people understanding its common purpose,
will the messianic cup of promise be filled.

NO BLESSING OVER THE
BROKEN MATZAH

I was five, perhaps six years old, when I found the matzah which my grandfather had placed in a linen napkin and hidden in the bedroom. I had glued my eyes on him from the moment he performed the yachatz ceremony, breaking the middle matzah into two unequal parts and replacing the smaller part in its original position. When he returned to the table, I looked forward to the search and retrieval. I knew, as did all my cousins around the Seder table, that he who found the concealed larger part, the afikoman, could hold out for any prize. That Passover night the Seder ran exceptionally long, and I was sleepy because of the cups of wine I had drunk and the lateness of the hour. I hid the napkinned matzah beneath the pillow of the bed and promptly fell into a deep sleep. I remember being roused by my mother, who, with some urgency in her voice, insisted that I return the matzah so that the services could be completed. As I did so I sensed that this was no child's play, that behind the hide-and-seek lay a more serious meaning. They were serious, and I, who knew where the broken matzah was, held some true power in my hands.

Through the years I sensed more and more the mystery of the yachatz act. Every other ritual gesture was preceded by a benediction—over the wine, the washing of the hands, the parsley, the matzot, the bitter herbs mixed with charoset. But there was no *berachah* recited over the *yachatz,* not even an explanation such as the one given before eating the Hillel sandwich. Rabbinic scholars sensed, as well, the oddity of reciting a Motzi over a *broken* piece of unleavened bread; they wondered why the middle matzah and not the other two were broken, and why it was broken into two uneven parts, with the larger part saved for the afikoman. Their explanations are largely legal, based upon the position of the Rambam, the Rif, and other sages. For others, the "stealing" of the afikoman was designed to keep the children awake with play. But none of the explanations satisfied me. As in the case of opening the door for Elijah, I knew that more than the amusement of children was meant.

WANTING WHOLENESS BUT NOT HAVING IT

In the outline of the Seder ritual the division of the middle matzah—*yachatz*—takes place early, before the great declaration, "This is the bread of affliction." The eating of the retrieved matzah comes after ransoming it from the children at the end of the Seder. The ritual of eating the afikoman is called *tzafun,* which means "hidden." It, too, is eaten in silence, without benediction, before midnight. After the afikoman no food or drink is to be taken except for the final two cups of wine. In some Haggadot there is a devotional prayer in Aramaic which announces, "I am ready and prepared to perform the commandment of eating the afikoman to unite the Holy One, blessed be He, and His Divine Presence through the hidden and secret Guardian on behalf of all Israel.

Brokenness is a symbol of incompletion. Life is not whole. The Passover itself is not complete. The Passover we celebrate deals with the past redemption of our people from the bondage in Egypt. That redemption is a fact of history, and it heartens us because through its recollection we know that our hope for future redemption is not fantasy. It did happen once and to our whole people. A small slave people witnessed the power of a supreme divine agency to snap the heavy chains around our hands, and to break the yoke upon our necks. It was no dream, this redemption. It happened, and at the Seder we relate the testimony of this act.

But it is towards the Passover of the Future that our memories are directed. *The redemption is not over.* There is fear and poverty and sickness. There is a trembling on earth. Around us are the plagues of pollution, and images of fiery nuclear explosions in the clouds, not like the cloud of glory and the pillar of fire which led our ancestors through the wilderness. The broken matzah and

Elijah's cup speak to our times, shakes us by the shoulders and shouts into our hearts, "Do not bury your spirit in history. Do not think it is over, that the Messiah has come and you have nothing to do but to wait, to pray, to believe."

THE PAST AND PRESENT TELL OUR FUTURE

The history of our liberation is not for the sake of gloating over the past but for the confirmation of our hopes. Even as we retrieve the past, the future is held before us. We begin the story of our past affliction with an appeal for present help and with an eye set upon the future. Three time dimensions in one opening paragraph: "This is the bread of affliction that our *ancestors* ate in the land of Egypt. All who are hungry, let them *come* in and eat; all who are in need, come and celebrate the Passover. Now we are here, *next year* in Israel. Now we are subjects, next year may we be free persons."

The silence before the breaking of the middle matzah and before the eating of the afikoman suggests that something secret is expressed in the ceremony. We know that the idea of a messianic era was considered a threat to regimes for whom there was no messiah but the emperor, no redeemer but Rome. To dream of an era of peace, an end to slavery, is a revolutionary critique of the status quo. Jews disagreed among themselves as to who the Messiah will be or when the Messiah will come, but one thing they all knew. *This* was not the Messiah, *now* was not the fulfillment of the messianic era. In silence, without benediction—*for one does not bless that which has not yet occurred*—they broke the matzah hidden between the two whole ones, anticipated its recovery, and, eating it, affirmed their belief in the Passover of the Future.

The hidden matzah is the greater part. The promise of the future is greater than the achievements of the past. It is no game to keep the child awake. It is the vision of the messianic times towards which we live and struggle. Rouse the child from his slumber. Without his find the Seder cannot be completed.

REMEMBERING SHIFRA AND PUAH

Passover we will be gathered around our tables with family and friends and ritual symbols, wine, matzah, bitter herbs, and parsley, to eat history and drink philosophy. And we will begin the narration of our root-experience with the question "Mah nishtanah ha-lailah ha-zeh mi-kol ha-leilot."

The answer is rooted in the three dimensions of the Passover; past, present, and future. We are pledged to know the past and to master it, to celebrate the present and to remember the future. The Passover of the Future is grounded in the conviction that hatred and persecution are not the destiny of our people and not the fate of humanity. We do not underestimate the capacity of men to do radical evil, but we refuse to submit to the melancholy judgment that hatred is the inexorable way of the world.

We know that there is Egypt in the world. The root of *Mitzrayim*, the Hebrew term for "Egypt," is *tzar*, which means "narrow," constriction, the tightness that grips us all. We rise in the morning to the headlines in the newspaper and fall asleep after the eleven o'clock news. Our minds are daily pounded with tales of violence, fear, betrayal, disaster. How then shall we not suffer insomnia? If we allow the shadows of television and the news to serve as the horizons of our conscience, the result is a darkened vision of terminal cynicism.

There is a pervasive cynicism in our culture, a "narrowness" that extends to our children and our children's children. Teachers in our schools report the anxiety of the children. Children are bombarded by stories of greed, narcissism, the terror of the streets. Children eavesdrop. They hear only of AIDS, poisonous atmosphere, acid rain, the thinning ozone layer, the proliferation of drugs, the terrors of an addictive culture.

Pity the children who grow old before their time, wrinkled with distrust, the juices of idealism dried up. They do not believe that the future will be better than the past. Who are their heroes? the models of human behavior they are to emulate? The major heroes our society offers them are Dirty Harry and Rambo.

The Jewish child additionally inherits tales of treachery. I myself was raised by a family escaped from Poland, their memories filled with anecdotes of pogrom, persecution, betrayal. Around the Passover table, we read, "In every generation they rise to destroy us." I heard it as a statement confirming the eternal recurrence of anti-Semitism. It placed a stone upon my heart. Is that statement our immortal heritage?

In 1965, I was invited by the West German government to visit Germany, free to interview people, to see for myself the rehabilitation of Germany from its Nazi past. Two interviews stood out from that month-long visit. One came shortly after I visited Dachau. It was with a distinguished clergyman, D. Otto Dibelius, bishop of Berlin-Brandenburg, and later president of the World Council of Churches. I asked him what he did during the Nazi years, what he said after Krystalnacht. I cannot forget his answer. "You must remember, Rabbi, that I was pastor of my flock, that I had one overriding responsibility and that was to protect the church. Had I spoken out for the Jews, I would have jeopardized the church. That I could not do." I was saddened and angry. I said something to him about there being forty-five million Protestants in Germany, that Hermann Goering died a Lutheran and Adolph Hitler a Catholic, and that not even a single S.S. man, not even a single Gauleiter, was excommunicated by the church. What of the moral lesson of Jesus? What of the biblical mandate not to stand idly by the shed blood of your neighbor?

I left the Berlin home of D. Otto Dibelius angry and depressed. The following day, I met with another churchman, Pastor Heinrich Grüber. He had risked his life ferrying Jews out of Germany. He had repeatedly protested the persecution of Jews, was arrested, and was sent to Sachsenhausen, where his teeth were knocked out by Nazi guards. He spoke bluntly. "Dear Rabbi, if there had been a hundred ministers and priests in Berlin marching in the streets, if a hundred of us had been willing to be imprisoned, the fate of your people and our country would have been quite different."

Listening to Grüber I recalled a sentence Dietrich Bonhoffer, the Protestant theologian, wrote: "Only he who cries out for the Jews has the right to sing Gregorian chants." Pastor Grüber was a valuable counterforce to the corporate, ecclesiastical narcissism of Bishop Dibelius. I knew that Dibelius was profoundly wrong, and it triggered my search for evidence that even in hell there were good people.

To find you must want to look. Goodness is not as much on the surface as evil. But where to look? In the sixties there were only rumors, whispers, a few scattered footnotes that during the Nazi era there had been people—non-Jews from every walk of life, lawyers, doctors, businessmen, peasants, sewer workers, maids, nuns, and priests—ordinary folk who risked life and limb to protect a persecuted people, our hounded sisters and brothers.

There were a few articles and a rare book that mentioned this phenomenon. Most episodes were buried in footnotes. But not until I met and befriended blood-and-flesh human beings of moral courage—Jeanne Damann, Heinrich Graebe, Alex Roslan—and some of the Jews they had rescued, did I begin to understand how important Jewish testimony was for the therapy of a traumatized world and how important it is to search out goodness with the same zeal that Beate Klarsfeld and Simon Wiesenthal hunt down evil. Meeting some gentile rescuers helped me. It confirmed my Jewish theological stance on the moral capacity of human beings. It offered empirical illustrations of the biblical belief in humanity as created in the image of God.

I met and heard the witnesses. I heard the testimony of goodness. What does it mean that this man, this German man, could take into his home this frightened couple? What does it mean that this Polish family could harbor three Jewish children abandoned in the Warsaw Ghetto.

What does it mean that this simple Dutch family (Aart and Yotte Vohs) could hide thirty-six hunted souls in the cellar of their own house? Holland is a flat country, without mountains and forests in which to hide the pursued. What does it mean that in a country brutalized by the Nazis, the Dutch resistance movement cried out to every Hollander, "The deportation of all Jewish citizens . . . is the final link in the long chain of inhuman measures. . . . It means the complete annihilation of the Jews. . . . The Netherlands has been deeply humiliated . . . we must prove our honor is not lost and our conscience not silenced . . . we ask our fellow Netherlanders to sabotage all preparations and executions of mass deportation." Of forty thousand Jews who hid from capture, fifteen thousand were successfully hidden and their lives saved.

Goodness moves me. Nothing confirms my belief in God more than the existence of goodness in His creatures. You don't prove God's reality by logic, you prove God by human behavior. What does it mean that these people, not my coreligionists, not members of my people's mishpachah, transcended their circle and made themselves into "hiding places."

These questions I add to the Passover *mah nishtanah* at my Seder. Why, in every country that the Nazis occupied, were there the apathetic passive collaborators with tyranny, but also non-Jews who took Jews into their homes, falsified passports, shared their meager rations? Why were there traitors to human conscience but also men and women with the sense of responsibility to protect them, to lie to the Nazi predators and the local informers so easily bribed by a bottle of vodka or a carton of cigarettes for betraying the hidden Jews?

I am moved by the exploits of the rescuers, by the moral courage and heroism and by the utter simplicity with which they respond to the question "Why did you do it?" They typically reply, "What else could I do?" or "What could I say to my young son should he ask me, 'Papa, what did you do then?' " or "What would you have done?"

"What would I have done?" It is a question for our times. Would I risk my career, my family? Would I take into my home this pregnant woman? Would I remove their excrement and hide their waste from the pursuing predators?

I knew then and I know more now that we Jews own a holy testimony, that we Jews have in our history a double memory, a memory of evil and of goodness, that we Jews have an invaluable witness for the post-Holocaust world. I knew that it was important to search out these ordinary people of extraordinary character, to extend to them a hand of friendship, to have them know our gratitude for their moral courage.

We owe our children a healthy heart. I want my children and grandchildren and yours to know the ugly truth that there is evil in the world, killers of the dream. "Not to know what happened before you were born is to remain a child forever" (Cicero). But I want them to grow up knowing as well that there were and are heroes in our times. I want them to know not only the maledictions of anti-Semitism, but also the benedictions of others. I would not hide from them the harsh and bitter facts of anti-Semitism, but I would have them know that out there in the world are also friends and allies. I want them and their Christian friends to know the faces, voices, and deeds of goodness. Why should our children know only the names and deeds of the exploiters and sadists? Why should their minds and hearts be deprived of the examples of lived idealism? A post-Holocaust generation needs heroes, needs the supportive knowledge that strengthens trust, that quality which scholars like Erik Erikson identify as the source of our vitality. Not Pollyannish naivete, but the positive "ratio of trust over distrust" is the energy out of which hope, morals, and morale are formed.

This Passover evening is different. It celebrates a vision that breaks the fetters of fatalism, that offers hard, empirical evidence of human character that can alter history. The Passover of the past redemption offers confidence in what history can yet be. In our people is that sacred record of human decency, trust, and goodness that is indispensable for the regeneration of a post-Holocaust civilization. We cannot live on maror, on bitter herbs, alone. Maror must be tasted, but charoset, the sweetness of trust and hope, must be added.

When we relive the Exodus, chew the bitter herbs, and raise the cup of Elijah, let us recall for our children the moral heroism of Shifra and Puah, the two Egyptian midwives who refused to submit to Pharaoh's decree to drown every Jewish male. As the Bible records, Shifra and Puah feared God and "they let the children live." Recall as well, with your families and friends, the extended hand of Pharaoh's daughter, who against her father's edict rescued a Jewish child who grew up to be the teacher of redemption.

The cynic is bound to the notion that every tomorrow is a

repetition of yesterday. Men and women of faith believe in the Passover of Tomorrow. Shifrah and Puah are the ancestors of the non-Jewish rescuers who would not submit to the decree of genocide. We Jews are witness to an idea that has much to contribute to the sanity of the world. We Jews are the witnesses, but the therapy is for humankind. We who are pledged to help these rescuers live out the remainder of their lives with dignity and with recognition; we who mean to immortalize their acts by translating into curricula for public and private schools the meaning of moral heroism, the cultivation of character, have a sacred purpose. Goodness deserves immortality. Around our tables, raise a cup of wine, and sing a prayer for the Passover of the Future, "From slavery to freedom, from sorrow to joy, from mourning to festivity, from bondage to redemption, from darkness to light."

The Holy One observed the chaos and emptiness. "How long shall the world exist in darkness?" And God said, "Let there be light." With the poet we sing, "Let us side with the sun."

THE MIRACLES OF
PASSOVER

How am I, a believing Jew raised in a world of scientific culture, to speak to my grandchildren about miracles? They who are taught to explain events in terms of natural cause and effect, how are they to understand the record of speaking serpents and donkeys, rivers turned into blood and frogs, seas split? They ask at different stages of their life, "Did it really happen? Could it really happen?" And I am caught between affirmation and denial of a literal proposition.

I remember one of my Hebrew school teachers putting us to the test: either the prophet spoke the truth or he was a liar. Faced with such either/or options, we are forced into the affirmation of fundamentalist literalism or the negations of literal scientism. The story either happened or did not happen; miracles are real or imaginary. It is an uncomfortable choice which turns us into naive fideists or sour atheists.

There are large segments of the rabbinic tradition that relieve me from the double bind. The tradition enjoys a healthy skepticism, the incredulity of the pious. Here, for example, we read in the Bible of Aaron and Hur on top of a hill, holding aloft Moses' tired arms during the battle between Amalek and the children of Israel: "When Moses held up his hand, Israel prevailed; when he let down his hand, Amalek prevailed" (Exodus 17:11). There it is, a miracle of divine intervention, plain and simple. But the rabbis cannot abide such a literal interpretation. "Did the position of Moses' arms determine the outcome of the battle?" To them it smacks of magical legerdemain. No, they insist, what the Bible means to inform us is that when Israel raised its eyes heavenwards, they were inspired to victory, and when they cast their eyes downwards, they were defeated. The rabbis transformed a literal account of a miraculous intervention into a metaphoric narration of faith. The biblical story is not evidence of God's triumph over the laws of nature, but an account of the natural power of faith over adversity.

We meet a parallel rabbinic deflation of a supernatural miracle in the Book of Numbers. The children of Israel, wandering in the desert, are attacked by biting serpents. God Himself tells Moses to construct an image of a fiery serpent made of brass and hoist it atop a staff, so that "if a serpent had bitten any man, when he looked unto the serpent of brass, he lived" (Numbers 21:9). Despite the unambiguous biblical account of what prima facie appears to be a miracle, the rabbis are incredulous. "Could the copper serpent cause death or life? It means that when the Israelites, in gazing at the serpent, looked up on high and subjected their hearts to their Father in heaven, they were healed, but if they did not do this, they pined away."

The explanation cited by the commentator is found in the Talmud (*Rosh Hashanah* 29a). Again the biblical story of a literal miracle is transformed into a celebration of faith.

Such commentaries understand miracles differently than they are conventionally understood. What are *nissim ve-nifla'ot*—miracles and wonders? They are signs, *otot,* events of significance; events to be held aloft, ensigns, standards marking occurrences that have special meanings. *Nissim,* signs, are set up to gain our attention. They are extraordinarily ordinary happenings that have significance beyond the surface of natural events. The significance is not in the literal raised arms or raised brazen serpent, but in their meaning.

The rabbinic interpretations suggest a world of poetic truths, moral truths that are buried by a prosaic literalism. The Nile turning into blood is not Moses' magic. The redness of the water avenges the innocent blood of the Jewish infants drowned in the Nile. The frogs that choke the Nile are the worshipped gods of fertility, thus instructing a moral symmetry for the Egyptian policy of infanticide. This measure-for-measure (*middah ke-neged middah*) interpretation focuses on the moral meaning of the ten plagues and is less interested in questions of their facticity. The cause of the event may be as prosaic as dust, but moral faith breathes the life of meaning into them. Literalism, scientific or religious, misses the spiritual and moral dimensions of story and history.

A passage in the *Mechilta* (on Exodus 17:5) reports that the Israelites complained about three things: the incense, the ark, and the rod. When the people said that the incense was a means of punishment, for it had killed Nadab and Abihu, the Bible showed it to be an atonement for the people. When they complained that the ark was but a means of punishment, for it smote Uzzah (II Samuel 6:7), the Bible showed how it was a blessing for David and the people (II Samuel 6:11–12). When they complained that the rod was only a punishment, for it brought ruin upon Egypt, the Bible showed how it had saved the children of Israel.

It is not to the rod of Moses that the rabbis call our attention. The rod has no intrinsic supernatural powers. The rod is an instrument that can save or destroy, relative to the moral intention of its use. For when the same rod that was used to split the sea was used by Moses to strike three times against the rock, forcing it, against God's will, to yield water, it led to the punishment of Moses. The same pans of incense that killed Nadab and Abihu and the 250 rebels against Moses and Aaron restrained the plague against the people and saved them (Numbers 17:13). There is no magic in genuine miracles, only moral meaning.

The "signs" of God are found not in the reports of the changes in the natural order of things, but in nature's orderliness. God is discovered in the intelligibility of the universe rather than in its capriciousness. For its intelligibility enables human beings to exercise their intelligence and will to hallow creation. The evening service (*Ma'ariv*) begins with the praise of God who with wisdom orders the cycles of time and varies the seasons. Significantly it is followed with a prayer that emphasizes the wisdom that the House of Israel shares through God's teachings. The miracles that are daily with us are in us and are revealed through us when we use our God-given moral wisdom to protect and enhance His creation.

CHANUKAH: TO MAKE A SOMETHING OUT OF SOMETHING

The second blessing over the Chanukah lights praises God for performing miracles "in those days at this season." A rabbinic observation questions the propriety of this benediction for the *first* evening. For if the miracle refers to the small amount of oil in the sanctuary lamp that lasted seven days beyond its normal capacity, why speak of miracles on the first night? After all, on the first night there was sufficient oil present, and its burning was natural enough. That part of the blessing on the first evening appears superfluous. The benediction for miracles, then, should only be recited on the second night.

One commentator explains that the reason we recite the blessing for miracles even on the first night is because there are all kinds of miracles in the world. Creation, for example, is a miracle in which something is created out of nothing. Theologians call such an act "creatio ex nihilo," or in Hebrew *yesh me-ayin*. But there are other miracles that refer to acts that create something out of something (*yesh me-yesh*). The first night's blessing over the oil that was present illustrates the second type of miracle, one that makes something out of something; something sacred out of some ordinary material already existing. Those kinds of miracles require human initiative and activity. Humans do not create the world out of nothing. The world is given to us. But humans can change the world, shape it according to whatever image is in our heart and mind. And when the transformation is done for the sake of God and goodness it is miraculous.

On the first evening of Chanukah, before the match is struck to light the candle, we are literally in the dark. We cannot make out faces or things in the unlit room. There are obstacles all about us, partitions, walls, pieces of furniture. When the candle is lit we see that nothing in the room has changed. Things are as they were in the dark. But with that instant illumination we experience a revelation. In the flash of that momentary light we know where things are, what obstacles are to be avoided. In that moment we are oriented to the world about us. Nothing new has been created except our awareness of the environment that gives us greater opportunity to choose, to know where to stand and where to move. We can make something out of something. Our capacity to discover wonders and signs is a gift for which we offer thanks thrice daily, "evening, morn, and noon." "Thou gracest the human being with knowledge and givest him to understand."

In many cultures miracles signify strange, mysterious, unnatural events like a man walking on water or flying in the air. But in the language of our tradition, Hebrew, the word for miracle is *nes*. It means "sign," from whose root the term "significance" is derived. To witness the miraculous is to observe in an ordinary event extraordinary significance, an event so important that it cries to be raised up and celebrated. The victory in the second century over the Greek-Syrian forces that sought to extinguish Jewish freedom is a *nes*, a signpost in our history that points to the direction of our lives. Chanukah is the celebrated significance of the Jewish ideal of religious freedom.

The world in which we live is real. The swords and spears and elephants of the Greek-Syrians were real, as were the strengths of the Maccabeans. Miracles are experienced through the capacity of human beings to turn the real into the ideal. Miracles create something out of something, something transcendent out of something ordinary. The paragraph added to the *Amidah* and the grace after during the eight days of Chanukah celebrates the significance of transformation, "for You have delivered the strong into the hands of the weak, the many into the hands of the few."

The sense of sign-significance applies to our daily lives. We cannot often in our lives create or alter the "given," change the diseases, accidents, misfortunes dealt out to us. We can, more often than we expect, make something out of them, create something out of something. Negative experiences can be converted into affirmations of life. Adversity may be used to refine the human spirit, to bring forth courage and compassion never suspected. The triumph of the human spirit over tragedy is a divine-human encounter, a creation of something of transcendent meaning formed out of something common.

What happened on the fifth day of Iyar in our time—the day of Israel's independence—reaffirms the miracle, *nes,* that took place on the twenty-fifth of Kislev over two thousand years ago. The Chanukah lights remind us that miracles are as real as the transforming power of ideals.

CURSING HAMAN,
BLESSING MORDECAI

Rebbe Raphael, the disciple of Rabbi Pinchas, explains that there are two ways to serve God. The first way is to seize hold of one's evil qualities and crush them, "for one who slays the beast reaches prayer and *devekut* [clinging unto God]." This way is called "let Haman be cursed." The other way is that of Rebbe Shneur Zalman, which is to contemplate the greatness of the Creator and labor towards *devekut,* in which process evil would be nullified by itself. This way is called "let Mordecai be blessed."

It is told that when Rebbe Abraham the Angel saw Shneur Zalman off on a journey, he advised the latter in these words: *Fohr, fohr, kuk nit oif die ferd*—"Ride, ride, pay no attention to the horses." These words were interpreted to mean that we should not spend all our efforts attempting to banish the animal traits in man, but instead to ride the horses by speaking words of wisdom. "For a little light will drive away darkness." This is the way of blessing Mordecai.

Among his autobiographical fragments, Martin Buber recalls an intense conversation with a fellow Jew over the action of Samuel the prophet, who in God's name slew Agag, prince of the Amalekites, and prophesied God's rending the Kingdom of Israel from King Saul (I Samuel 15). All of this because Saul spared Agag's life. "And Samuel hewed Agag in pieces before the Lord in Gilgal." Buber cannot believe that this was the message of God to Samuel. Samuel must have misunderstood God.

Buber does not doubt the revelation of God, only whether he

who hears understands the meaning of the message. Did God really mean for us "to wipe out the memory of the Amalekites" (Deuteronomy 25:17–19)? For Buber, "nothing can make me believe" the rightness of the Agag-Samuel story. No more than the philosophers are able to believe that God can violate the laws of logic is Buber able to believe that God can call for genocide. Like Buber, the patriarch Abraham was equally confident that God cannot wipe out the righteous with the wicked. "Cannot" does not impugn God's power, it expresses the conviction that God's character could not condone such unfair action.

The passage from the Book of Samuel is read on *Shabbat Zachor,* the Sabbath preceding the festival of Purim. For some Jews, Purim is a troubling festival. There is something wild, pagan, vindictive about enumerating out loud the ten sons of Haman and their public hanging. A custom developed which had the reader of the Megillah mention all the ten names in one single breath so as not to appear to relish their downfall in detail. So, too, the acrosticon of the plagues is employed by Rabbi Judah to gulp down the ten plagues rather than articulate each disaster brought upon the Egyptians.

Are these Jewish commentators oversensitive to the fall of the enemy? We are not supernatural angels that we should repress our rage against our enemies. Does it not run counter to natural anger to suppress our anger and follow the proverb "Rejoice not when thy enemy falls, and let not thy heart be glad when he stumbles"?

Buber's incredulity resonates a Jewish sensibility. There is something troubling about the children's Purim singing of Haman and his sons, for whom "we'll have a little hanging party." The words are more than child's play. It has the sound of lynching about it.

Is the section on Agag and Samuel, read on *Shabbat Zachor,* the best-chosen biblical reading for the Haftarah of the Sabbath before Purim? I am better instructed by the sages of the Talmud who dared to envisage different destinies for the children of our villains. Whatever happened to Sennacherib and Nebuzaradan, the destroyers of the Temple, and to the descendants of Haman? In Talmud *Sanhedrin* 96b, the rabbis inform us that Nebuzaradan became a righteous proselyte for whom we Jews offer daily prayers in praise of their choice and behavior. The descendants of Sisera, the military foe of the children of Israel (Judges 4), studied Torah in Jerusalem. The descendants of Sennacherib became teachers instructing Torah to the multitudes, among whom are numbered Shemaiah and Avtalyon, the teachers of Hillel. The Holy One led the descendants of Nebuchadnezzar, destroyer of the Temple, under the wings of the Shechinah. And what of the descendants of villainous Haman? "They studied Torah in Benei-Berak."

Thus the finest Jewish revenge against the despoilers of life is in the change of heart and mind in the children and children's children of the enemy. Purim is in the victory of the righteous descendants over evil ancestors. When the sins of the fathers are overcome by the virtues of the sons and daughters, God is victor and Israel rejoices.

We come from a tradition wedded to the imperatives of balanced memory. Not to forget the treachery of the Midianites and the Amalekites, nor the hatred of the Edomites and the Egyptians. But as well to remember: "Thou shalt not abhor an Edomite, for he is thy brother; thou shalt not abhor an Egyptian, for thou wast a stranger in his land" (Deuteronomy 23:8). Jewish memory is not the indiscriminate playing back of all the recordings of the past. Jewish memory calls for the art of selective intelligence to focus events which sustain morale and inform our future attitudes and actions.

On *Shabbat Zachor* I think of Haman's descendants studying Torah in Israel, and I substitute for the Haftarah from the Book of Samuel another prophetic section. "On this day shall Israel be third with Egypt and with Assyria, a blessing in the midst of the land—whom the Lord of hosts shall bless, saying, 'Blessed be Egypt My people, and Assyria the work of My hands, and Israel Mine inheritance' " (Isaiah 19:24).

SHAVUOT: IN QUEST OF SPIRITUALITY

As in all things, there are fashions in words. Some are out, some are in. These days "religion" is out, "spirituality" is in; "supernaturalism" is out, "transcendence" is in. "Religion" conjures up images of a starched tuxedo shirt, stiff, proper, publicly impressive but privately unwearable. "Spirituality" suggests a free-floating chemise, worn without the restriction of ties, the pomp of shirt studs, or the discomfort of ivory buttons pressing against the trachea. "Religion" is formal, organized, external. "Spirituality" is spontaneous, internal, expressive. Martin Buber preferred "religiosity" to "religion." "Religiosity," he thought, "induces sons, who want to find their own God, to rebel against their fathers; religion induces fathers to reject their sons who will let their fathers' God be forced upon them."

There is more than faddishness in the rise and fall of a people's vocabulary. The present preference for "spirituality" protests the impersonalism and coolness of "establishment religion." It opposes the sameness of prayer, the rabbi as paginator, the dutiful responsiveness of the congregation, the soloistic concerts of the cantor, the predictability of the service. "Transcendence" is similarly critical of the flat naturalism that seeks to reduce the wonders and surprises of the world into immanent, horizontal terms. At the same time, "transcendence" would avoid the eerie, otherworldly quality associated with the "supernatural."

The Hebrew term *kedushah* is conveniently translated "holiness." A Latin proverb warns, *omnis traductor traditor*, "everything translated is traitorous." Jews feel the treason of translation in the marrow of their bones. They know that a shofar is not a horn, tzedekah is not charity, the shul is not a sanctuary, a kohen is not a priest, a beadle is not a gabbai, a shammes is decidedly not a sexton. "Phylacteries" derives from the Greek, meaning an amulet to guard against threatening evil—a far cry from a pair of tefillin wrapped around the arm. It's not that English or Latin or Greek is an alien tongue, but that too frequently translation inadvertently spreads disinformation. The soul of a people and its religious experience expresses itself truest in a language of its own.

Consider the term *kedushah* and its derivative forms in *Kaddish* and *Kiddush*. In Leviticus 19, *kedoshim tihyu* is translated as "ye shall be holy." When Rudolph Otto, the distinguished Lutheran scholar, wrote his modern classic, *The Idea of the Holy*, in 1950, he drew his illustrations from Polynesian, Hindu, and Christian sources, but strangely made no references to what biblical scholars call the Holiness Code of the Jewish Bible (Leviticus 19–20). It turned out to be a revealing omission. The Jewish biblical conception of *kedushah*, "holiness," simply does not fit into Otto's scheme of things. For Otto, the holy is *mysterium tremendum et fascinans*, an awe-inspiring, mysterious experience eliciting emotions from creatures "submerged and overwhelmed by their own nothingness." Before the tremendous mystery of the holy, I am nothing. "Mystery," etymologically, refers to closing or shutting one's eyes. The Buddha statues portray the saint with heavy-lidded eyes, closed to the illusory world of *maya*. Before the holy, what can truly be understood and what can honestly be said? Before mystery, the appropriate response is silence. In many ways, the current use of "spirituality" is closer to Otto's idea of the holy than to the biblical and rabbinic notion of *kedushah*.

The biblical Holiness Code opens with a startling imperative addressed not to isolated spiritual virtuosi but to the entire congregation of the children of Israel: "Ye shall be holy, for I, the Lord your God, am holy" (Leviticus 19:2). The Jewish ideal of holiness is personal, communal, and moral. Far from indicating distance between God's holiness and human holiness, the imperative presupposes moral intimacy. The people are addressed as co-sanctifiers with the One who sanctifies *asher kiddeshanu be-mitzvotav*, through His commandments. The Holy One is emulatable because

He created the human being in the divine image, with the potentiality of holiness. The holy God of the Bible is not eerie, wholly other, inaccessible, unfathomable. God speaks plain language. Holiness is imitable through human activity. We can walk with holiness, internalize His mercy and righteousness, because this Holy God "is sanctified through righteousness" (Isaiah 51:16). To live humanly is to exalt God. To injure His creatures is to desecrate Him. In human death, God's holiness is reduced. The novelist Agnon suggested that the *Kaddish* prayer comforts Him, and the purpose of the minyan (quorum) is to replenish the holiness that was diminished by the death of His co-sanctifiers.

"Spirituality" in our time is often biased towards the transcendence of our mundane world. "Spirituality" would favor withdrawing from the battle, from confrontation. But in biblical *kedushah* there is little to suggest muteness before the mystery of God, less yet the deference of obsequious silence. By virtue of their knowledge of God and moral competence, patriarch and prophet are entitled, even mandated, to question His ways. The biblical heroes know what is good and what the Lord requires of them—"to act justly, to love mercy, to walk humbly." They will not play possum before God's mystery. They confront the Judge of all the earth and challenge His ways. Muteness before mystery frequently masks the less noble motive: to deny the holy imperative to act. Silence is not always harmless meditation. It is not infrequently used to disguise a passive acquiescence to evil. In the eyes of *mysterium tremendum* the close encounters of biblical heroes with God are viewed as acts of lèse-majesté; but in the eyes of the biblical God they are courageous imitations of God's integrity.

Jewish holiness is not a global, abstract feeling of awe or mystery, an uncanny meditation on an isolated mountaintop. Jewish holiness takes one out of solitariness into community, out of the cosmetics of beauty into the grime and the dust of the marketplace. Halachically and philosophically, acts of *kedushah* require community. No *Kaddish,* no *kedushah,* no communion without community. Holiness is lived in and through community. The Jewish idea of holiness is not an idea, an intellectual abstraction. Mahatma Gandhi argued against the Jewish cry for a national homeland by insisting that the true Palestine "of the biblical conception" was not a geographic tract but sacred "in their hearts." In his response to Gandhi, Martin Buber insisted that holiness is not a metaphor of the mind: "This land is holy; but it is not the holiness of an idea, it is the holiness of a piece of earth. That which is merely an idea and nothing more cannot become holy; but a piece of earth can become holy just as a mother's womb can become holy."

Holiness is not invested in objects, it is lived in relationship. The lulav, ethrog, Passover roasted egg and shankbone are symbols, not intrinsically holy. The wine of the *kiddush* is not sacramental wine. The *Motzi* over the challah is not intrinsically holy. The wine and the bread are not mysteriously transubstantiated. Unfinished, the wine may be poured out, the bread discarded. Both are blessed for sustaining life and rejoicing the heart. The high priest and his household, even the altar in the Holy of Holies require atonement. No one and nothing on the face of the earth is unblemished, inerrant, perfectly holy. Holiness is not a "what," it is a "with." Jewish holiness is in relationship with the broken vessels of society: the poor, the stranger, the fatherless, the widow. *Kedushah* is being humanly holy. It takes place in the marketplace, the prison, the hospital, the convalescent home.

The Vilna Gaon—scholar, saint, pietist—on the eve of the Day of Atonement sought *musar* from the Dubner Maggid. He asked for words of chastisement so as to humble his soul and prepare himself for the fast-day. "What can I say to you?" the Dubner asked. "You, who are the pride and light of our people, and who study and pray day and night." Still the Vilna Gaon insisted on words of *musar*. The Dubner finally spoke to him. "You are learned and pious; but you study and pray here in the house of study, among your holy texts. Would you remain unblemished in the marketplace, where men and women compete ruthlessly to sell their products, where corruption is rampant, and price-fixing common? Would you be holy then? In a world of mud and muck, where people are fallen into pits, it is easy to keep one's cloak clean by refusing to enter the pit." The Vilna Gaon accepted his chastisement. He knew how extraordinary are the ordinary dictates of holiness.

The most celebrated verse in the Holiness Code locates holiness in love: "Love thy neighbor as thyself" (Leviticus 19:18). Scholars debate whether love of neighbor is primary or secondary to the biblical imperative to love God with all your heart, mind, and might. But most commentators recognize the complementary character of the two loves. Love the world in God, love God in the world. The vertical and horizontal converge in the oneness of holiness. It is the neighbor living alongside you, not the stranger in a foreign land, that commands attention. It is not the global humanitarianism that rhetorically embraces humankind that is formulated in the verse. It is this very neighbor who barbecues, parks in my driveway, owns barking dogs, and plays rock and roll music to whom I am to relate.

"Spirituality" emphasizes feelings. The humanly holy of Judaism includes but is not exhausted in feelings. To feel is not yet to do. So the rabbinic tradition translates love into understandable, concrete, doable acts. To love one's neighbor is *bikkur cholim,* to visit with him in his sickness; it is *nichum avelim,* to comfort him with your presence in his mourning; *hachnasat orchim,* to offer hospitality to others; to rejoice the bride and groom; even to choose an easy death for the criminal sentenced to capital punishment.

Asked where the Holy One lives, Menachem Mendel of Kotzk answered, "Wherever God is let in." An extraordinary ordinariness, a sanctity of the pedestrian inheres in the Jewish way of holiness. Holiness is played out in the marketplace, in keeping just scales and honest weights, in not keeping the wages of a hired servant overnight. Jewish holiness does not direct us to the study of esoteric books or the practice of ascetic religious behavior. The first question we are asked on the ultimate Day of Judgment, the Talmud *Shabbat* conjectures, is not about introspective, subtle, sophisticated meditative exercises. The first question asked is, "Did you do business honestly?" But the new longing for spirituality in our era tends towards self-absorption, an interiority oblivious to the mundane external world. It covets peak experiences above and beyond the prosaic. It misses the ordinary signs and signals of the miraculous about which our daily prayers speak, "Thy wonders and Thy miracles which are daily with us, evening, morn, and noon." It misses the piety that sees godliness in the diurnal transactions with a piece of bread, a newly bought garment, fragrant spices, a wise human being.

When the rebbe urged his disciples to think of God when they prayed during their business hours, several objected. "How can we think of matters of prayer in the midst of business?'' "Why not?'' the rebbe replied. "You manage to think of matters of business in the midst of praying.''

There is a notion of "spirituality" that opposes the Jewish idea of holiness. It flirts with absorption with the Wholly Other. It suggests we are to lose ourselves in the other, to achieve a unity through fusion. Thou art me and I am Thou. But for *kedushah*, holiness is to be approximated, never to be achieved. Only God is holy. Human beings are to strive to become holy. They are not meant to be holy. The boundaries between human and divine holiness are not to be transgressed. The mystical union is not accomplished by the loss of self surrendered to the mysterious Other. I am I and Thou art Thou. Holiness requires the dignity of separation, not the dissolution of merger.

Jewish holiness is not reserved for rarefied moments in the sanctuary. Ezra brought the Torah to the market square on Mondays and Thursdays. What better place to hear the words of holiness than when men and women are selling and buying their wares, fixing their prices, asking their profit? *Kedushah* does not translate easily into "holiness," and not yet into "spirituality." It is experienced through realizing the holy (*kodesh*) locked in the potential (*chol*). "What is holier—Sabbath, tefillin, or study?" a Hasidic master was asked. He answered carefully: "Holy is whatever we are doing at that moment."

IT IS NEVER TOO LATE

The last word has not been spoken,
the last sentence has not been written,
the final verdict is not in.
    It is never too late
    to change my mind,
    my direction,
       to say no to the past
       and yes to the future,
       to offer remorse,
       to ask and give forgiveness.

    It is never too late
    to start over again,
    to feel again
       to love again
       to hope again.

    It is never too late
    to overcome despair,
    to turn sorrow into resolve
       and pain into purpose.

    It is never too late to alter my world,
    not by magic incantations
    or manipulations of the cards
    or deciphering the stars.

But by opening myself
to curative forces buried within,
to hidden energies,
the powers in my interior self.

In sickness and in dying, it is never too late.
    Living, I teach.
    Dying, I teach,
how I face pain and fear.
Others observe me, children, adults,
    students of life and death,
Learn from my bearing, my posture,
    my philosophy.

It is never too late—
    Some word of mine,
    Some touch, some caress may be remembered.
    Some gesture may play a role beyond the last
    movement of my head and hand.

Write it on my epitaph
that my loved ones be consoled,
It is never too late.

CLOSURE

What is left to be done after the dying is over?
After the earth has covered the grave
                the casket lowered
                the garment cut
                the tears shed
                the last *Kaddish* recited
                the farewells over
                the closure formed?

But there is no final closure in death.
Life and death are locked in embrace,
So intimately intertwined that the *keriah* of the cloth
cannot tear them apart.
Something important remains intact.

When the dying is over, another memory takes over.
Not obituary remembrance
Not the memory that records indiscriminately.
But memory that sifts through the ashes of the past
to retrieve isolated moments.
Memory is an act of resurrection
That raises up from oblivion forgotten moments.

Memories even of failure
are precious.
Broken memories are like the tablets Moses shattered,
placed lovingly in the holy Ark of remembrance.

Memories immaterial, disembodied ghosts
that endure.

What is left after death?
Pointers, ensigns, marking places
that raise us up to life and give us a changed heart.
A life lived differently, better, wiser, stronger than before.
What is left after death? The life of the spirit.
The life of the survivor.

STRANGE ENVY

Envy
Those who stand bent before the casket
   wiping away their tears.
Envy memories of
   Warm embraces, gentle humor,
   birthdays, anniversaries,
joyous meals around the Sabbath
   table.

Pity those who cannot cry
tears long
dried into resignation,
surrendering the promise.

Pity the dried-eyed sadness
of those who can only dream of that
which could have been, or should have been.

Pity those who regret what should have been said
   or left unspoken—
loves lost, joys missed,
hopes abandoned.

Pity memories in subjunctive moods—
"if only he had, if only she had, if only I had."

Envy the mourners
who with sweet-bitter nostalgia
slowly recite the *Kaddish*.

I AM OLDER NOW: A YAHRZEIT CANDLE LIT AT HOME

The *Yahrzeit* candle is different,
announcing neither Sabbath nor festival.
No benediction recited
No song sung
No psalm mandated.

Before this unlit candle
without a quorum, I stand
unstruck match in my hand.

It is less distant now,
the remembrance ritual of parents deceased.
I am older now,
closer to their age than before.
I am older now,
their aches in my body
their white hairs beneath my shaved skin
their wrinkles creased into my face.

It is less distant now
this ritual
once made me think of them
Now makes me think of me.

Once it recalled relationships to them
Now it ponders on my children's relationship to me.
Once I wondered what to remember of them
Now I ask what my children remember of me
what smile, what grimace
What stories they will tell their children of me.

It is less distant now.
How would I be remembered
How would I be mourned
Will they come to the synagogue
light a candle
recite the *Kaddish*.
It is less distant now
Once *Yahrzeit* was about parents deceased,
Now it is of children alive.
Once it was about a distant past,
Now it is about tomorrow.

HOLDING ON AND
LETTING GO

Hold on and let go.
On the surface of things
   contradictory counsel.
But one does not negate the other.
The two are complementary, dialectical
   two sides of one coin.

Hold on—death is not the final word
The grave no oblivion.
Hold on in *Kaddish, Yahrzeit, Yizkor.*
No gesture, no kindness, no smile
   evaporates—
Every kindness, every embrace
has its afterlife
   in our minds, our hearts, our hands.

Hold on and let go.
Sever the fringes of the tallit of the deceased
the knot that binds us to the past.

Hold on
Not enslaving memory that sells the future
   to the past
nor recollection that makes us passive,
listless, resigned.

But memory that releases us
   for new life.

Lower the casket, the closure meant
to open again the world
of new possibilities.

Return the dust to the earth
not to bury hope
but to resurrect the will to live

Artists, aerialists
on a swinging trapeze
   letting go one ring to catch another
   to climb to higher heights.

Hold on and let go
   a courageous duality
   that endows our life
   with meaning.

      Neither denying the past
         nor foreclosing the future.

The flow of life
   the divine process
   gives and takes
retains and creates.

Old and new yesterday and tomorrow
   both in one embrace.

The Lord giveth and the Lord taketh
   Blessed be the name of the Lord.

LIFE AND DEATH

What is left to be done after the dying is over?
After the earth has covered the grave
                    the casket lowered
                    the ribbon cut
                    the tears shed
                    the last kaddish recited
                    the farewells over
                    the closure formed?

But there is no final closure in death.
Life and death are locked in embrace,
So intimately intertwined that the "Keriah" of the cloth
cannot tear them apart.
Something important remains intact.

When the dying is over, another memory takes over.
Not obituary remembrance
Not the memory that records indiscriminately.
But memory that sifts through the ashes of the past
to retrieve isolated moments.
Memory is an act of resurrection
That raises up from oblivion forgotten moments.

Memories even of failure
are precious.
Broken memories are like the tablets Moses shattered,
placed lovingly in the holy Ark of remembrance.

Memories immaterial, disembodied ghosts
that endure.

What is left after death?
Pointers, ensigns, marking places
that raise us up to life and give us a changed heart.
A life lived differently, better, wiser, stronger than before.
What is left after death? The life of the spirit.
The life of the survivor.

Acknowledgments

Many of the chapters of this book are revisions of articles that have appeared elsewhere under different titles:

Jewish Apartheid
  Moment, December, 1985.
The Pendulum of Pluralism
  HUC Commencement Address, May 16, 1983.
Love with a Bear Hug around my Soul
  Jewish Journal, January 22, 1988.
From Either/Or to Both/And
  University of Judaism, *University Papers*, January, 1982.
Letting Go/Holding On
  American Jewish Committee, December, 1988; *Christian Century*, December, 1988 (published as "Remembering the Rescuers: Post-Holocaust Recovery").
My Goldfish and AntiSemitism
  Baltimore Jewish Times, August 12, 1988; *Jewish Journal*, September 9, 1989; *Brotherhood*, Winter/Spring, 1989.
Fiddler on a Hot Tin Roof
  Baltimore Jewish Times, February 23, 1990.
Caught between Sesame and Wall Streets
  Baltimore Jewish Times, February, 1988 (published as "An Embarrassment of Riches").
Raised in an Addictive Culture
  Reconstructionist, March, 1989.
Countering the Attraction of Cults
  Moment, November, 1974 (published as "What Hurts the Jews").

Sex and the Single God
  Reconstructionist, November, 1981.
The Hyphen Between the Cross and the Star
  Jewish Journal, November 25, 1987; *Reconstructionist,* July/
  August, 1988.
Riteless Passages and Passageless Rites
  Moment, 1984 (published as "Helping Rabbis Be").
The Stranger in Our Mirror
  Baltimore Jewish Times, April, 1989.
Kiddush: Jewish Philosophy Squeezed in a Cup of Wine
  Baltimore Jewish Times, January, 1989 (published as "Why
  Wine for Jewish Rituals"); *Jewish Voice,* April 14, 1989; *Greater
  Phoenix Jewish News,* September 29, 1989.
Ha-Motzi: Social Ethics in a Loaf of Bread
  Baltimore Jewish Times
Space and Time
  Sh'ma, October, 1989.
Creation and Creativity
  Sh'ma
As Servants or as Children?
  Baltimore Jewish Times
Concealments and Revelations
  Baltimore Jewish Times, May 20, 1988 (published as "The True
  Revelation of Shavuot").
Imagining Zaydeh's Sukkah
  Jewish Journal, September 23, 1988.
Commentaries on the Seder
  Jewish Journal, March, 28, 1988
Elijah's Cup is Empty
  Baltimore Jewish Times, April 18, 1986
Remembering Shifrah and Puah
  Inaugural Reception Address, JFCR/ADL, April 4, 1989
To Make a Something out of Something
  Baltimore Jewish Times, April November, 1989.